Queen Bees

Queen Bees

Six Brilliant and Extraordinary
Society Hostesses Between the Wars

Siân Evans

www.tworoadsbooks.com

First published in Great Britain in 2016 by Two Roads
An imprint of John Murray Press
An Hachette UK company

1

A CIP catalogue record for this title is available from the British Library

Hardback ISBN 978 1 473 61802 2
Trade Paperback ISBN 978 1 473 61803 9
Ebook ISBN 978 1 473 61804 6
Audio Digital Download ISBN 978 1 473 63143 4

Typeset in Sabon MT Std by Palimpsest Book Production Limited,
Falkirk, Stirlingshire

Printed and bound by CPI Group (UK), Croydon, CR0 4YY

Hodder & Stoughton policy is to use papers that are natural, renewable
and recyclable products and made from wood grown in sustainable
forests. The logging and manufacturing processes are expected to
conform to the environmental regulations of the country of origin.

Hodder & Stoughton Ltd
Carmelite House
50 Victoria Embankment
London EC4Y 0DZ

www.hodder.co.uk

For my father, David Meurig Evans.

Contents

Dramatis Personae

Lady Nancy Astor, née Nancy Witcher Langhorne, 1879-1964. Energetic Virginian-born political pioneer, and militant teetotaller.

Lady Sibyl Colefax, née Sibyl Halsey, 1874-1950. Determined collector of the great and the good, and a successful interior designer.

Mrs Laura Mae Corrigan, née Laura Whitlock, 1879-1948. Impervious to snubs and snobs, the Wisconsin-born queen of malapropisms and consummate party-giver was a heroine in World War Two.

Lady Emerald Cunard, née Maud Alice Burke, 1872-1948. San Francisco-born hostess whose sparkling wit attracted the cultural elite, she became a key figure in the Abdication crisis.

Dame Margaret Greville, aka 'Mrs Ronnie', née Margaret Helen Anderson, 1863-1942. The illegitimate daughter of a Scottish millionaire, she courted princes and politicians for her own Machiavellian ends.

Lady Edith Londonderry, née Edith Chaplin, 1878-1959. London's pre-eminent society hostess and a passionate activist for women's rights, who sported a tattooed snake on her ankle.

Introduction

*'Existence is a party. You join after it's started,
and you leave before it's finished.'*

Elsa Maxwell, 1883–1963

Between the two world wars, a number of spirited, ambitious women from differing backgrounds used their considerable charm, their intelligence and their fortunes to infiltrate and influence the upper ranks of British society. By cultivating the *prominenti* in fields as diverse as politics and court circles, theatre, science and the arts, each great hostess sought to create her own 'set', a virtual forum where she could bring together the most important, interesting and illuminating people of the day.

Six particular 'Queen Bees', each born in the Victorian era, had profound effects on British history. As a result of the social revolution wrought by the First World War, they slipped through the filters that previously would have barred them from the highest social circles. Each was able to reinvent herself as an independent, often influential focus on the political, social and cultural elite. To be a great hostess was a career choice for these resourceful and energetic women at a time when their formal opportunities for making a mark on the outside world were limited.

By creating convivial and welcoming homes, and providing

I

lavish and enjoyable hospitality, they consciously attracted the most stimulating and dynamic people of the day. They had a profound and radical effect on the many aspects of the inter-war era, from the idiocies of the Bright Young Things to the abdication and the Munich Agreement.

Throughout history, there have always been certain women who have been keen to shape the society of their times by using their influence, charm, contacts and humour. Whether queens or mistresses, aristocrats or bluestockings, they have furthered their own, their families' or their friends' interests, to achieve their aims or to provide themselves with intellectual and cultural stimulus. Through the use of 'soft power', society hostesses have brought together the famous, the notorious, the gifted and glamorous, the talented, beautiful and wealthy, creating their own milieus in which their own interests and talents could shine in reflected glory. They have used their opulent salons and elegant drawing rooms to marshal their own cliques, to launch the careers of bright young people with no background, to advance the interests of their protégés and allies, to matchmake and scheme, to gossip and to pass hints to the well-connected of their acquaintance, and to place scurrilous stories about their rivals.

The inter-war Queen Bees who appear in this book came from very mixed backgrounds. Three of the six – Lady Nancy Astor, Mrs Laura Corrigan and Lady Emerald Cunard – were American in origin, and only Nancy could make any claim to gentility. Their British-born contemporaries and rivals were Lady Sibyl Colefax, Lady Edith Londonderry and Mrs Margaret Greville; of these, only Lady Londonderry was of high birth. Despite their diverse origins, all of them were determined and ambitious 'social mountaineers'. Each one initially gained an established position within the hierarchy of British society through making an advantageous marriage; once they had a 'name', they were able to harness their intelligence, their wits and their resources to pursue their own passions.

Their areas of operation varied, and inevitably their social circles often overlapped, resulting in rivalries. Nancy Astor and Edith Londonderry both moved in aristocratic circles, as a result of their marriages to influential and wealthy career politicians. They were both brought up as political conservatives, but subsequently developed radical social ideas of their own, and used their contacts and powers of persuasion to achieve their aims, with far-reaching consequences.

Lady Cunard and Lady Colefax, on the other hand, favoured the artistic, musical and literary scenes that flourished across Britain, America and Europe between the wars. Sibyl Colefax and Maud Cunard (or Emerald, as she later preferred to be known) competed fiercely with each other to attract both the intelligentsia and celebrities to their tables, as well as fostering the burgeoning relationship between Edward VIII and Mrs Simpson, an affair that was to have such dramatic consequences for the royal family.

Conversely Mrs Margaret Greville, known variously as 'Maggie' or 'Mrs Ronnie', was a great friend of the old guard at Buckingham Palace, but became involved in the complex world of international politics through her curiosity and her early misplaced enthusiasm for Hitler and his 'little brownshirts.' Her complete antithesis and despised social rival, Mrs Laura Corrigan, was widely dismissed as a frivolous, foreign millionairess with a knack for social gaffes, whose entire *raison d'être* appeared to be organising novelty parties with glittering prizes for the Bright Young Things, so that she could indulge her own fantasies of being a circus ringmaster.

However, it was brave Mrs Corrigan who defied all expectations, remaining in Paris when the Nazis occupied the city and dedicating her considerable fortune to funding her charitable work by putting herself at considerable personal risk during the Second World War.

The Queen Bees of London society benefited from advantageous marriages that gave them wealth and brought the necessary social mobility that went with it. The rigid class distinctions that had existed in the nineteenth century were sufficiently permeable after the Great War to allow these women to rise to positions of influence. Naturally, many women of that era were obliged by their social position and that of their husbands to entertain their contemporaries on the grand scale, by offering and receiving hospitality, 'matching cutlet for cutlet' in the telling phrase of Lady Violet Greville, Margaret's formidable mother-in-law. However, the six characters under consideration here actively made it their life's work to surround themselves with a distinctive coterie, to bring together diverse individuals they felt should meet under their roofs. They often cited altruistic reasons, although one cannot avoid the inevitable conclusion that each Queen Bee also enjoyed a little reflective lustre from attracting the most desirable individuals to their homes.

Tellingly, each of these six women seems to have been driven by a volatile childhood or unhappy experiences. Both Lady Londonderry and Maud Cunard lost a beloved parent while still young. Sibyl Colefax's restless mother was estranged from her father, and she grew up living under sufferance in other relatives' homes, shuttling between India and London, or eking out a pittance in out-of-season Continental resorts. Margaret Greville was well aware of the stigma of illegitimacy that hung like a cloud over her early years, spent in an obscure boarding house in Edinburgh. Laura Mae Corrigan was born in rural poverty in the American Midwest and was driven by a childlike determination to have the well born dance to her tune. Nancy Astor's father redeemed the family's fortunes after the American Civil War, but she too appreciated the impermanence of apparently secure fortunes, and made a disastrous early marriage to an alcoholic that coloured many aspects of her later life.

As a result of their early years, each Queen Bee sought to create a social circle of her own as an adult, a set of friends and acquaintances over whom she could have some control. They were aware of the importance of making a good marriage, and notably each one married a man who could provide what she required from a lifelong partnership, even though the husbands tended to be very different in character from their wives.

Although they tended to lack formal education, the society hostesses were clever, curious and largely self-taught. Coinciding with the moment when women were first allowed some access to the professions, after the end of the Great War, several of the hostesses became high-profile role models through their pioneering careers outside the home. The eldest of the six, Mrs Margaret Greville, an astute businesswoman and one of the wealthiest people in Britain, was fifty-five years old before she was allowed to vote in the general election of 1918. Nancy Astor was a mother of six children and forty years old when she was elected Member of Parliament for a Plymouth constituency in 1919. The youngest, Laura Mae Corrigan, was forty-three when she launched her charm offensive on London in 1922. All of these women were already mature before they embarked on the most influential years of their lives.

The reach of women like Nancy Astor, Mrs Greville and Edith Londonderry was considerable; they were celebrities in their own age, travelling extensively, forging valuable personal connections in America, India and Europe. They exerted considerable influence on the government and the legislature, and demonstrated through their own example that women could have careers and roles beyond those traditionally ascribed to them. Their diverse activities affected the royal family, the aristocracy and international relations. Lady Astor and Lady Londonderry used their influence to improve the lives of women of all classes, by implementing legislation designed to protect their interests, such as banning the sale of alcohol to under-eighteens, by improving maternal and infant mortality rates through the provision of trained midwives funded by the state, and by proving through the aegis of the Women's Legion that women could work outside the home. By contrast, Emerald Cunard, Sibyl Colefax and Laura Corrigan provided much-needed patronage and stimulus, which enhanced the rich and varied cultural life of Britain. Even Mrs Greville, notorious for her apparent snobbery and cultivation of the rich, discreetly funded a scholarship programme for nearly four decades which enabled hundreds of ambitious young people from poor backgrounds to gain professional qualifications by studying at night school.

The six Queen Bees of the inter-war years helped to shape the course of British history. They had stamina, energy and determination; they also enjoyed proximity to power and collecting celebrities. Their hospitality was legendary; above all, they were excellent company and knew how to throw fabulous parties. As Oswald Mosley wrote in his autobiography: 'It was all enormous fun. The cleverest met together with the most beautiful, and that is what social life should be.'

I

Origins

———

The six society hostesses who came to dominate London society were born between 1863 and 1879, at the height of the Victorian era. They were the products of their era and their diverse upbringings, but what marks them out from their contemporaries was the way in which each woman transcended her origins, using her intelligence to reinvent herself.

The oldest of the hostesses, who was to become Mrs Margaret Greville, was born Margaret Helen Anderson, in a discreet rented house in St John's Wood, London, on 20 December 1863. The two Scots of notably modest origins who claimed to be her parents, Helen and William Anderson, were far from Edinburgh, where they both lived, when Helen's child was born. The registrar who recorded the birth assumed they were married, but in fact Helen and William shared nothing more than a coincidence of surname, and the same employer. They were involved in an elaborate plot to legitimise the baby, and to spare Helen the stigma of being an unmarried mother.

Helen Anderson worked as a humble domestic servant in Edinburgh in the early 1860s. She became the mistress of the entrepreneurial bachelor brewer William McEwan, and in 1863 she discovered she was pregnant. Mr McEwan had a trusted employee at the brewery, the cellarman William Murray Anderson, who was married with a family of his own. William Anderson was willing to help solve Helen's predicament, and so the two Scots moved to London together to await the baby's arrival, pretending to be husband and wife. After registering the birth and following the child's christening in April 1864, William Anderson returned to his marital home in Edinburgh, and he remained working in the brewery till the mid-1890s. It seems that Mr McEwan bank-rolled the deception, so that Helen Anderson might appear to be a respectable widow, whose husband had died in London, leaving her with a small daughter of uncertain age, when she returned to Scotland. Records are scarce, but by 1868 Mrs Anderson was running a boarding house at East Maitland Street in Edinburgh, an enterprise presumably funded by Mr McEwan. Meanwhile, Helen's family lived at 102 Fountainbridge in the same city, across the street from William Anderson's household at number 107, and they all worked at Mr McEwan's brewery, apparently amicably.

Little Margaret's true origins were probably suspected by many in Edinburgh, but Mr McEwan had deep pockets. His private account books show that he made irregular but generous payments to a 'Mrs Anderson' for the next two decades; he also funded young Margaret's education, even providing dancing lessons. So when, in 1885, Mr McEwan, now an extremely wealthy and well-connected Liberal MP for Central Edinburgh, and apparently a confirmed bachelor aged fifty-eight, announced he was marrying the respectable middle-aged widow Mrs Anderson, aged forty-eight, who ran a boarding house in the city with her daughter, eyebrows were raised and lips pursed in Morningside drawing rooms. The press were very careful always to refer to Miss Anderson as Mr McEwan's 'stepdaughter'. Nevertheless, the newly married McEwans and Margaret relocated to London, removing themselves from Scottish censure. As Margaret was to advise her friends sagely in later years, 'Never comment on a likeness.'

William McEwan did not formally adopt Margaret, but he dropped hints in the right circles that his 'stepdaughter' would inherit the bulk of his massive fortune, and she was launched into London society. He moved in rarefied circles; as a Privy Councillor, he knew many senior statesmen and landowning families. He was also familiar with the Marlborough House set, the associates and friends of the self-indulgent Prince of Wales, the future Edward VII, who had no compunctions about seeking the financial advice – and informal loans – of self-made millionaires.

It was believed that a young woman's wedding day was the most important of her life. Aspiring social climbers had to use whatever assets they might possess to attract a desirable mate, and one of the most desirable attributes a marriageable young woman might offer was a substantial fortune provided by a parent, benefactor or protector. In the case of Margaret Anderson, all three roles were combined in Mr McEwan. He was keen to secure his daughter's future by arranging her marriage into a good family. An aristocratic title was a highly desirable acquisition for ambitious families whose wealth came from 'trade'. Conveniently, there were a number of upper-crust British families whose impressive escutcheons and rolling acres urgently needed shoring up with ready cash. As a result, many a marriage was discreetly arranged or tacitly encouraged between the parents of sons set to inherit venerable titles and daughters who could provide newly minted banknotes. Any attrition caused by a rapid scramble up the social ladder could always be alleviated by the soothing poultice of money.

The McEwans and Margaret Anderson, now in her mid-twenties, had moved to 4 Chesterfield Gardens, London, in the late 1880s; living at number 7 in the same street were Lord and Lady Greville. He had been Prime Minister Gladstone's Private Secretary and moved in high Liberal circles, as did Mr McEwan. The two neighbouring households became acquainted. The Grevilles' eldest son and heir, Captain the Hon. Ronald Henry Fulke Greville, or Ronnie to his friends, was considered quite a catch; easy-going and charming, handsome, fond of horse-racing and a great friend of the Prince of Wales. Despite their grand title and extensive property in Ireland, the Grevilles were perennially short of cash. In order to keep Ronnie afloat in the high-spending Marlborough House set who hung around the Prince, it was imperative that he found a wealthy wife.

However, Margaret Anderson, the girl living just across the street, was not Ronnie Greville's first choice. He pursued Virginia Daniel Bonynge, who was a rich, beautiful and good-natured American; to add to her attractions, her step-father, William Bonynge, a Californian gold-miner and finan-cier, had planted a dowry worth $4 million on her. Unfortunately, William Bonynge was locked in a vicious vendetta with a former business associate, John McKay, and the fight became so ugly and notorious on both sides of the Atlantic, with slanderous stories about their wives deliberately placed in the press and spread around the London clubs by the protagonists, that the matter came to a head in a violent fist fight in a San Francisco bank in January 1891, a skirmish that was reported with evident enjoyment in the press:

Mr Mackay [*sic*] struck when Mr Bonynge was not looking. Then they had it. Chairs turned over, inkstands flew and the ink made long, black streaks on the wall. It was a regular possum and wildcat fight. President Heilman said, 'Gentlemen! Gentlemen! This will never do!'

Despite the two-year courtship, the Grevilles decided against the marriage; Ronnie resolved to look for a bride with a similarly wealthy stepfather but a less volatile background. He also needed a wife who could thrive in the slightly louche company that surrounded the Prince of Wales, who was to become King Edward VII. Ronnie found the perfect partner much closer to home; Margaret Anderson, the illegitimate daughter of a millionaire, brought up in an Edinburgh lodging house, who could charm and entertain the highest in the land yet knew the value of keeping secrets. Almost exactly three months after the fist fight in San Francisco, Margaret married Ronnie.

Lord and Lady Greville presumably knew that their future daughter-in-law was not the only child of a deceased manual labourer from Selkirk who had died in London at an unspecified date in the mid-1860s, the cover story that concealed her true parentage. They would not have allowed their eldest son and heir to marry someone so far below their social strata. Margaret wasn't a member of the peerage, but she was pre-eminent among the 'beerage', the daughters of self-made entrepreneurs, who were successfully marrying into grander but cash-strapped families. The glamorous wedding took place on 25 April 1891, and the subsequent marriage was very happy; Ronnie provided Maggie with elevation into the highest social circles. One of Ronnie's best friends from his army days was George Keppel, who was married to Alice, a beautiful Scot. The Grevilles and Keppels became firm friends. Alice went on to become the future king's much-loved mistress, and the Grevilles became part of his inner circle. In return, Maggie provided pleasure-seeking, dandyish Ronnie with a well-padded lifestyle, including a luxurious home in Mayfair and ample opportunity to indulge his hobbies, such as horse-racing and, in time, motoring. Meanwhile, she adopted the slightly 'racy' name of 'Mrs Ronnie', and began to establish herself as a hostess of note on the London circuit.

Once they were married, she persuaded Ronnie to resign his commission with the Life Guards and take up politics. With support from his friend Winston Churchill, Ronnie won Bradford East for the Conservatives in 1896, and he represented the constituency for ten years. Mrs Greville was accustomed to mingling with politicians, having observed her father in action; politics brought out her Machiavellian streak, and even the Prime Minister, A. J. Balfour, commented that her conversation was 'a sort of honeyed poison'. Unlike her husband, she was ambitious and craved proximity to power. Mrs Greville's god-daughter Sonia was in no doubt that she was a formidable character:

> In any generation, Maggie would have been outstanding. The daughter of a shrewd old Scottish brewer, from her earliest years she had taken an interest in his business, mastering the intricacies of its processes and management until eventually she won for herself a seat on the Board through her own business acumen. Always, she had loved power, in her youth sipping it, in small draughts, in her father's office in Edinburgh; later (with his money behind her), savouring it, in its social context, in the drawing-rooms of Europe [...] she had married Papa's greatest friend, Ronnie Greville, eldest son of Lord Greville, a charming unambitious man whom she moulded affectionately into

any shape she pleased [...] when no child of her own materialised, she took up her pursuit of power again (preferably, beside a throne), firmly conducting Ronnie through the lobbies of politics.

Through making a glittering marriage to Ronald Greville, young Margaret Helen Anderson had reinvented herself. She had transcended her murky beginnings and risen above the speculation about her true parentage to become a woman of status and substance. It is significant that, immediately following her marriage in 1891, the new Mrs Margaret Greville started to keep press clippings about herself, supplied by a professional cuttings agency; it was as though her life had begun anew, and she was now poised to make a name for herself.

The future Lady Sibyl Colefax was born in Wimbledon on 4 December 1874, in a house owned by her uncle by marriage, Walter Bagehot, the noted journalist and essayist, editor of *The Economist* and author of *The English Constitution*. Sibyl's father, William Halsey, had returned to his civil service posting in India by the time of her birth. In 1875 William's wife, Sophie, and their new daughter joined him at Cawnpore, and Sibyl's early years were spent in India. She had a brother and sister, Willie and Ethel, respectively eleven and ten years older, but they were at boarding school in England, so she effectively grew up as an only child. Her early years were not happy; her parents were fundamentally incompatible and the marriage was stormy. She described her childhood simply but eloquently: 'My father worked, my mother wept, and I played on the floor and knew nothing.'

Until Sibyl was six, she and her mother flitted restlessly between India and Europe. Summers were spent at Simla to avoid the worst of the heat; there Sibyl encountered Lockwood Kipling, the curator of the museum and principal of the school of art at Lahore. He missed his own two children, Rudyard and Trix, who, like so many of the 'children of Empire', were at school in England. He liked this intelligent but rather solitary little girl, encouraging her interest in art and literature, and she remained friendly with the Kipling family for the rest of her life.

After the sensory exuberance of India, with its vibrant colours, sounds and smells, Sibyl disliked cold, gritty and monochrome London when she and her mother returned in 1880. Sophie promptly left her daughter in the clutches of her rather formidable sisters, known as the 'Victorian aunts', while she escaped to Europe in a borrowed fur coat, in search of adventure. Fortunately the day-to-day care of Sibyl was handed to a servant called Mary Jordan, who had been her grand-mother's maid. Mary provided warmth, security and affection for the little girl, a compensation for the lack of love from her parents. Sibyl referred to many of her relatives as 'grim', and as soon as she had the chance she cultivated her own intense friendships. She viewed family as a lottery but recognised that, with discrimination, one could create one's own social circle.

Sophie returned from Europe at Christmas 1880 and moved with all three children into her sister's house on Wimbledon Common. Sibyl was now on the fringes of artistic London; she knew May Morris, daughter of William Morris, and Margaret Burne-Jones, whose own parents were the painter Edward Burne-Jones and Alice Kipling. Another aunt, Emilie Barrington, was known as 'The Egeria of Melbury Road', a reference to a nymph of classical mythology who advised the king of Rome. Emilie had failed to enter the Royal Academy to study art, so she ruthlessly pursued famous artists and sculptors, like a lepidopterist completing her collection. In 1879, with her husband Russell, and her widowed sister Eliza, Emilie bought a house next door to the painter and sculptor G. F. Watts in Melbury Road, Kensington, a very short walk from the homes of eminent painters Holman Hunt and Lord Leighton. For two decades Emilie hounded the artistic elite of west London, 'dropping in' on Watts while he was working in his studio, and buttonholing Lord Leighton through her friendship with his sister. Sibyl visited Melbury Road often, and Aunt Emilie's relentless lion-hunting was a useful object lesson in how to create a salon. Scraping an initial acquaintance with a famous person was not impossible, but the successful hostess needed a sympathetic and congenial atmosphere in which her quarry would meet others of their own or (preferably) superior rank and achievement.

Family relationships remained strained; in December 1882 Sibyl's mother, Sophie, returned briefly to India, omitting to tell Sibyl of her plans until just before her departure. 'As the train moved out I knew for the first time the agony of sorrow – the sense of desertion – which I can feel even today', she wrote in later years. Sibyl was sent to a boarding school, which she enjoyed because for the first time she had company of her own age, but then the mercurial Sophie changed her mind and engaged a French governess to teach her at home. Fortunately Mademoiselle Bigot was young and lively; now Sibyl had a companion and chaperone to take her to musical concerts and plays, and her cultural horizons expanded.

By 1889 both Halsey parents and all three children were reunited uneasily under one roof at Warwick Gardens. William had retired from the Indian civil service in 1883, and a subsequent trip to Australia to try to make a fortune had come to nothing. He now found it difficult to readjust to life in Britain after decades in India, a common problem with returning 'expats'. Sophie avoided her husband by travelling extensively in Europe, taking Sibyl with her as a companion. For a number of winters they lived in cheap and obscure hotels on the French Riviera, eking out a limited budget.

In the spring of 1894 Sophie finally agreed that she and Sibyl should go to Florence, a decision that was to change her daughter's life. Idle Sophie preferred to lie in bed in the mornings, while solitary Sibyl, now nineteen, used those hours to explore the Renaissance city on foot. Fortunately, a group of older British visitors took her under their wing; they were 'doing' Florence and had a particular interest in its art, culture and architecture. The group included the writer Lytton Strachey, Roger Fry and his wife, the art expert Herbert Horne and the knowledgeable art historian Bernard Berenson. The group held idyllic picnics in the Tuscan countryside and explored the Duomo and the Uffizi, the galleries and palazzi, talking all the time of their theories, their discoveries, their favourite artists. Sibyl was enchanted.

> Once I had fallen in with my Florence friends it was different. They opened all the windows of the world to me [...] that Spring in Florence and on the hillsides of Tuscany settled once and for all what I really wanted. To be able to turn to books great and small. To listen to enchanting talk, gay, learned, frivolous [...] that I realised was the first real part of growing up. To those friends and those beginnings I owe so much.

Considering Sibyl's lifelong enthusiasm for creative and cultured people, her choice of Arthur Colefax as a husband seems at first uncharacteristic. They met in May 1897, when she was twenty-two and he was thirty-one. Arthur was a reticent Yorkshireman, logical and disinclined to flights of fancy. By contrast, Sibyl was mercurial in speech, with a distinctive artistic and theatrical bent. A former grammar school boy who won a scholarship to Oxford, Arthur read Natural Sciences and was awarded a first-class honours degree. He completed a PhD at Strasbourg, where he learned to speak and read German fluently, quite a rarity among Victorian Englishmen. Arthur's first love was the law but, ever cautious, he had opted for the regular life and reliable income of an academic, until he unexpectedly heard of a law scholarship that allowed him to pursue his true vocation. He was called to the Bar in 1894 and embarked on a successful career as a barrister specialising in international patent law, using his linguistic skills and scientific background.

Arthur and Sibyl finally became engaged in January 1901; to Sibyl, Arthur represented the solidity and reliability she had lacked as a child. The new Mr and Mrs Colefax were respectable rather than wealthy, and Arthur's fluctuating income was to concern them throughout their marriage. They married in Knightsbridge in July 1901, and honeymooned in Somerset, before returning to 85 Onslow Square in South Kensington, their home for the next eighteen years. After her rackety upbringing in a succession of other people's houses, Sibyl finally had a house of her own. It was here that she first displayed her distinctive skill in designing interiors, installing panelling in the downstairs rooms and painting it in light colours, introducing attractive walnut furniture in the drawing room, creating a mahogany dining room and a comfortable sitting room furnished with antique rugs, and with a view over the garden. All these elements she was to repeat with great success in her later homes, and in her eventual career.

The consummate political hostess the future Lady Londonderry was born Edith Helen Chaplin on 3 December 1878. Her mother died when she was only four years old, so Edith was brought up at Dunrobin Castle, Sutherland, the home of her maternal grandfather, the third Duke of Sutherland. She retained a romantic passion for Scotland throughout her life, and it was a factor in her burgeoning if unlikely relationship with Britain's first Labour Prime Minister, Ramsay MacDonald, the illegitimate son of a crofter.

Aside from her aristocratic origins, there was much about Edith that many found appealing. She was tall, handsome and poised, with a rather commanding presence, and sported a tattoo of a snake on one ankle, a *risqué* adornment for those times. Edith was very athletic and fond of the outdoors life; in addition, she was an excellent horsewoman, who would occasionally shock convention by riding astride her mount rather than side-saddle, as was thought more seemly for young ladies of her caste. She was a keen shot, adored field sports and had great organisational and inspirational abilities, as she was to prove in her later years.

Her grandfather's London home was Stafford House in the Mall, an extremely grand mansion close to Buckingham Palace. In time Edith's Aunt Millicent became Duchess of Sutherland and was able to create her own social milieu, entertaining a band of like-minded aristocrats known as 'The Souls'. Aunt Millie was an intellectual with a love of culture and literature, who held advanced ideas about the welfare of the working classes and believed in the necessity of greater equality between the sexes. Millicent was only eleven years older than her young niece, and it was at her glittering receptions at Stafford House that Edith acquired a taste for exerting 'soft power' through one's social life.

Playing the Tory hostess was a role for which blue-blooded Edith always seemed destined, initially in loyal support of the political ambitions of her husband. They met in 1897, and in 1899, at the age of twenty, Edith married Charles Vane-Tempest-Stewart, Viscount Castlereagh, eldest son of the sixth Marquess of Londonderry. He was considered to be quite a catch, but his cousin Winston Churchill referred to him frankly as 'that half-wit Charley Londonderry'.

Charles was one of the most eligible bachelors of his day, tall, slim and handsome. An excellent horseman, he had joined the Royal Horse Guards (known as 'The Blues') in 1897. The Londonderrys' fortune was considerable: they owned 27,000 acres in Ireland and 23,000 acres in England, and their income was mainly from mining coal, a commodity much in demand in the late Victorian and Edwardian eras. The family owned Wynyard in County Durham, a palatial neo-classical mansion where they hosted large house parties, entertaining guests with game shoots and visits to the racecourse. Magnificent Mount Stewart, overlooking Strangford Lough in Northern Ireland, was the Londonderrys' main provincial residence; here they spent Christmas, Easter and Whitsun, occupying themselves with shooting, wildfowling or sailing. They also had a large estate in north Wales, Plas Machynlleth. Their London base was Londonderry House, a monumental aristocratic town house on Park Lane designed by the Wyatt brothers. The main stairway rivalled that of nearby Lancaster House, with a large skylight, rococo chandelier and two individual flights of stairs leading up to the Grand Ballroom. This was modelled on the Waterloo Chamber at Apsley House, home of the Duke of Wellington. Like the Iron Duke, the Londonderrys had a taste for grandeur, French furniture and sculptures by Canova.

Sociable, good-humoured and curious, Edith was quick to establish her own group of friends in London society. Among this group, she retained her childhood name of Circe, the name of the Greek goddess of magic who was able to transform humans into animals. Consequently, her coterie became known as The Ark, each adopting humorous nicknames supposedly representing their characters. However, the name they chose for their hostess's husband, Charley the Cheetah, had a double-edged significance. He was a serial and dedicated philanderer whose personal charm seems to have got him off the hook many times. His amorous activities were well known; Charles was consistently unfaithful to Edith from the very start, even conducting an affair with Lady Westmorland during the early days of their engagement. Edith forgave him when it came to light, writing to him, 'Myself, I don't care because I know it is all nonsense [...] Darling, you know I don't mind one little bit.'

He seemed to have a lifelong particular penchant for American women. Charley and Edith's wedding took place on 28 November 1899, but shortly afterwards she discovered that he had been having an affair with a vivacious married American actress, Fannie Ward from St Louis, later known as the 'Perennial Flapper'. Fannie gave birth to Charley's daughter Dorothé on 6 February 1900, a mere ten weeks after the Londonderrys' marriage. Charley also had a lengthy and passionate affair with the American heiress Consuelo Vanderbilt, who was unhappily married to the ninth Duke of Marlborough, his second cousin; the couple ran off to Paris together, to the delighted horror of British society. His longest and most serious extra-marital relationship was with Eloise Ancaster, from New York State, the wife of the Earl of Ancaster. Charley would even enfold notes to Eloise in the letters he sent to Edith, asking her, 'You might send the enclosed to Eloise [...] Put a stamp on and just send it off. That would be very sweet and dear of you.' Both Edith and Charley referred to Eloise as his 'wife', so much was she a constant presence in their lives. He assumed that all parties would accept the situation, and Edith chose once again to excuse her husband, saying, 'I don't blame you because the women hunt you to death. You are so beautiful.'

Perhaps Edith was reluctant to challenge Charley's infidelities because she knew from observation how nasty a soured marriage could be. Her father-in-law, the sixth Marquess of Londonderry, had married Lady Theresa Chetwynd-Talbot, a daughter of the Earl of Shrewsbury, in 1875. Theirs was an arranged marriage, and typical of the advantageous matches made within their social class at that time. It was not unknown for members of the upper classes to indulge in romantic affairs, whether platonic or physical, once both of them had done their duty by providing several children, 'the heir and a spare'. However, absolute discretion was expected on the part of all participants. It was important to avoid scandal by hiding illicit affairs from gossipy contemporaries and social rivals and, even worse, one's own servants.

Within a decade of her marriage, by 1884 Lady Theresa had fallen in love with the Hon. Henry Cust, a notorious 'ladies' man'. Irresistibly charming, it is believed that he was the real father of Lady Diana Manners, daughter of the Duchess of Rutland. Henry was simultaneously enmeshed with Gladys, Countess de Grey, who found and stole a cache of love letters written to him by Theresa Londonderry. Jealous Gladys entertained her friends by reading out selected extracts, but when this palled, she bundled up Theresa's letters and had her footman deliver them to Lord Londonderry in person. He read them, rewrapped them and left them on Theresa's dressing table with a note attached which read, 'Henceforth we do not speak'.

According to salutary accounts of the time, for the next three decades, until his death, Lord Londonderry uttered barely a word to his wife except when absolutely necessary. Polite society had some sympathy, but Lady Londonderry had transgressed, not only by having an affair but also by being caught out in a way that humiliated her husband. However, the truth was less sensational: by the late 1890s the husband was once again writing to his wife with some affection, and he added numerous codicils to his will to ensure she would be well provided for after his death. They were never to be truly close again, and a palpable *froideur* existed between them in private, but the proprieties had to be observed nevertheless and the couple still met their social obligations, entertaining at the highest levels. Year after year, wearing the famous Londonderry jewellery, flashing with diamonds, arch-Tory society hostess Theresa welcomed the great and the good to one of the Parliamentary balls for which Londonderry House was famous, standing at the top of the famous stairs, flanked by her husband and the Prime Minister of the day. For patrician women of Theresa's generation, duty, rank and protocol were the glue that held society together. No wonder she was likened to 'a highwayman in a tiara'.

It was a spirited American woman, born Nancy Langhorne, who revolutionised British politics. Through her marriage to Waldorf Astor she became first the doyenne of Cliveden, the magnificent Italianate house in Buckinghamshire, and later the first woman to take up her seat as an MP in the House of Commons. Queen Victoria would not have approved; indeed she had deplored the sale of Cliveden to an American millionaire, who was to be Nancy's father-in-law. William Waldorf Astor had inherited a vast fortune from his father in 1890. He no longer felt safe in America, as his children had been threatened with kidnap, and he wished to live as an English gentleman. With his wife, Mamie, and their children Waldorf, John Jacob and Pauline, he leased Cliveden in 1892, and the following year the Astors bought it for $1.25 million, worth approximately $41 million today, or £28 million.

Oblivious to royal disapproval, the Anglophile Mr Astor had his magnificent collection of Italian art and antiques shipped to Cliveden. Money was no object to this connoisseur, and he paid for Old World treasures with his New World dollars. He added to the grounds a 200-foot-long carved stone balustrade dating from the seventeenth century that he had bought from the Villa Borghese in Rome. He installed Italian statues and Roman sarcophagi, and planted gardens, trees and topiary. In 1897 William commissioned a huge and exuberant fountain from the American sculptor Thomas Waldo Story; combining marble and volcanic rock, the Fountain of Love seethes with *risqué* Belle Epoque carved figures. Among the modifications to the interiors of the house was the installation of a complete, ornate eighteenth-century room from the Chateau d'Asnières, outside Paris, where Madame de Pompadour had lived. Covered with carved and gilded *boiseries*, it became Cliveden's elegant French Dining Room. Territorial and tetchy by nature, William had a wall topped with broken glass built around much of the estate to deter curious locals; they responded by giving him the nickname Walled-off Astor.

The family divided their time between Cliveden and their town house, 2 Temple Place, in London. However, their happiness was short-lived, as Mamie Astor died shortly before Christmas 1894. Without his beloved wife's moderating influence, William Astor became gradually more doctrinaire and eccentric. He would invite guests to stay for the weekend, but impose a schedule that dictated exactly what they could and could not do while under his roof. His children were similarly ruled with a rod of iron. Ironically William Astor had far more in common with Queen Victoria than either of them might have supposed. He disapproved thoroughly of the Prince of Wales's rather fast 'Marlborough set', with its worldly members such as Mr and Mrs Greville and their great friends George and Alice Keppel; indeed, Astor described her as nothing more than a 'common strumpet', who was not welcome at his house.

When in 1899 he became a British subject, his decision was reviled by the American press, and he took to sleeping with two loaded revolvers beside him, in case of assassination attempts. William Waldorf Astor was determined to infiltrate the higher echelons of British life; in 1892 he bought an influential magazine, the *Pall Mall Gazette*, and turned its editorial tone from Liberal to Conservative. He appointed the ubiquitous playboy and Tory MP Harry Cust as its editor.

William's eldest son, Waldorf Astor, was introverted and shy, like his father, but he also had a strong social conscience and was drawn to public service. He was popular with his contemporaries at both Eton and Oxford, where he joined the Bullingdon Club, hunting with the Bicester and rowing, but this affected his health as he strained his heart. He returned to Cliveden to pursue the life of a country gentleman, shooting and hunting in winter, helping to run the estate, making short trips abroad. In addition, in 1905 he was diagnosed with TB, for which it was recommended he spend several months a year abroad. In December 1905 young Waldorf met Nancy Langhorne Shaw on a transatlantic crossing and was smitten. But by the time she met Waldorf Astor she was also a twenty-six-year-old divorcée with a six-year-old son, Bobbie, in tow.

Nancy was the daughter of Chiswell Dabney Langhorne, a former tobacco planter whose estate, run with slave labour, had been adversely affected by the American Civil War. He became a tobacco auctioneer, then a railroad contractor and made a substantial fortune, which he invested in Virginian real estate. With his wife, Nancy Witcher Keene (who was of Irish extraction), and their five daughters and two sons, the Langhornes moved to a house called Mirador, near Charlottesville.

Like her sisters, Nancy was beautiful and spirited. She was small, slim and blue-eyed, with aquiline features and an acerbic wit. She was highly competitive at sports, a fine horsewoman and an excellent mimic. Nancy was sent to a finishing school in New York, then stayed with her eldest sister, Irene, a great beauty who married the artist Dana Gibson, who used her as his model and muse for the Gibson Girl pictures. Through her sister Nancy met Robert Gould Shaw II, a handsome Bostonian of distinguished background. She married him on 27 October 1897, when she was only eighteen.

The marriage went awry almost from the outset; Robert

had concealed from his naive and inexperienced fiancée the fact that he was an alcoholic. On the second night of the honeymoon Nancy ran away and returned to her family home, Mirador. Mr Langhorne sympathised, but encouraged her to return to her husband, which she did with some reluctance. After the birth of their son Nancy and Robert separated, and in 1903, after six years of marriage, they were divorced, as Robert wanted to marry his pregnant mistress. Nancy was granted custody of little Bobbie, and Robert was 'enjoined and restrained from interfering with Mrs Shaw' by the judge. Two days after his divorce Robert remarried, and Nancy was free.

Traumatised by her experience and now harbouring what would be a lifelong aversion to alcohol, Nancy side-stepped the stigma of divorce by travelling to Europe. In 1904 she and her younger sister Phyllis rented a hunting box in Leicestershire. Nancy and Phyllis were dashing and skilful horsewomen, and they became popular with the local hunting fraternity. Nancy met Edith Cunard, the sister-in-law of Maud. Edith initially suspected the dashing Virginian's motives, saying, 'I suppose you've come over to England to take one of our husbands away from us?' The freshly divorced Nancy replied, 'If you knew what difficulty I had getting rid of my first one, you wouldn't say that', and as a result the women became good friends. The American sisters were particularly valued as an asset at the dining tables of their hunting friends, where their vitality enlivened many an otherwise predictable evening.

Nancy's sparkling personality and ready wit captivated Waldorf Astor when they met on board a transatlantic ship in the autumn of 1905, and they were engaged within four months. They shared the same birth date, 19 May 1879, but were completely different in character: he was quiet and conscientious, tactful and thoughtful; Nancy was volatile and spirited, prone to saying exactly what she thought. Throughout her life she vacillated between being an opinionated and manipulative extrovert with a mischievous capacity to provoke outrage and a deeply sincere and spiritual individual who genuinely cared about people less fortunate than herself.

Waldorf dreaded telling his autocratic father about his love for Nancy, but William accepted his son's choice, declaring, 'If she's good enough for you, Waldorf, she's good enough for me.' As proof of his sincerity, he gave his son's fiancée a spectacular tiara that cost $75,000, the centrepiece of which was the famous Sancy diamond, weighing 55 carats; it is now in the Louvre. This gem had belonged to James I and his son Charles I, and was worn by King Louis XV of France at his coronation. As the bride had been married before, Waldorf and Nancy's wedding took place with little fanfare on 3 May 1906 at the elegant All Souls Church, Langham Place. As a wedding present William gave them Cliveden, and an endowment of several million dollars; Nancy referred to her indulgent father-in-law as 'Old Moneybags'.

Nancy's manner was frank and acerbic, and could be alarming. Edwin Lee, the family's butler, once informed a new member of staff that Waldorf Astor was 'every inch a gentleman', but his verdict on the mistress was: 'she is not a lady as you would understand a lady.' Despite their personality differences, the marriage was successful. Rose Harrison, her maid, described Nancy as 'hot-blooded by nature', and she had five children with Waldorf, as well as her son from her first marriage. However, both Nancy and Waldorf were intensely private and fastidious by nature, and disliked sexual innuendo or vulgarity of any type. They were also inclined to keep their emotions in check in front of servants. Nancy was resolutely faithful to Waldorf and jealous of other women's attentions. Before his marriage, Waldorf had been friendly with both Queen Marie of Romania and the Astors' near neighbour Ettie Desborough, but Nancy made it very plain where his loyalties lay and saw off both her rivals.

Adventurous Maud Burke took a more elastic approach to her marriage vows. The future Lady Cunard was born in San Francisco on 3 August 1872, and details of her early life are sketchy, as many public records were destroyed in the great earthquake of 1906. Her father was of Irish extraction, but he died when Maud was in her early teens. Her mother, who was half-French, was petite and pretty, and expertly cultivated a clutch of male admirers, who competed to provide for her and her daughter. One of Mrs Burke's protectors was William O'Brien of the Nevada Comstock Lode, one of the most important and productive silver mines in the USA. It was suspected by some that little Maud was actually O'Brien's child, as she resembled him and inherited a large sum of money after his death. She never explained the origins of her apparent wealth.

Another of Mrs Burke's gallant protectors was Horace Carpentier, who had been a general in the American Civil War. His fortune was made by buying and selling land; he encouraged Maud's burgeoning passion for both music and great writers, introducing her to Balzac, Shakespeare and the poets of the ancient world. Her favourite novel throughout her life was *Pamela; or, Virtue Rewarded*, by Samuel

Richardson, which she first discovered in Carpentier's library. It is a tale of a virtuous low-born heroine who overcomes many vicissitudes to triumph by marrying the aristocrat who had attempted to seduce her, and being accepted and admired by the upper classes.

When Maud was eighteen, her mother married a stock-broker called Charles Tichenor, but instead of joining their household, Maud moved into the home of her 'guardian', Carpentier, a somewhat unorthodox arrangement even by modern standards. She continued to travel with her mother, and while they were staying in London in May 1894, Maud met the Irish novelist George Moore. She admired his work, and she swapped two of the *placement* cards at a formal luncheon at the Savoy so that they would be seated next to each other. By the end of the meal, the forty-two-year-old bachelor was smitten by the pretty young blonde American in a dress of pink and grey shot silk; she told him, 'George Moore, you have a soul of fire!' He ardently pursued Maud across Europe, but marriage was out of the question as both mother and daughter had a more advantageous match in mind. George Moore realised that she needed to find a wealthy titled husband in order to establish a salon, which was her true ambition. He wrote:

> she had a course and a destination, and I knew well it would have been selfish to delay her. Wiser by far it would be to seek a husband for her, a springboard from which she could leap [...] I mentioned a name and her eyes brightened. 'Do you think so?' Then I knew my hour had sounded.

While in New York, Maud attracted the attentions of Prince André Poniatowski. He was the grandson of the late

King of Poland and possessed a keen business brain. Maud returned to her home town, and when the Prince wrote to her from Paris to say he was planning to visit San Francisco, Maud was sure he was coming to propose marriage. Unwisely she dropped the hint to friends, but was mortified when a local newspaper speculated about their engagement, and the Prince vigorously denied it. In fact, he had fallen for a star of San Francisco society, Beth Sperry, the sister of Mrs Harry Crocker; the Sperrys and the Crockers regarded the Burkes as nobodies.

To save face, Maud countered that her 'guardian', Horace Carpentier, did not approve of Prince André and had threatened to disinherit her if they married. By the time the Prince's true engagement was announced, Maud and her mother were in New York, three thousand miles from the source of their embarrassment. The whole experience was a salutary lesson; personal charm could only take an ambitious young woman so far without either classy antecedents or a considerable fortune, preferably both. What Maud needed was a husband, a wealthy one, whose own social standing would propel her almost effortlessly into the upper strata of society.

With her ability to charm older men, such as Carpentier and Moore, twenty-three-year-old Maud Burke made an immediate conquest of Sir Bache Cunard, aged forty-three, when she met him on the rebound in New York. He was the third Baronet Cunard, the grandson of the Canadian founder of the great shipping line and heir to the family business. Being extremely wealthy, he took little active part in running the family firm, devoting himself to the traditional pursuits of the English squire, playing polo or fox-hunting with hounds at his country estate, Nevill Holt, a romantic fifteenth-century manor house in Leicestershire.

Despite the two-decade age difference and their total lack of common interests, Bache was determined to marry his 'Pocket Venus'. Maud appears to have been similarly keen, although her motivations were inevitably different. Bache's sister wrote to Maud shortly after the engagement was announced, pleading with her to call it off on the grounds that her brother was best suited to bucolic rural pursuits, while his fiancée needed the vitality of city life. Maud refused, saying, 'I like Sir Bache better than any man I know.' Even on the eve of her wedding, she chose the word 'like', not 'love'.

The wedding took place on 17 April 1895, with a ceremony in New York; the Burkes were keen to renounce any ties with San Francisco. Sir Bache and the newly minted Lady Cunard spent a few days in New York, then set sail for England. As was customary among the titled classes, arrangements were made to launch the newcomer in society, and on 22 May 1895 Lady Cunard was among the group of débutantes 'presented' at Buckingham Palace.

Country life with Sir Bache was a far cry from Maud's metropolitan pursuits in San Francisco, New York, Paris or London. Ever since he had inherited Nevill Holt from his brother in 1877, Sir Bache had remorselessly pursued the fox across rural Leicestershire and Rutland with his hunting chums. From his home Sir Bache could hunt six days a week without missing breakfast or dinner. He had a nasty accident in 1887 when hunting with the Maharajah of Cooch Behar, being knocked unconscious in the field, but that didn't deter him, and neither did marriage. By the 1890s it was becoming easier to entice people to stay in the country for the weekend, because of the development of the railways, so an invitation to Nevill Holt from the Cunards was prized by the sporting fraternity.

Meanwhile, Maud dropped any pretence of enjoying getting muddy and hot on the hunting field; as soon as she was pregnant, she devoted herself to filling her drawing room with interesting people. She produced a single daughter, Nancy, born on 10 March 1896, and was determined not to repeat the experience, saying in later years, 'Motherhood is a low thing, the lowest'. She ensured that the child was brought up largely by nursemaids and nannies, and taught by governesses. In time Nancy came to feel resentful towards her mother for the neglect she experienced as a child.

While Sir Bache hunted vermin, Maud collected scalps, using Nevill Holt as her bait. As George Moore wrote, 'You have come into this life to shine in society, to be a light, to form a salon and to gather clever men around you.' Well read and witty, she lured the artistic and the creative, particularly the writers and musicians whom she met on her occasional forays to London. Her favourite house guests included handsome Harry Cust, A. J. Balfour, Herbert Asquith, F. E. Smith, Somerset Maugham, the Duchess of Rutland, Vita Sackville-West, Lord Howard de Walden and Jennie Cornwallis-West, the mother of Winston Churchill. Her old flame George Moore visited regularly after meeting her again in London in 1898.

A certain amount of latitude in marriage was understood among the country house brigade. Lady Cunard always had a number of admirers and flirtations, and some of these appear to have been genuine and reciprocated. When Lord Alexander Thynne was killed in the Great War, love letters from Lady Cunard were found among his papers. Meanwhile George Moore was a constant and ardent admirer; he spent a large part of the summer of 1904 staying at Nevill Holt, and became close to Nancy Cunard, then aged eight, a friendship that endured till his death. There were some who speculated that Moore was Nancy's real father, including Nancy herself, but that seems unlikely, considering the timing and location of the Cunards' marriage. Nevertheless, he continued to send love letters: on 26 January 1905 he wrote from Dublin, 'dearest Maud, you are all I have, it is through you I know that I am alive [...] My heart is overflowing – I must stop writing. When can I see you?'

Nevill Holt was a romantic, venerable stone house in an idyllic setting, with a loggia and porch, a terrace, an oriel window, walled gardens, rolling lawns and avenues of beech trees. Maud transformed the rather stark interiors so that they were attractive and appealing to her sophisticated guests, with vast Chinese bowls full of pot-pourri, hot-house plants, the latest books, subtle textiles, Oriental rugs, Russian cigarettes, writing materials and American standards of comfort. Fashionably dressed visitors came and went constantly, entertained in summer by games of tennis and croquet on the lawns, and in winter by endless games of bridge in front of the roaring log fires. Laughter, gossip and intrigues added colour and zest to Lady Cunard's otherwise rather provincial married life.

Maud had to get to know the country set who lived nearby; for a spirited and well-travelled young woman with a taste for culture, and a lack of interest in field sports, they could be trying, as the overriding interests of her upper-class neighbours were hunting, shooting and parochial matters. Before long she was planning her escape. The Cunards did not have a London home, but Maud wanted to spend time in the capital, so she cultivated people who would invite her to stay. She deliberately timed these trips so as to avoid Sir Bache and his hunting friends. Whenever he was shooting or fishing in Scotland, she would fill Nevill Holt with her friends, the musical, artistic and literary. One sultry evening, during a heatwave, one of her more theatrical guests threw open his bedroom window and sang the Valkyries' cry from Wagner's *Lohengrin*. A similarly musical wit a few rooms away answered with a fluting phrase from *Gotterdämmerung*, and within minutes the entire place was alive with operatic yodelling. Lady Cunard described Sir Bache's reaction to such romantic tomfoolery: 'When my husband came back he noticed an atmosphere of *love*. "I don't understand what is going on in this house, but I don't like it," he said.'

Maud Burke from San Francisco had transcended her obscure origins through marriage. As an American woman, she was difficult for the class-conscious English society to 'place', but she had passed the test of being presented at court as a débutante, and her husband's title, fortune and household surname provided protective camouflage. If she had stayed in the States and married an American man, she might have found it much more difficult to gain acceptance among her native elite. Some Americans were prepared to travel the world to find a niche in society where they could establish themselves as women of influence, and Laura Corrigan was one of them.

She was born Laura Mae Whitrock on 2 January 1879, the daughter of Charles Whitrock and his wife, Emma, *née* Sitherwood. Accounts of Laura's early life are sketchy, but the family were humble. Some claimed that her father was an odd-job man, others said a lumberjack, and in later years Laura was known to demonstrate a level of dexterity with an axe unusual in a society hostess. Her home town was Waupaca, Wisconsin, a small town that in its first census of 1880 registered 1,392 inhabitants. The town is located on the banks of a river and both were named after Sam Waupaca, the chief of the indigenous Potawatomi people. Waupaca's main industry was the Pioneer Foundry, first established in 1871 by John Roche, supplying iron castings to customers in Chicago. It was a rural backwater with harsh winters, and Laura tired of small-town life and moved to Chicago when a young woman. She was ambitious and took a number of jobs, from waitressing at the Hotel Blackstone on Michigan Avenue and working as a telephonist to a freelance role as a society reporter for a Chicago newspaper. She met a Canadian physician, Duncan R. MacMartin, who was the house doctor at the Hotel Blackstone, and they married. But Laura and Duncan were not to stay together; in 1913 they were guests at a party given by James Corrigan. He owned a luxurious summer home on Dry Island, one of the archipelago of 1,864 islands lying along the American–Canadian border where Lake Ontario meets the St Lawrence river. The Thousand Islands, as the area is still known, attracted American and Canadian millionaires, who would buy a small island and have a palatial summer home built on it. The heirs to the Singer sewing machine fortune, John Jacob Astor and Helena Rubinstein, were among those who had elaborate homes here.

The Corrigans were extremely wealthy; James's father was the steel man Captain James C. Corrigan, known also as Jimmy. He had been born poor in Canada, but through perseverance he had established one of the richest steel companies in America with a financial partner, Judge Stevenson Burke. He married Ida, and they had three daughters and a single son, James Junior, who was born on 7 April 1880 and was adored and cossetted. The Corrigan family lived on prestigious Euclid Avenue in Cleveland, a street described by Mark Twain as: 'one of the finest streets in

America [...] none of your poor white trash can live in that street. You have to be redolent of that odor of sanctity which comes with cash. The dwellings are very large, are often pretty pretentious in the matter of architecture, and the grassy and flowery "yards" they stand in are something marvellous.'

By the end of the nineteenth century, nearly 260 mansions lined this prestigious street, with their back gardens running down to Lake Erie. Between 1880 and 1930 Euclid Avenue was known as 'Millionaires' Row', as captains of industry such as John D. Rockefeller had houses there.

However, in 1900, when James Junior was twenty, the Corrigan family suffered an appalling tragedy. While James Senior watched from the shoreline in horror, his wife, Ida, their three daughters and a grand-daughter were drowned when their yacht, *The Idler*, sank on Lake Erie as the result of sudden storm. The only surviving members of the Corrigan clan were the father and son, who had not joined the expedition. Perhaps as a result of the loss of so many of his family, young James found it impossible to settle to the business, preferring to spend his time with a succession of lady friends and working as a barman. He took so little interest in the company that his father made a business decision that was to have far-reaching implications. James Senior appointed his book-keeper, Price McKinney, as his partner and renamed the firm the Corrigan-McKinney Steel Company. By the time he met the ambitious Mrs MacMartin, young James was leading the self-indulgent life of a playboy. Laura was to be the making of him.

2

The Edwardian Summer and the Successful Hostess

E dward VII, known popularly as 'Tum-tum' (though never to his face), was welcomed to the throne in 1902 by the majority of his British subjects, who recognised in him many of their own hedonistic impulses. His reclusive mother, Queen Victoria, the perpetually grieving widow, died in 1901, still blaming her eldest son for the death of her husband, Prince Albert. Edward had a well-deserved reputation as a *bon viveur*. He positively enjoyed good living, luxury, the new-fangled thrills of motoring, fast racehorses and even faster women. He had an eye for beauty, but he also enjoyed the companionship of women, their conversation and their friendship. His last and best-known mistress was Alice Keppel, known as 'La Favorita'. When his coronation was being planned, Edward insisted that Alice must be among his special friends in a screened-off section of the public gallery, above the ranks of peers and peeresses in Westminster Abbey. Inevitably, some wag designated the seating as 'the King's Loose Box'. The other ladies to be favoured in this way included Alice's great friend Mrs Margaret Greville, the world-famous actress Sarah Bernhardt and Mrs Arthur Paget, a beautiful American-born heiress and society hostess. Another guest, Theresa, Lady Londonderry, Edith's formidable mother-in-law, caused a sensation in the Peeresses' cloakroom by demanding a pair of forceps from behind the closed door.

The famous Londonderry Tiara had ended up in the water closet while she was using the facilities, and specialist tools were needed to retrieve it.

Edward VII benefited from the collusion of sympathetic hostesses, who could provide him and his mistresses with comfortable country house settings in which he could indulge his passions. Discretion was all, of course, and it was with his trusted inner circle of friends, the Marlborough House set, that he spent much of his leisure. Among his favourites were Ronnie and Maggie Greville, who entertained in luxury in their house, 11 Charles Street in Mayfair. As Mrs Greville's god-daughter recalled, 'Throughout most of Kingy's reign I can see her, small but forceful, making her way to the front of any company she was in'. The Grevilles occasionally rented a place in Surrey to entertain house parties, but they needed a country estate of their own for weekends, so that they could compete with their landowning contemporaries. In 1906 Mr McEwan bought the Surrey estate of Polesden Lacey for £80,000 and gave it to his 'stepdaughter' and her husband. It was just 22 miles from London, a very desirable property, at the centre of which was a handsome 1824 villa by Thomas Cubitt. The house had been redesigned and extended for the previous owner, and now Mrs Greville resolved to turn it into a house fit for a king.

Mrs Ronnie had been an early enthusiast for the new hotels that opened in London at the turn of the century. For the first time respectable ladies could dine in public with men in well-lit, comfortable restaurants within hotels, rather than in the rather louche 'private dining rooms' such establishments had previously provided. Inspired by the example of the Ritz Hotel on Piccadilly, near her Mayfair home, she engaged the same architects, Mewès and Davis, who had worked logistical and stylistic miracles on the hotel's congested and challenging site. They transformed Polesden Lacey, creating the epitome of modern luxury within a traditional country house. Their client required ample central heating, *en suite* bathrooms and endless hot water. She wanted a telephone switchboard, with extensions in each of the principal bedrooms and main rooms. The kitchens were state-of-the-art, to ensure that the quality of food and drink was sublime. By employing the very best staff, she ensured that the house was run like the very best hotel. The architects worked in a variety of historical styles, and the resulting interiors were sumptuous, with gilded *boiseries* acquired from an Italian palazzo, plaster ceilings copied from the best Tudor examples and museum-quality Chinese ceramics and Italian maiolica. The paintings were of the best quality, and no expense was spared to provide the *arriviste* Mrs Greville with the sort of authentic setting that the daughter of a long-established aristocratic family might consider her natural habitat.

Margaret intended that Polesden Lacey should be fit to entertain the King. But before the metamorphosis was complete, tragedy struck. In March 1908 her charming forty-four-year-old husband was diagnosed with throat cancer, and had to have an operation to remove his larynx. Ronnie survived the surgery but succumbed to pneumonia and was dead within a week. Margaret had genuinely loved him, and his loss was devastating. After a period of mourning she started to socialise again, often accompanied by Mr McEwan, who was a widower, Margaret's mother having died in 1906. Her great triumph was to have Edward VII to stay at Polesden Lacey in 1909, with her dear friend Alice Keppel, who was Edward's mistress. The King complimented Mrs Greville on her 'genius for hospitality'.

For any ambitious would-be hostess, it was vital to have an impressive home in the country, for weekend entertaining, as well as a place in London. When he handed over the keys to Cliveden in 1906, William Waldorf Astor had breezily assured his son and new daughter-in-law that he would never return. Consequently, Nancy transformed the formal High Victorian interiors from the 'splendid gloom' of her father-in-law's era into a more welcoming house, with comfortable chintz-covered furniture and curtains, modern books and flowers in every room. The suits of armour were sent down to Hever Castle in Kent, where Waldorf's father was busy creating another idealised historic house. However, in 1907 the Astors' first son was born and named William Waldorf after his grandfather, who announced he would visit Cliveden after all in order to see the latest addition to the clan. The couple were apprehensive, but he accepted their modifications, saying, 'The first joy of possession is to change everything around and remould it nearer to the heart's desire.'

Cliveden was a very grand and largely self-contained estate. White Place, its home farm, supplied fresh produce to the house and its occupants. At its height there were fifty outdoor staff, including gardeners, stable hands and coachmen, estate workers and groundsmen. The indoor staff numbered around twenty and included housemaids and kitchen staff, a valet and three footmen, a ladies' maid, a French chef, a head housekeeper and the butler. The outdoor staff lived with their families in estate cottages, while the domestic staff lived inside the west wing of the house. Former servants helped when required for large social events such as banquets and balls. As befitted their rank and wealth, the Astors' household was run to exacting and formal standards. Until the advent of the Great War, the butler and footmen powdered their hair and wore formal livery, including knee-breeches, while serving dinner.

Cliveden was set on a steep wooded hill looking to the Thames on one side and across terraces and gardens on the others. The ground floor contained a vast front hall, a drawing room overlooking the river, a panelled library, a Louis XV dining room, Lord Astor's study and Lady Astor's boudoir. There were forty-six guest bedrooms, and the Astors liked to entertain great groups of visitors for the weekend. Nancy would impulsively invite additional guests to join them at the last minute, which often caused chaos in the extensive kitchens. In order to fit everyone around her dining table, she dictated that each diner should only be allowed eighteen inches of the table's perimeter to accommodate their place settings and persons. Burly Winston Churchill complained that, while he could get his knees under the Astors' table, he could not then move to sample any of the thirty courses served at dinner. The Cliveden butler discreetly sought the advice of the High Priest of his fraternity, the Head Steward at Buckingham Palace. 'Two foot 6 inches per guest', came the Delphic reply. Thereafter Cliveden guests were allocated enough elbow room to wield their cutlery in comfort.

Nancy's manner as a hostess was refreshingly natural and informal by the standards of Edwardian England. She rarely appeared in front of her guests before lunchtime, leaving them to make their own amusements in the morning, but was frank and funny when she did appear, and would galvanise any group with her immense energy and charm. She was a startlingly effective mimic and a skilful raconteur, with a great sense of fun; midway through a meal she would suddenly pop a pair of celluloid stage dentures into her mouth and imitate Margot Asquith.

The guest list of those who visited Cliveden in the Edwardian era reads like a combination of *Who's Who* and Burke's Peerage. Literary guests abounded, such as J. M. Barrie, the author of *Peter Pan,* and Rudyard Kipling. Foreign royalty were as welcome as their British relations; the unassuming and popular Crown Prince Gustav of Sweden was such a favourite that he was lent the Astor family holiday home at Sandwich in Kent for his honeymoon when he married Lady Louise Mountbatten. King Edward VII had a particular penchant for pert American beauties; on one occasion Nancy Astor side-stepped his request to play bridge with the knowing reply 'I'm afraid I can't tell a King from a Knave', exactly the sort of suggestive remark he appreciated.

'Edward the Caresser', as he was known, admired American women for their *brio* and worldly wit, and he liked pretty Lady Cunard too, who joined his social circle in Marienbad. The King was 'taking the cure' at the German spa town, supposedly purging the overloaded royal digestive system through saunas, baths, massages and epicurean meals. Maud dined with the King and his entourage, but she made the error of attempting to amuse the table by discussing a racy novel by Elinor Glyn, *The Visits of Elizabeth,* in which a naive young girl is puzzled by the nocturnal creaking of corridors in a country house. A fellow guest at the table was an unmarried woman, and such frank talk in front of an 'innocent' was a singular breach of etiquette. The King cut her off by turning away and pointedly changing the subject; he was a veteran corridor-creeper himself, but he observed the proprieties in public. Maud was reprimanded afterwards by an equerry, and hid in her hotel for a few days after this gaffe. It was the first time she made herself *persona non grata* with the royal family, but it would not be the last.

Maud seized any opportunity to travel; she made frequent trips to London to attend the opera, sometimes taking her daughter with her, and in 1906 they travelled to America in some style on a Cunard liner to see Horace Carpentier, who was now living in Saratoga. In the summer of 1910, as soon as Sir Bache returned from a trip to Scotland, Maud went to Munich with George Moore to hear Wagner. It was evident that Maud was keen to avoid Sir Bache at any cost.

Travel for its own sake also captivated the Colefaxes. During the Edwardian era Sibyl and Arthur took advantage of the long Bar vacations to explore Europe. They travelled *en famille* throughout the Low Countries, Germany, the Italian Alps, northern Italy, Tuscany, Umbria and the Balkans. They also rented houses in the country, once their two sons had been born: Peter in March 1903 and Michael in June 1906. Through a very distant cousin of Sibyl's, Eliza Wedgwood, and her neighbour Lady Elcho the Colefaxes met notable writers and intellectuals, such as H. G. Wells, James Barrie and the Webbs. Sibyl also cultivated Lawrence Johnston of Hidcote, whom she first met in 1906; he was a reclusive man obsessed with creating his astonishing garden, and he shunned company, except for those who shared his passion for horticulture. Sibyl tackled him like a project, reading extensively on the subject and visiting other exceptional gardens. She conversed with Johnston from a position of genuine knowledge, and they remained friends for life.

In contrast to Sibyl's rather lonely, isolated and tense childhood, she and Arthur were keen for their children to have an idyllic upbringing, and they were allowed more liberty than most children of the era. The Colefaxes liked country house life and often stayed with wealthier friends such as the diamond millionaire and philanthropist Alfred Beit, and his brother Sir Otto Beit, who in 1906 inherited Alfred's lovely house called Tewin Water in Hertfordshire. Through Arthur's work, the family were becoming well connected. Molly Harmsworth, later Lady Northcliffe, was one of Michael Colefax's godmothers, and Sibyl and Arthur often stayed with the Northcliffes at Sutton Place in Surrey. When Lord Northcliffe bought the *Observer* in 1905, it was the Colefaxes who introduced him to the man he subsequently appointed as the paper's editor, J. L. Garvin, at an intimate little dinner at their home. Sibyl wanted to establish for herself a virtual colony of intelligent, entertaining friends, much as she had found by accident that spring in Florence.

The Colefaxes continued to explore Europe, visiting Spain in 1908 and Greece and Turkey in 1909. In 1911 they sailed from Liverpool to Canada, where Sybil was struck by the number of upper-class women who did their own cooking and cleaning, servants being a rarity. They stayed at the Canadian home of their friends the Northcliffes. In her diary Sibyl noted the financial success of entrepreneurs of all stripes in the New World – her nascent business skills were burgeoning.

Edward VII died in 1910, and the widowed Margaret Greville attended his funeral, as she had his coronation. The new King, George V, had disapproved of his father's infidelities and was scrupulously faithful to his own wife, Queen Mary. George was aware that Mrs Greville had facilitated the King's affair with Mrs Keppel. While Alice tactfully left for a lengthy tour of the Far East, Mrs Greville met and struck up a friendship with Queen Mary that was to have far-reaching repercussions for the royal family. The two women shared a love of beautiful objects, paintings and furniture, and their knowledge of the fine and decorative arts was largely self-taught. In addition, Mrs Greville continued to take an interest in politics; both her husband and her father had been MPs. In fact, in the early twentieth century, four of the husbands of the six Queen Bees were or became Members of Parliament.

Waldorf Astor's decision to go into politics was initially due to his indifferent health. Having been advised in 1908 to abandon all strenuous physical exercise, his social conscience led him to a new career. In 1910 he was elected Conservative MP for the Sutton division of Plymouth, and he subsequently concentrated on promoting Anglo-American relations, agriculture and health. Nancy and Waldorf were an effective working partnership; she would campaign on his behalf in Plymouth by the simple method of knocking on doors and appealing to the startled householders: 'My husband is standing for Parliament. Will you vote for him?' As well as having a large family, Nancy threw herself into entertaining the wealthy and the influential, both at Cliveden and at their London base, 4 St James's Square.

Despite her apparent *joie de vivre*, Nancy suffered from bouts of ill-health during the early years of her marriage. Child-bearing was a considerable strain on women of the era, even well-off ones. Regardless of how many staff and servants they might employ once the child was born, antenatal care was still fairly rudimentary, and obstetrical procedures were primitive; in addition, in an age before antiseptics and antibiotics, the process of giving birth carried the risk of puerperal fever, which killed many otherwise healthy women. Nancy and Waldorf had a large family of five children together. William Waldorf was born in 1907, (Nancy) Phyllis Louise in 1909 and (Francis) David Langhorne in 1912, but after the births of these three children Lady Astor lacked all vitality and was prescribed bed rest by her doctors, which left her depressed and restless. However, in 1913 she discovered the writings of Mary Baker Eddy; the American founder of Christian Science had published *Science and Health with Key to the Scriptures* in 1875. With the zeal of the convert Nancy Astor read an extract from this book every day for the rest of her life. She was convinced that all sickness was mere 'error', and that people could cure themselves through willpower alone. She saw infirmity of any sort as due to a lack of faith, an attitude that was later to alienate her own ailing husband and family. Christian Science was a philosophy that suited Nancy Astor's natural self-belief and innate determination. She was unstoppable in her energies, and unshakeable in her beliefs.

As Waldorf's Parliamentary career developed, they entertained on an impressive scale, giving several balls a year for five hundred guests at a time and dinner parties for sixty. Most weekends they would have twenty or thirty house guests staying at Cliveden, the elite of London society or the upper circles of the political world. Like Nancy, Waldorf was teetotal, even though his father William stoutly declared that he had drunk wine every day of his life since the age of seven, and insisted that his robust health was due to his reliance on stimulants. Nevertheless the Astors provided excellent wines for their visitors, but canny guests could ensure preferential treatment, thanks to the ministrations of the expert butler, Mr Lee, who was happy to provide alcoholic refreshments for house guests in their rooms, and was well-rewarded with tips.

Lavish hospitality was also on offer at the Londonderrys' luxurious homes, where political entertaining was in their blood. Despite being handsome and charming, their eldest son, Charley, was not considered especially intelligent or politically astute by his contemporaries. He never forgot that he was a direct descendant of Robert Castlereagh, the architect of the settlement at the Congress of Vienna in 1815, which brought a negotiated peace to Europe after the Napoleonic Wars. Along with his spectacular wealth, Charley had inherited a belief that, like his illustrious ancestor, he was a natural statesman and diplomat, born to lead. He entered Parliament as the Tory MP for Maidstone in 1906, a post he held till he inherited his father's title in 1915, gaining nine years' valuable experience of Parliament.

Meanwhile Edith devoted herself to raising a family, producing five children over two decades: Maureen was born in 1900, Edward (known as Robin) in 1902, Margaret in 1910, Helen in 1911 and Mairi in 1921. She also supported her husband's career, learning the social duties expected of her as a grand Tory lady, by observing Lady Theresa, doyenne of massive political receptions at Londonderry House. However, Edith was not a natural conservative; she was developing a robust political consciousness of her own, and she clashed with her intimidating mother-in-law. Edith supported the Suffragists, led by Millicent Fawcett, who believed that they should use legal and constitutional means to achieve votes for women. (The Suffragettes, on the other hand, stated they would use any means possible to achieve the same end.) Edith had written a letter to *The Times* in April 1912, in reply to a seething diatribe against women's suffrage, and Edith's mother-in-law, Theresa, was appalled at what she called 'a young hound running riot'. As Edith recorded afterwards, 'henceforth my attitude in home circles was regarded with grave misgivings[7]'.

While the Suffragists attempted to engage in reasoned political debate and won some sympathy among the elite, the more militant Suffragettes were deplored by the establishment because of their strident demands for votes for women. They were willing to confront politicians face to face, which was considered unseemly, and Winston Churchill was a particular target. On two occasions, when he was staying at Rest Harrow, the seaside holiday home owned by the Astors at Sandwich in Kent, protesting Suffragettes attempted to block the road to deny him access, but he managed to avoid them. It was ironic that this should happen at one of Nancy's houses, since she was later to become the first female MP to take her seat in Parliament.

Arthur Colefax was briefly the Conservative MP for a Manchester constituency in 1910 but lost the seat in 1911, when the Liberals triumphed in a general election. He was considered as a candidate for the seat of Hythe in 1912 but was passed over in favour of Philip Sassoon, who later befriended a number of the hostesses. Meanwhile Arthur 'took silk', becoming a KC in 1912; his career was thriving, and he joined the Athenaeum and Garrick clubs. With their new-found prosperity Sibyl fulfilled a long-held ambition to buy a comfortable and roomy house in the country, where she could entertain their theatrical and musical friends for weekends. In 1912 they acquired Old Buckhurst, in Kent, a Tudor property that had been converted into an attractive, idiosyncratic house. Sibyl decorated and furnished the place with imagination and natural taste, and also tackled the garden, relying on the advice of Lawrie Johnston of Hidcote. The Colefaxes' income was still unreliable as they were largely dependent on Arthur's legal fees, so Sibyl always budgeted carefully for the improvements she made to their houses and the copious entertaining of their ever-growing coterie of friends.

No such financial restrictions curbed Mrs Greville's plans. She became one of the wealthiest women in the country, but sadly it was through the death of her father. Frail and elderly, William McEwan had been knocked down by a horse-drawn carriage while crossing the road near Hyde Park, and on 12 May 1913 he passed away at his London home. Maggie was with him at the end, and mourned him sincerely. The relationship between McEwan and his supposed stepdaughter was extremely close, and it is significant that he left her an estate worth £1.5 million, the equivalent of about £65 million today. He also included two-thirds of the voting shares in McEwan's brewery, a significant bequest as he had two nephews working in the business, sons of his sister Janet Younger, and might have left the shares to them. Maggie also inherited his grand Mayfair home, 16 Charles Street, formerly the home of the Earls of Craven.

Margaret Greville was now fifty years old; she was extremely rich, but she had no husband or children, no close relatives, and both her parents were dead. In that era widows were expected to live quietly, perhaps retiring to the country with deferential staff, employing a sedate paid companion, indulging their pets, socialising a little with the local gentry – perhaps an occasional supper party or a game of bridge. However, Margaret Greville was made of sterner stuff, and she was resolved that once her year-long period of mourning was over, she would return to the fray and re-establish herself as one of London's leading society hostesses. She invested in pearls and diamonds (jewels deemed suitable to be worn with mourning by Queen Victoria, the acknowledged authority on the subject) and threw herself into cultivating the political elite of London. She also commissioned extensive improvements at her father's former home, 16 Charles Street, once again employing her favourite architects, Mewès and Davis.

While Mrs Greville was targeting the establishment, Lady Cunard was planning her escape from the squirearchy. At the Munich music festival in 1910, Maud and George Moore were both injured and narrowly escaped death under the wheels of a runaway car that ploughed into the crowd, killing two and injuring many. Perhaps this event made Maud consider her life to date, and her future. Despite the social status and financial security it provided, her sixteen-year marriage to Sir Bache had become unbearable, and in August 1911 scandal erupted. Early one morning some estate workmen using ladders to repair the stable block's clock tower at Nevill Holt spotted Lady Cunard through her open bedroom window, and she was not alone. One of the house guests, the conductor Thomas Beecham, was with her. For a married woman of any class, being caught in bed with a man who wasn't her husband transgressed every social taboo. Even worse, the witnesses were Sir Bache's employees. Like Caesar's wife, the squire's lady had not only to be above reproach but also to be seen to be so, to command the respect of the lower classes for the upper crust. Maud could no longer continue her old life, even if she wanted to. Once more Lady Cunard set out for London, taking Nancy with her, but this time she had no intention of returning.

Maud had fallen in love with Thomas Beecham; now she created a new home in London near him. Because the Asquiths were in residence at 10 Downing Street, 20 Cavendish Square was vacant. Lady Cunard rented it from her friends and had it redecorated at extravagant expense. The drawing room was littered with rare books, bibelots and antiques, and the interior was redecorated in fashionable Ballets Russes style; Beecham's orchestra had played for Diaghilev's dance company when they took London by storm in 1911. Lady Cunard adopted the strong colours and exotic finishes used to such great effect by the ballet's designer, Léon Bakst. She acquired a dining table with an inlaid lapis lazuli top, and elegant Louis Quinze furniture, whose gilded frames shone against the walls of emerald green. Lady Cunard created a remarkable interior, like a theatrical set, against which to set her players. Here she could entertain to her heart's content the pretty, the smart, the intelligent, the powerful and the *risqué*. It was an eclectic mix of people, and, unlike more traditional hostesses of that era, she found it most stimulating to mix people from diverse walks of life. Lord Berners, Winston Churchill, Mrs Patrick Campbell, the Londonderrys and Somerset Maugham might find themselves rubbing shoulders with the Prince of Wales and, of course, Thomas Beecham.

Beecham's grandfather had founded the company manufacturing the eponymous liver pills, and established the family fortune. However, Thomas Beecham, born in 1879, had fallen out with his father, Joseph, because he had confined Thomas's mother to an asylum. The resulting family rift meant that for a number of years father and son were estranged, and Thomas struggled financially while establishing himself as a conductor. Wealthy Lady Cunard had considerable charms for him, including her financial generosity.

Thomas Beecham had married a resonantly named American, Utica Celestia Welles, in 1903 and they had two sons, born in 1904 and 1909. Thomas first encountered Lady Cunard at a dinner party in London in late 1909. She was six years older than him, but they shared a passion for music and their friendship developed. She invited him to stay at Nevill Holt; his first visit there was 16 August 1910, and during the following year he stayed there on seven further occasions, the last visit being on 14 August 1911. Beecham ended the love affair he was currently conducting with a married woman called Maud Foster in order to embark on the burgeoning love affair with Lady Cunard; as all three of them were married, discretion was essential.

But within three months of the revelations at Nevill Holt there was a further scandal. In October 1911 Beecham was named as co-respondent in a divorce case. While he and Mrs Foster were still having an affair, Thomas had written her an exuberant letter describing a reconciliation with his father. The letter was hidden in a stocking, where it was discovered by the housekeeper, who handed it to Mr Foster. A second letter came to light, and Mr Foster petitioned to have their marriage dissolved on the grounds of adultery. Even legal representation from Charles Dickens's son, Henry Dickens KC, could not convince the judge that Thomas and Maud had been just good friends. Beecham's handsome appearance was probably against him; the *News of the World* enthusiastically described him as looking like 'a smart French army officer, being tall and slim, with neatly trimmed, glistening black hair, a thick black moustache and chin-beard, and large, dark expressive eyes'. The judge agreed to a decree nisi, and Beecham was left with a hefty bill for the costs, a sum of £695 (more than £45,000 in today's values) as well as his own expenses.

Beecham separated from his wife, Utica, in February 1912, moving into his club, but she refused to divorce him. However, his professional career went from strength to strength; in May 1912 he was named as one of the conductors for Diaghilev's Ballets Russes. He conducted the thrillingly modern *Scheherazade* by Rimsky-Korsakov seven times, with the astonishing dancer Nijinsky as its star. It was the sensation of musical London. Following this triumph, he and Lady Cunard holidayed together in Venice. She had comprehensively 'burned her boats' in leaving her husband to live in London near her lover. The events of 1911 and 1912 had proved that she would not be the exclusive recipient of Beecham's affections, but that did not deter her.

George Moore was outraged by Maud's affair with Beecham; he had loved her faithfully since before her marriage, and had remained single. In 1911 he had moved permanently from Ireland to London to be closer to her. Moore's letters from that era are querulous and resentful; her decision to leave her husband, not for him but for some married musical Lothario, obviously rankled. 'Why you should wish to hear my impressions of the music it is difficult to think, for you know many musicians who can talk about it better than I can [...] I did not remain till the end of the concert because I wished to fly from your world, which is not my world', he wrote on 21 January 1913. Moore did not want to join Maud's new social circle, which now nearly always included her lover, but insisted on seeing her on her own. 'I thought you might be coming to dine with me. You didn't because you feared you mightn't be amused all the while, and of course life is intolerable if it be not always at concert pitch', he wrote in January 1914. The antipathy was mutual; Beecham was always dismissive of Moore's prior claim on Lady Cunard. In 1957 he remarked that Moore was the sort of person who 'didn't kiss, but told' – in other words, a romantic fantasist.

While Joseph Beecham arranged a season of Russian opera in London for his son to conduct, and provided a smart town house for him in Belgravia, Maud did everything possible to further his career, persuading her fashionable and aristocratic friends to take boxes when he was conducting. A Drury Lane season of opera opened in May 1914, with *Der Rosenkavalier,* brilliantly conducted by Thomas Beecham without a score, a *tour de force*. He also conducted the first nights of Diaghilev's productions of Rimsky-Korsakov's *Le Coq d'Or* and *La Légende de Joseph* in June 1914. Margot Asquith, the Prime Minister's wife, in black tulle and diamonds was among the many VIP guests who joined Lady Cunard's box at yet another fashionable musical sensation.

It was Maud who arranged for Joseph Beecham to be created a baronet in the King's birthday honours of 1914, by exerting pressure on her landlord, Prime Minister Asquith, who found it impossible to resist her constant cajoling. The composer Delius wrote to his wife saying, 'Lady C – who had brought it of course all about, is exultant'. Duff Cooper also recorded in his diary that Joseph Beecham had paid £4,000 to Lady Cunard, £5,500 to Edward Horner, a relation by marriage of Asquith, and £500 to Lady Diana Manners.

Lady Cunard's exploitation of her establishment contacts to benefit her lover's father was impressive, but Mrs Greville's overtures to the royal family were positively Machiavellian. Just over a year after the death of her father, on 25 May 1914, she wrote a personal letter to King George V, and it survives in the Royal Archives, a handwritten masterpiece in manipulation. Mrs Greville outlined her concerns about what might happen to her enormous wealth and her country estate after she was gone, and wondered disingenuously whether she should leave a bequest to a member of the royal family:

the fact is that I am alone in the world, I love Polesden Lacey, I have nobody to bequeath it to and I can never forget King Edward's kindness to me, he helped me to face life. He was an angel to me and if Your Majesty would consent, I should feel so happy if one of his descendants lived here. I made a will last March extract (copy) of which I enclose […] if Your Majesty disapproved of what I have done, to save trouble when I am gone I could revoke it − I left the sum of £300,000 to go with the place and an additional £50,000 for possible alterations […] it is so sad to have nobody and I just can't bear to think Polesden may have to go the same way.

King George V rapidly revised his former disapproving attitude to Mrs Greville. Within three weeks of receiving the letter, on 14 June 1914, he and Queen Mary visited Polesden Lacey for the day, to discuss her proposal. He recorded in his diary:

Mrs Ronny [*sic*] Greville gave us tea, she showed us all over her lovely house and gardens, a most charming place. She told me confidentially that she intends leaving the place to one of my sons with at least £300,000 to keep it up, to be selected by me and to belong to him and his descendants for ever. He will indeed be a lucky boy.

The 'lucky boy' was the second son, Prince Albert, as his elder brother, the Prince of Wales (known to his family as David), would inherit the Duchy of Cornwall, which would provide him with a substantial income. In addition, when David became King he would have a number of royal residences in which to live: Windsor, Sandringham, Balmoral and, of course, Buckingham Palace. But dutiful Prince Bertie, shy, slightly knock-kneed and hindered by a bad stammer, would be set up for life by a bequest of this generosity, a vast and prosperous country estate and the modern cash equivalent of approximately £15 million for its maintenance. Unsurprisingly, the King and Queen subsequently regarded Mrs Greville with great favour, and all members of the royal family, especially young Bertie, were encouraged to cultivate her at every opportunity. Mrs Greville took great delight in her royal rehabilitation, using it to re-launch her career as the best-connected hostess in London society. Satisfied with the success of her negotiations, she left the decorators in occupation at 16 Charles Street and set out for her summer holiday. She was joining a house party of lively friends at a beautiful mansion called Clingendael in the Netherlands. It was July 1914, and there was barely a cloud in the sky.

The intrepid, well-connected and well-travelled Colefaxes were among the first to get an inkling of the disaster that was about to engulf Europe. For their summer holidays in 1913 they had visited Sarajevo, then a sleepy backwater of the Balkans. It was completely by chance that a year later they were staying with the Northcliffes at Sutton Place on Sunday 28 June 1914. Sibyl remembered enjoying an idyllic tea on the sunlit lawn under the cedars when a telegram arrived addressed to Molly Harmsworth from her husband, Lord Northcliffe, the press baron, who had returned to town earlier that afternoon. It read: 'The Heir Apparent to the Throne of Austria and his wife were murdered at Sarajevo at 2.30 today, signed N.' That small group of people were among the first in Britain to hear the news of the assassination that signalled the start of the Great War.

While Lady Cunard dedicated herself to advancing the career of her lover Thomas Beecham, her daughter Nancy was devising her own social life. She was 'presented' at court and was launched on a social life in 1914, the last season before the war. Nancy often clashed with her mother; she always resented having been suddenly transplanted from rural Leicestershire to London. She missed her father and felt sorry for his isolation because of Her Ladyship's affair. Maud saw Nancy as a decorative adjunct to her social life, but Nancy became a truculent and difficult teenager. Asked during a parlour game who she would most like to see next enter the room, she replied, 'Lady Cunard, *dead*'.

Highly strung and volatile, when she was eighteen Nancy witnessed a tragedy that probably affected her subsequent mental health. On the evening of 2 July 1914 a group of fifteen well-heeled young people boarded a pleasure launch at Westminster to sail up the Thames for a midnight supper party. The dance music was provided by a small band selected from Beecham's orchestra. The party-goers included Lady Diana Manners and her future husband, Duff Cooper, Raymond Asquith (the eldest son of the Prime Minister), Iris Beerbohm Tree (Nancy's best friend), Count Constantin Benckendorff (the son of the Russian Ambassador) and Sir Denis Anson, a hot-headed young aristocrat who had inherited his title just a month before. At 3 a.m., near Battersea Bridge, Denis Anson suddenly took off his jacket and his watch and dived into the Thames, probably as the result of a bet. He was swept away by the strong tide, and one of the musicians, William Mitchell, jumped in to save him, as did Count Benckendorff. The Russian was picked up by a launch, but the other two men were lost, and their bodies were not found for several days. Nancy arrived home at 6 a.m. severely traumatised, and had to be put to bed. The casual loss of two of their number horrified the *jeunesse d'orée*, the wealthy and cultured crowd with whom Nancy Cunard was mixing, but worse was to follow; within a month Britain found itself dragged into a conflict that would decimate the youth of that generation.

3

The Great War

———

When the news first broke in Britain that the Austrian Archduke Franz Ferdinand and his wife had been shot by an opportunist Serbian nationalist after their chauffeur became lost in Sarajevo, on the evening of 28 June 1914, there was little reaction at first. The Court Ball was postponed, and several embassy dinner parties were cancelled, but the incident was largely dismissed as an isolated murderous act in a rather obscure corner of Central Europe. King George V had a slightly better grasp of the possible implications, but typically viewed it as another anarchic attack on the institution of monarchy, observing sagely that it must have been a dreadful shock for the Austro-Hungarian Emperor.

Country Life briefly abandoned its usual fare of articles such as 'The Heron as Pet' or 'Are Salmon Colour-Blind?' to run an editorial on 4 July 1914, speculating that 'Doom and woe shadow the Royal Family of Hapsburg [sic] as they did the characters of Greek tragedy', but overall the upper classes were more concerned with the issue of Home Rule for Ireland and the outcome of the annual cricket match between Eton and Harrow.

Osbert Sitwell, who was in the army, noted that throughout his life to date many members of royal families and foreign heads of state had been assassinated, so he and his fellow officers initially overlooked yet another skirmish in the Balkans. However, he was aware that throughout the summer of 1914 there had been unprecedented signs of restlessness among four of his army friends. One yearned to join a polar expedition; another was mulling over a transfer to an African regiment; the third wanted a ranch in South America; while the fourth dreamed of exploring China. Coincidentally, Sitwell wrote, there was a craze in London for consulting a celebrated palm-reader, but she was dismissed as a charlatan when, time after time, she appeared to 'dry', unable, she explained, to see any indication of the future in the palms of her young male clients. Meanwhile, as Sitwell recorded, the parties continued:

> The whole of London still seethed with a feeling of summer and gaiety. The children of the rich feasted, and from the ballrooms, wreathed in roses where they waltzed to the deep-hearted rhythm of the Rosenkavalier Waltz, the sons could not see the ruins, the broken arches and cut and twisted trees which were all their future [...] no-one mentioned the possibility of war.

On 28 July, Austria declared war on Serbia, and Winston Churchill, the First Lord of the Admiralty, ordered the British Fleet to war station. By the beginning of August the situation had escalated, and it seemed that Britain could not avoid being drawn into a Continental war; the Foreign Secretary, Sir Edward Grey, warned that 'it can but end in the greatest catastrophe that has ever befallen the Continent of Europe at one blow'.

The outbreak of the Great War seems to have caught the British establishment largely by surprise. It was so little antici-pated that the Prime Minister's own daughter, seventeen-year-old Elizabeth Asquith, had left for a holiday in the Netherlands with Mrs Ronnie Greville and the Keppels on 25 July, only nine days before hostilities were declared. The house party included the Duchess of Rutland, her daughter Lady Diana Manners, Harry Cust (widely believed to be Lady Diana's father), Lord and Lady Ilchester, Lady de Trafford and her daughter, Sir Fritz and Lady Ponsonby and their children, and the charming royal fixer and Mrs Ronnie's relative by marriage, Sir Sidney Greville. Clingendael, the exquisite mansion in which they were all staying, picturesquely spanned a canal and had rose-garlanded stables, a Japanese garden and an observatory. Amply staffed and provided with a fleet of chauffeur-driven motors, Clingendael was an idyllic setting for this large group of wealthy friends. They had known each other since before the reign of their favourite monarch, Edward VII, and still enjoyed each other's company. As in the old days, George Keppel had devised an itinerary of expeditions and amusements for every day, from barge trips and picnics to visits to cheese factories and picture galleries, arrangements described by Harry Cust as 'George's summer manoeuvres'.

However, it was 'summer manoeuvres' of another type that brought an abrupt halt to the fun. First Elizabeth Asquith received a telegram from Margot, her stepmother, urgently recalling her to Britain. She made the return trip by boat with a number of young Englishmen who had been summoned to rejoin their regiments, but still very few people seemed alert to the situation. Then, out of a clear blue sky, it seemed, on Sunday 2 August the British newspapers carried reports that the Germans had crossed the frontiers of France and Luxembourg. Urgent telegrams were despatched to holiday-makers on the Continent, and the dash began for the Channel. In complete contrast to the leisurely and luxurious outward trip, the house party packed and hurried to the coast.

By the following day, Bank Holiday Monday, the international crisis was on everyone's minds as the nation played cricket, paddled or watched their children build sand-castles. That evening the boat from the Hook of Holland arrived at Harwich, carrying 780 exhausted and stressed passengers instead of the usual 100 holiday-makers. Alice Keppel, needless to say, had been provided with two cabins by the purser; the old King's mistress could still turn on the charm when necessary.

When war was declared, there was a great reaction of patriotism and jingoism. Recruiting efforts were apparent everywhere; music-hall singers warbled, 'We don't want to lose you, but we think you ought to go'. Men signed up with their friends and fellow workers from factories, mills, great country estates and small towns. Those who were among the first to go to France were full of misplaced optimism. Osbert Sitwell heard some of the most confident telling their batmen to pack their evening clothes as they would be needed when the officers got to Berlin within weeks. By the late autumn of 1914 all four of Osbert's ambitious and restless friends were dead.

The jingoism and confidence expressed as Britain went to war soon dissipated. Within six months, as the opposing forces dug in during the long wet winter of 1914–15, there was a growing awareness of the heavy toll the war was taking on the men fighting at the front. The British public who had cheered the men signing up in the autumn of 1914 were appalled by the stream of maimed figures returning from the battlefields of France. The casualty figures were grim; and thousands of wounded and traumatised soldiers were sent back to Britain for treatment and recuperation. Many died from their injuries *en route,* but those who survived were sent to recuperate in hospitals or private homes. This was an era before the government-funded National Health Service, so the wounded were reliant on the Red Cross or the philanthropy of wealthy individuals who set up hospitals. Within weeks of the conflict starting, the Duke of Devonshire gave over the ground floor of his opulent London home as the temporary headquarters of the Red Cross. Women of all classes wanted to support the war effort; Queen Mary was tireless in her charitable activities, and the hostesses were quick to follow the royal example, offering their own homes as hospitals and convalescent homes.

Mrs Greville turned over most of Polesden Lacey for use as a convalescent home to King Edward VII's Hospital for Officers. It was run on luxurious lines; she retained the use of the east side, and her private apartments on the south side, for her own use, while the patients lived on the west and north sides of the house, with a resident staff of nurses and orderlies. Mrs Greville continued to entertain her circle of ambassadors, peers and politicians at Polesden, and showed King George V and Queen Mary over the site in 1915 when they visited to raise morale. Throughout the war Queen Mary would visit the injured in a variety of hospitals and convalescent homes; she would sometimes manage three or four in an afternoon. On one such visit, overhearing one of her entourage muttering, 'I'm tired and I hate hospitals', the Queen replied crisply: 'You are a member of the British Royal Family. We are *never* tired, and we all *love* hospitals.'

Nancy Astor was playing tennis at Cliveden when she first heard that war had been declared. Within months the tennis court had been replaced by a state-of-the-art hospital built by the Canadian Red Cross to accommodate 200 soldiers. Waldorf paid the salaries of ten medical officers, twenty nurses and a staff of orderlies. Winston Churchill visited the hospital on 3 May 1915; the Astors knew the Churchills from the early years of their marriage, though Nancy's later relationship with the politician was often stormy. King George V and Queen Mary also visited on 20 July 1915.

Nancy took a genuine interest in the recovery of the patients, 24,000 of whom passed through the hospital. She was no ministering angel, but galvanised the patients into putting up a fight. She could be generous and inspiring – she offered a gold watch to one badly injured Canadian soldier who was in the hospital at Cliveden, if he recovered, and when he survived four operations she was as good as her word.

Sadly, not all those who were treated at the hospital survived. The Cliveden War Cemetery is a melancholy memorial, a peaceful and elegant sunken garden in the Italian style on the side of the hill, surrounded by trees, and ornamented with Roman sculptural fragments such as broken columns. It was originally created in 1902 as a neo-classical garden, but was consecrated as a burial ground and contains forty-two graves from the Great War, including those of two nurses.

Dominating the site is an impressive symbolic bronze statue of a female figure with outstretched arms, representing Canada; Nancy was the model. There is also an eloquent memorial to the Cliveden staff who joined the services but never came back. The Octagon Temple, the family mausoleum, which stands on a scarp looking out over the Thames, bears a bronze plaque on the exterior, listing the names and regiments of fifteen men who had been employed by the Astors but who lost their lives in the Great War.

Waldorf Astor applied for active military service in 1914, but he was rejected because of his weak heart and respiratory problems, so he continued as an MP and also became an inspector of ordnance factories with the rank of major, an unpaid and unpopular job. Nancy supported his burgeoning political career and became an astute and very well-connected hostess in London. In 1916, when Lloyd George became Prime Minister, Waldorf was made a Parliamentary Secretary along with Philip Kerr, who was to become a close friend to both the Astors. Under Nancy's influence Kerr converted from Catholicism to Christian Science. Many said that he was in love with her, but Nancy always insisted he was primarily Waldorf's friend rather than her own.

Between 1914 and 1918 the Cliveden estate was dedicated to the war effort. The gardeners transformed the flower beds into vegetable plots, and the lawns were turned over to grazing sheep and poultry-keeping. Most of the menfolk had signed up or had joined reserved occupations, and the domestic staff were almost entirely female. No alcohol was served for the duration of hostilities; Nancy was resolutely teetotal, but she had previously provided drinks for her guests. Meanwhile, her energy was phenomenal: she sailed through her two wartime pregnancies, giving birth to her fifth and sixth children: Michael in 1916 and John Jacob II in 1918. 'My vigour, vitality, and cheek repel me. I am the kind of woman I would run from', Nancy said of herself. On the contrary, she was extremely attractive to men; the hot-blooded widower Lord Curzon pursued her for years. She enjoyed his company but was unwilling to have an affair, so their relationship was one of ardent friendship. He was a frequent visitor to Cliveden, but in 1915 his unreciprocated affections moved on to Mrs Grace Duggan and, when she was unexpectedly widowed, George Curzon proposed marriage, and Grace accepted. Curzon's long-standing lover, the notorious novelist Elinor

Glyn, spotted their engagement notice in a six-day old copy of *The Times* and stalked out of Curzon's country house, Montacute, never to return. Nancy Astor was relieved by Lord Curzon's remarriage and she took a close interest in his three motherless daughters, the celebrated Curzon sisters, who were to play such key roles in British society in the 1920s and 1930s.

The Londonderrys also threw themselves into supporting the war effort by offering their London home as a hospital. In addition, 'Captain Charles Castlereagh MP' was in Paris by 29 August 1914, acting as aide-de-camp to General William Pulteney, who commanded the Third Army Corps in France. Charley served under him for a year before rejoining his own regiment, the Royal Horse Guards, becoming second-in-command in 1916. He acquitted himself honourably at the first Battle of Ypres, the Somme and the Battle of Arras, but was appalled at the carnage he saw and felt a great sense of loss over his dead and wounded friends. His first-hand experience of the horrors of war influenced many critical decisions in his later life.

In February 1915 Charley's father, the sixth Marquess, was desperately ill with pneumonia. His wife, Theresa, dubbed by war correspondent and former British Army officer Charles à Court Repington 'the ferocious Lady Londonderry', sent a note asking to see him. The couple had exchanged barely a word in thirty years, after a jealous rival, Gladys de Grey, had sent him a bundle of stolen love letters Theresa had written to Harry Cust. This was Lord Londonderry's last chance for reconciliation, but he refused and died without seeing his wife. Three years later, when Lady Londonderry was gravely ill, her nemesis Gladys similarly sent a telegram asking for forgiveness. Once again, the answer was no.

Edith led a radical public campaign to mobilise women during the war. She had lunched with her disapproving mother-in-law at the end of August 1914 and the conversation turned to her support for votes for women, which was ridiculed. The (unnamed) editor of a famous newspaper who was present apparently offered her a wager of £5 that at the end of the war there would be no Suffragettes, as 'War will teach women the impossibility of their demands and the absurdity of their claims'. Edith accepted the challenge; it was the spur she needed. By the autumn she had launched a drive to enlist female volunteers in order to free up men for military service. Edith campaigned persuasively for women with knowledge of agriculture and an aptitude for rural life to work on the land, a radical idea. The press largely agreed that it was the duty of fit and willing women to volunteer their labour in order to help shorten the war.

The Women's Legion was very successful; at first it tackled the shortage of farming labour, by recruiting female volunteers to help bring in the harvest and to care for livestock. The organisation acted as an employment agency, placing willing women workers where they were most needed. They undertook the management of horses, animal husbandry, milking, thatching and muck-spreading, weeding, fruit-picking and ploughing. Edith wrote in later years:

> The effect of regular work and wearing sensible clothes and thick shoes was immediately seen. Many girls and women that I thought would be far too delicate or highly strung for the work turned out to be the best; this applied not only to agriculture but to all sections of the Legion.

As President of the Women's Legion, Edith adopted a military-style uniform, which disconcerted servants at the smart houses of her London friends; she was sometimes redirected 'downstairs' to see the housekeeper, as it was assumed from her outfit she was collecting for the Salvation Army. Edith took such misunderstandings in her stride; these were exceptional times. She wrote numerous press articles exhorting women to put their energies into war work and was not deterred by the many anonymous letters and insults she received. So successful was her initiative that, as the war advanced, women filled other critical roles previously the preserve of men:

> Women cooks were replacing the male Army cooks at home and these women were gradually put into uniform. Next in order were the Army Service Corps girls and the Royal Flying Corps drivers of the Women's Legion, and dispatch-riders appeared in neat uniforms wearing breeches. As the war progressed the Legionaries were followed in 1917 by the regular Women's Armies – the WAAC, the WRAF and finally the WRNS [...] There were also women police; women 'bus conductors; all the land girls, foresters, and munition workers; there were railway girls, and the drivers of the Royal Mail vans... by the end of the war 80 per cent of the labour in this country was carried on by women. A training such as these women had undergone during the terrible years revolutionised all previous ideas. Not only had their dress become rational and useful, but they themselves had risen to the occasion, their outlook had broadened, they were sure of themselves and of their vocations, and knew that they had 'made good'.

> Queen Mary was very complimentary about the valuable work the Women's Legion was undertaking when she

inspected them in March 1918. As a result of her war work, Edith was the first woman to be appointed as a Dame Commander of the Order of the British Empire in the Military Division, when the honour was inaugurated in 1917. In the same year Charley was recalled from the army because his services were required by the new Prime Minister, Lloyd George. He had been an MP for nine years, but was obliged to give up his seat when he inherited his father's title in 1915. Because of his valuable Parliamentary experience and his knowledge of Northern Ireland, he was appointed a member of the Irish Convention, a short-lived attempt to head off the growing crisis over the issue of Home Rule.

Edith and Charley offered Londonderry House to be used as a hospital for wounded servicemen. Most of the building was taken over, leaving only two rooms on the ground floor and the top floor for the family's use. Edith was fully occupied running the Women's Legion, so the day-to-day provisioning of the hospital was managed by her cook, Mrs Harris, and her housekeeper, Mrs Guthrie. The nursing was organised by a succession of matrons, but Edith helped to care for some of the shell-shocked soldiers, whose behaviour was often alarming. Some patients were also fond of adding graffiti, make-up or props to the neo-classical statues that adorned the gallery, one of their wards. The marble figure of Apollo sporting a Glengarry cap, or an Aphrodite enhanced with rouge and lipstick, lifted the patients' morale. Air raids over London were similarly treated as a joke, and the wounded would limp and hop to the balconies of Londonderry House to watch the pyrotechnics. By 1918, when the Zeppelin air raids were more frequent and deadly, the patients and staff were forced to shelter in the cellars.

Writing in the late 1930s, Edith recalled fondly how, despite other commitments, Londonderry House became a wartime meeting place for her friends. Every Wednesday evening she held a dinner party. In jest, Londonderry House had been renamed The Ark, a reference to the Biblical tale. The friends created the Order of the Rainbow, recalling the divine signal that the floods were over. The members of the Order were each given the name of a creature or a mythological or magical figure. Edith was known as 'Circe the Sorceress'; Winston Churchill, now the Secretary of State for War, was 'The Warlock'; and Edith's husband was 'Charley the Cheetah'. Despite the jovial nicknames, the clique were very well informed. Lord Balfour, First Lord of the Admiralty ('Arthur the Albatross'), related the story of the Battle of Jutland to the Ark the same night that radio reports of it reached London and two days before accounts appeared in the newspapers. Other members included Sir Edmund Gosse ('The Goss-hawk'), J. M. Barrie (Barrie the Bard) and Nancy Astor (who was 'Nancy the Gnat', appropriately enough). On Wednesday evenings pre-war sartorial rules were abandoned, and invited guests attended in either day wear or evening clothes. Politicians and aristocrats rubbed shoulders with artists, writers and convalescing officers, as well as the more bohemian set, all fuelled by champagne. The Ark was one of the first salons in wartime London to dispense with formality, and Edith inaugurated supper buffets rather than structured dinner parties, so that refreshments were available to guests whenever they arrived.

Meanwhile Edith tolerated Charley's mistresses with fortitude; she would advise him on how to treat them, and even bought small presents for him to give them. For many years she was loyal to him personally, and very keen to advance his political career. However, it must have rankled that he did not adore her enough to leave other women alone. For Edith her marriage was a love match, like that of her own parents, and a complete contrast to the frosty emotional wastelands occupied by Charley's parents. Her husband was careful to tell her that she mattered more to him than any of his 'girls', and although it was hurtful, she chose not to see his entanglements with other women as a threat to their relationship. However, as she was socially successful, personally popular and very good-looking, it was perhaps inevitable that she would look outside her marriage for emotional fulfilment and admiration.

As the war dragged on, the British royal family were acutely aware of the public mood, and anxious to distance themselves from their German relations. The King's first cousin by marriage, Prince Louis of Battenburg, was hounded from his post as the First Sea Lord in October 1914. In 1915, after British ocean liner RMS *Lusitania* sank, with the loss of 1,198 lives, the level of hostility against Germany rose. The King maintained that he was British to the core, despite his German grandfather, but he was angered by H.G. Wells's remark about 'an alien and uninspiring Court'. 'I may be uninspiring, but I'll be damned if I'm an alien!' In 1917, a low point in the war, he decided to change the family name to Windsor, and cousin Louis adopted the surname of Mountbatten.

Meanwhile, King George patriotically banned sugar and alcohol from the royal residences for the duration. Queen Mary, who was fond of a glass of hock and a light touch with patisserie, would often motor over from Windsor to see her new friend Margaret Greville for tea. A lady-in-waiting would telephone Polesden Lacey to announce the royal visit. '*Dear* Queen Mary, always so welcome, but always so little notice!' purred Mrs Greville smugly. The importance of the tea table as a forum for exerting 'soft power' was recognised by *Vogue* magazine in October 1916:

> Socially, as every woman knows, the tea hour is invaluable [...] possibilities lie in the tea-table for expressing her own delicate personality, and gently making evident any aesthetic, original or discriminating qualities she may possess.

The Queen enjoyed visiting Polesden, and she was also keen to advance the relationship between Mrs Greville and her second son, Bertie, who was currently serving in the Navy but who would inherit the estate one day. Mrs Greville invited Bertie to dinner and to stay for weekends when he was old enough; their first lunch together was in March 1918, and afterwards Margaret wrote to his mother in rapturous terms, saying: 'He is delightful, such charming eyes, manners and complexion [...] fancy a delightful young radiant being like that being so charming to me.'

Mrs Greville always enjoyed the company of young people, especially the children of her friends, and she liked them to call her 'Mrs Ronnie', an informal, slightly sporty nickname with pronounced Edwardian overtones. The Keppels were frequent visitors to Polesden, and stayed with their old family friend for Christmas of 1916, bringing with them their daughter Violet and her young fiancé, Captain Osbert Sitwell. It soon became apparent that the engagement had been a mistake (not least because both parties preferred their own sex). However, in Violet's discarded beau Mrs Greville found a presentable, aristocratic young chap who was excellent company. Their friendship was genuine, if unorthodox; she was a fifty-three-year-old, traditionally built Scottish widow of great wealth, and he was a charming and well-mannered twenty-six-year-old Guards officer of indeterminate sexuality, with a titled but penny-pinching and eccentric father. It was a relationship that benefited both Osbert and Mrs Ronnie, and was to last until her death.

Mrs Ronnie was sociable, and entertained with select gatherings at her newly refurbished London house, 16 Charles Street. The general mood of national austerity deemed it distasteful to hold ostentatious events, but there were opportunities for hostesses to invite the great and good to mingle discreetly. She held weekly dinner parties on Wednesday evenings at her Mayfair home, where the dining room held some of her exquisite paintings. A select band of guests would gather around a single long table, laden with museum-quality early silver and decorated with sumptuous flowers sent up from her country house. The produce was also from the Home Farm. In addition, Mrs Greville often invited her favourites to stay at Polesden Lacey for long weekends; she prided herself on maintaining high standards of comfort and hospitality throughout the duration of the war.

Mrs Greville was prominent among the London-based hostesses in wielding influence in political circles. In February 1918 the dinner guests of Lord Wimborne, the conservative politician and first cousin of Winston Churchill, were forced to take cover because of an air raid. They amused themselves while the bombardment continued by drawing up a 'Cabinet of Ladies' to replace the male politicians, who they thought were exhausted by the war. Minister for Propaganda was Lady Cunard, the Chancellor of the Exchequer was Mrs George Keppel, and the Financial Secretary was Mrs Ronald Greville.

The Great War ground on, and both Nancy and Waldorf

were busy with their myriad concerns: his Parliamentary career, the hospital and estate at Cliveden and their young family. But Waldorf's days as an MP were numbered. His eccentric father, William Waldorf, was living in romantic Hever Castle in Kent, a medieval structure reputedly haunted by the ghost of Anne Boleyn. By 1910 he had spent £10 million on renovating the castle, including a village in Tudor style to house his guests. At night he would pull up the drawbridge, and shut out the modern world. William was living the life of an English gentleman of former centuries; all he needed now was an aristocratic title. He started making discreet enquiries with that end in mind.

On 1 January 1916 Waldorf was telephoned by a journalist asking him how his father's ennoblement would affect his own political ambitions. This was the first inkling Waldorf had that his Anglophile father had now acquired a title. W. W. Astor had secretly courted the upper echelons of the Conservative Party, donating generously to various charities: more than £26,000 to the War Fund, £41,000 to Lord Rothschild's Red Cross and £6,000 to Queen Mary's Fund for Women. Now he was Baron Astor of Hever, a hereditary title that would pass to Waldorf when William died, ending his role as an MP. Waldorf was outraged, and vowed to change the law so that he could remain a Member of Parliament. The new Baron was offended by his eldest son and heir's ingratitude and disloyalty, and changed his will so that on his death Waldorf would receive nothing. This estrangement was to have far-reaching consequences for the family; it was also to alter the political history of Britain.

The disposition of another American millionaire's fortune was to have enormous consequences for the Corrigans of Cleveland, whose vast fortune had been created by the entrepreneurial steel magnate James Corrigan Senior. When he died in 1908, his only son and heir, also called James, discovered to his shock that he had been left just a little over £3,000 in unrestricted funds. His father's 40 per cent share of the steel company he had founded, worth millions of dollars, was held in trust until James Junior turned forty, in 1920. Price McKinney, the company's former book-keeper, had been appointed the trustee of James's fund. Resentful and under-occupied, James spent the next five years gaining a considerable reputation as a playboy. Sources differ as to where and when he first encountered the resourceful and ambitious Laura Mae Whitrock. The professional party planner Elsa Maxwell, who knew Laura well in Paris in the 1930s and liked her, claimed that she had been working as a telephone operator at a hotel in Cleveland. According to Elsa, James was a guest at the hotel and had been drinking heavily; he had made a blind date for the next day with the attractive-sounding telephonist who tried to put through his calls. Other sources claim that Laura, with her respectable physician husband Dr MacMartin, was invited to James's house-party in 1913, when he was recovering from a sensational court case. A nineteen-year-old girl from Pittsburgh sued him for $50,000 for breach of promise after Corrigan promised, but failed, to marry her following the death of his father.

Whatever the truth, Laura later described their first encounter as 'love at first light'; she quickly divested herself of Dr MacMartin, and married James Corrigan on 2 December 1916. His wedding present to her was a Rolls-Royce worth $15,000, complete with a chauffeur. Laura had arrived in some style. But snobbish Cleveland society was unimpressed by the marriage of the thirty-seven-year-old playboy with a scandalous history and his divorced bride, who was from a working-class background and a small back-woods industrial town. Polite matrons disapproved and avoided Nagirroc ('Corrigan' spelt backwards), their grand home on Euclid Avenue, and even James's business contacts were ambivalent about socialising with the couple. Laura Corrigan resolved that she and James deserved to find a better milieu, where they and their millions would be better appreciated. She set her sights on New York.

The family life of the Colefaxes was less volatile and decidedly less affluent than that of the Corrigans and the Astors, but the years of the Great War were nevertheless busy and sociable ones for them. Sibyl and Arthur had two young sons, and she divided her energies between 'her boys' and a growing desire to create a social circle rich in artistic and creative people. She used Old Buckhurst as a weekend place to entertain her friends. It was not as grand as the rural retreats of other society hostesses, more of a 'house in the country' than a 'country house', but Sibyl took immense satisfaction in decorating it. Once war broke out, she found it difficult to hire gardeners. She applied for and was allocated a number of German prisoners of war, who were supposed to be employed on farm work. Sibyl put them to work to create a wild garden.

She particularly enjoyed the company of theatrical and musical artistes, who would motor down after the curtain fell on their West End stages on Saturday evenings, joining the literary, artistic and political guests already in residence. The August 1914 guest list included Kathleen Scott, widow of Scott of the Antarctic, the Austen Chamberlains and the philanthropic Beits, who were millionaires. Later guests included the Prime Minister, Herbert Asquith, and Bonar Law. There were publishers and media moguls such as the

Northcliffes, William Heinemann and Sir Frederick Macmillan. The influential owner of *Country Life,* Edward Hudson, and his architectural editor, Henry Avray Tipping, were also visitors. Accomplished writers included Desmond MacCarthy, Lytton Strachey and Rudyard Kipling, the son of Sibyl's old friend from Simla days. The novelist Enid Bagnold, who in 1920 was to marry Sir Roderick Jones, Chairman of Reuters, was another visitor. Celebrated actresses included Gladys Cooper, and Ivor Novello played his evocative wartime song 'Keep the Home Fires Burning' on the piano.

Sibyl was also making a mark among more avant-garde literary circles in her London home in Onslow Square. In December 1917 she organised a charity fundraising evening, with guests reading their poems aloud. The readers included Aldous Huxley, T. S. Eliot and the Sitwells. Meanwhile Arthur Colefax, who was too old for active service, had volunteered to be the head of a scientific department within the Ministry of Munitions, a role for which his background and profes- sional experience made him well suited. However, the post was unpaid, and he turned down lucrative patent cases at the Bar to fulfil what he saw as his patriotic duty. Consequently, by the end of the war the Colefaxes were less financially secure than they had been at its outset, and they had to face the reality that it was too expensive for them to maintain both a London house and one in the countryside.

Economies were also forced upon Sir Bache Cunard, now estranged from his extravagant wife, Maud, who was living in London in some style. He no longer wanted to entertain and so moved into a substantial house called The Haycock in the village of Wansford, 20 miles from Nevill Holt, where he was to live alone for the next eleven years. His daughter Nancy described him as 'manually an ingenious, gifted man in all his manipulations of wood and iron', and in the war his practical skills were useful when he organised and ran a munitions factory at The Haycock. Nancy would occasionally visit him; she was fond of her father, but they had very few interests in common apart from her mother, hardly a happy topic of conversation. A number of Lady Cunard's contemporaries disapproved of her behaviour. Consuelo Vanderbilt Balsan, a fellow American similarly unhappily married to a British aristocrat, remarked that Maud 'took a house in London, for it was her ambition to have a political salon in the tradition of the eighteenth century. Ruthlessly determined to success, she bent a conspicuous talent to this end.'

Meanwhile Lady Cunard exercised her deep-rooted elitism, attracting politicians and aristocrats, artists, writers and musicians, creating a milieu in which her beloved Thomas Beecham's career as a musical impresario could flourish. They both dreamed of reviving opera on the British stage. Substantial funds were required; Lady Cunard was generous with her own money, and she assiduously cultivated wealthy friends, from whom she wheedled further financial support. Maud always referred to Thomas as 'Mr Beecham' in public, but their relationship was no secret among their social circle. A review of a contemporary sculpture exhibition appeared in *Country Life* on 13 November 1915, and the two separate photographs used as illustrations on the same page happened to be busts of Lady Cunard and Thomas Beecham, a hint to those who suspected that they were a couple.

In the New Year's honours list of 1916, thirty-six-year-old Thomas Beecham was knighted, almost certainly owing to Lady Cunard's efforts. Later that year, following his father's death, he inherited both the baronetcy and the family fortune.

Lady Cunard always cared far more for Beecham than he did for her; she did not know that by autumn of the same year he was conducting a passionate affair with a soprano called Bessie Tyas, who was playing Mimi in *La Bohème* at the Aldwych.

Thomas Beecham's professional fortunes ebbed and flowed during the Great War; air raids had a deleterious effect on the box office, and some of the operas he was conducting, such as *Ivan the Terrible*, were considered too gloomy to attract the public. Beecham commented on the philistinism of the public: 'in London grand opera in English is supported by the rich and the poor. The middle classes know nothing about it. They have a meat tea, and then go to the pictures or the music-hall.' Fortunately, his patroness had a more positive attitude; Lady Cunard sifted through London society to pick out the nuggets. Her lifelong passion for art, music and literature led her to play Chopin and Beethoven on the piano with feeling and skill, and to read the dramas and novels of the greatest writers, modern and classical, and her cultural eclecticism informed her sparkling, scintillating conversation.

Her daughter Nancy Cunard had her own social circle now, and her best friend was Iris Tree. The two girls rented a studio together in Bloomsbury, near the Slade Art School, where they could entertain their friends, known as 'The Corrupt Coterie', with bohemian bottle parties. It was a more decorous age, but Nancy was already notorious for her wild behaviour, rebelling against what she considered her mother's hypocrisy. She resented Maud's attempts to charm her own friends, such as Osbert Sitwell and Lady Diana Manners. A dinner party hosted by Nancy for her friends at Cavendish Square on 12 December 1915 ended up with everyone very drunk. Lady

Cunard was horrified by the guests' behaviour when she returned to find her home full of sozzled youth. Nancy would often drink to excess; on 11 July 1916 Duff Cooper and his future fiancée called in at Cavendish Square to find Nancy suffering from a colossal hangover and still in her nightwear, having been extremely drunk the previous evening.

While Lady Cunard cultivated fashionable and creative London, her own daughter was coming to dislike her. Nancy was determined to break away from her mother's household and marriage seemed to offer an escape. She met an officer, Sydney Fairbairn, who had been wounded at Gallipoli. Maud was unhappy at her daughter's choice; she had hoped for a more prestigious match, but headstrong Nancy replied, 'I gave my word, and I must'. The couple chose 15 November 1916 to get married; unfortunately there was a smart royal wedding scheduled for the same day, that of Countess Nada Torby and Prince George of Battenberg. Nevertheless Maud attracted an impressive guest list for her daughter's wedding, despite the grander fixture across town; her guests included the ambassadors of France, Italy and Spain, the Duke of Rutland, his daughter Lady Diana Manners and Duff Cooper, Lady Randolph Churchill and Ivor Novello. Angular Nancy wore an unconventional gold-coloured dress; Maud chose the soft pink and furs that suited her *couleur de rose* complexion so well. As mother of the bride, Maud had a particularly fraught day; her estranged husband, Sir Bache Cunard, insisted on giving away their daughter. Her handsome and dapper lover, the recently knighted Sir Thomas Beecham, was in attendance, as was her disgruntled old admirer George Moore. There was a reception afterwards at Cavendish Square, then the new Mr and Mrs Fairbairn left for their honeymoon in Cornwall.

Lady Cunard's gift to the young couple was a house, 5 Montagu Square, but from the outset the marriage was not a success. Sydney and Nancy were fundamentally incompatible, and she subsequently remembered her brief period as a wife as one of the unhappiest times of her life. Seven of Nancy's poems were included in an anthology edited by the Sitwells, which was published in November 1916, but while her marriage lasted she felt unable to write, despite George Moore's encouragement. When Sydney rejoined the army in July 1918 and left for France, Nancy was relieved.

Nancy was friendly with Sybil Hart-Davis, the elder sister of Duff Cooper. With both their husbands serving in the war, in the summer of 1918 the two women rented a house together near Kingston Bagpuize, in Oxfordshire, with Sybil's two children, Nancy's maid and a cook. The house was often full of their friends, many of them in uniform. One was Peter Broughton-Adderley, a fellow officer of Sydney Fairbairn. Peter had first met Nancy in 1917, while he was on a five-day leave. In the summer of 1918 he sought her out again, staying at Bagpuize, and this time they fell in love. Then he returned to France, and in October 1918 Sybil had to break the news to Nancy that Peter had been killed in action. Nancy was heartbroken by her loss. When news of the armistice came just a few weeks later, she could not celebrate.

The end of the war caused complex reactions. For many it was the end of unbearable tension and strain. Margot Asquith, whose eldest stepson, Raymond, had been killed in battle in 1916, described feeling:

as numb as an old piano with broken notes in it. The strain of four years – waiting and watching, opening and reading telegrams upon matters of life and death, and the recurring news of failure at the Front had blunted all my receptive powers.

But on Armistice Day, 11 November 1918, many Britons danced in the streets, cheering and embracing total strangers; bells rang, maroons were let off and brass bands played. In the capital, revellers of all classes converged on Buckingham Palace. 'It was a wonderful sight, and more like a foreign carnival [...] Everyone in London, rich and poor, fashionable and obscure, were [sic] standing and shouting for the King, and many of the spectators had tears in their eyes', wrote Margot Asquith. The King and Queen made repeated appearances on the balcony to acknowledge the joyful crowds, the King still in the khaki uniform he had worn since the beginning of the war, the Queen with her diamonds and pearls, the gems of mourning.

Over 9 million men had been killed in the First World War, 942,135 of them from the British Empire. The conflict had started in Central Europe and spread rapidly across the rest of the Continent, involving Russia, Japan, Africa, the Near and the Far East, Australia and New Zealand, and North America. By its end, the war had engulfed the ancient regime that had controlled Russia, bringing about a Communist revolution and liquidating its royal family. The mighty Austro-Hungarian Empire had been decimated, and Kaiser Wilhelm had abdicated to live in exile in the Netherlands. America's international role as a mighty military force and as an influential power-broker was now established in a way that dictated that country's role throughout the twentieth century.

In Britain the Great War had very long-lasting effects. There was barely a home in the country that had not lost someone in the conflict. There were men returning from war who had survived the armed struggle but who found the peace impossible to bear; they were physically or mentally damaged in a way that affected their own lives and those of their families for decades. Of the previously wealthy, many had suffered the terrible burden of successive death duties as they lost sons and heirs. Increased labour costs led to a shortage of servants and brought about the closure of many of the very grand houses in London, some of which were now sold for new developments. But perhaps the greatest impact was psychological: the rules that had previously defined society and the pre-determined roles occupied by those in it were swept away by the devastation of the Great War.

4

The Aftermath: 1918–1923

The return of peace brought about huge social and political ramifications for all classes of British society.
Politically, the British Liberal Party had lost all credibility,
and Socialism came to be seen by some as an alternative
potential power. Many of the landed gentry had suffered
financially, and now had far less disposable income to spend
on modes of life they had previously taken for granted.

The 1920s saw a quiet revolution among the landowning
classes, and a sea change in the social life of London. Before
the Great War, the aristocracy had regarded entertaining their
peers as a crucial indicator of their importance and status.
High-born hostesses of this era included Lady Derby, Lady
Spencer, Lady Stanhope, Lady Waldegrave, Lady Shaftesbury
and Lady Lansdowne. But four years of austerity during the
hostilities, the increased taxation and death duties and the
drop in purchasing power of the pound to less than
50 per cent of what it had been worth in 1914 had adversely
affected their incomes. One by one, the great palatial London
houses were 'let go', sold and demolished to be replaced by
hotels, apartments and offices. The nobility retreated to their
country estates, often also diminished in scale. Even the Dukes
of Devonshire, Richmond, Portland, Beaufort, Rutland and
Somerset mostly relinquished entertaining on a vast scale in
London, preferring to lease a suitable property to 'do' the
London season or launch the next generation as required. As

the journalist Patrick Balfour observed: 'The older aristocracy was inclined to sell its London mansions, retire to the country and live on such of its estates and with such of its dignity as it could still preserve, thus ceasing to be *London* Society at all.'

Surviving sons of the upper classes returning to civilian life now began to go into business, in an attempt to keep afloat financially. Their attempts to infiltrate the City were regarded with a certain amount of scepticism by the stock-brokers, insurers and financiers already there. 'We want him for clerking, not for breeding purposes' was the verdict of one banker on a young applicant's aristocratic references. However, some sections of society had emerged from the war in a stronger and more influential position, including newspaper proprietors, capitalists, Socialists and the artistic avant-garde, which looked at the war with a jaundiced eye.

In particular, the role of women of all classes was re-assessed. On 6 February 1918 Parliament passed the Representation of the People Act, extending male suffrage and allowing most women over the age of thirty the vote for the first time, chiefly in recognition of their services to the state during the war. This swelled the electorate from 7.7 million in 1912 to 21.4 million in 1918. The following year the Sex Disqualification (Removal) Acts were also passed, giving women access to professions previously denied them. For the first time Parliament not only needed the votes of a previously unfranchised section of the population but allowed women to join the law-making elite. The first woman to take up her seat as an MP, a role she was to hold for twenty-six years, was Nancy Astor, though her Parliamentary career happened almost by accident.

In October 1919 Nancy's father-in-law, the first Viscount

Astor, died. His son Waldorf inherited the title his father had bought less than four years earlier. Waldorf was automatically elevated to the House of Lords, losing his seat as an MP for Plymouth, which he resented bitterly. He resolved to change the law from within the upper house, but meanwhile he petitioned the King. George V was a deeply conservative character, committed to precedent, to protocol and to wearing the correct insignia on all occasions. Waldorf's impassioned argument that the awarding of titles and honours enforced class distinctions singularly failed to impress the monarch, and his appeal was refused. (The rule was not overturned until 1963, when Anthony Wedgwood Benn was able to reject a hereditary title in order to retain his seat.)

Nancy sympathised: 'Some people find it hard to get titles; Lord Astor is finding it even harder to get rid of his.' Meanwhile, the Conservatives in Plymouth urgently needed a replacement candidate. Waldorf's brother John Jacob Astor was suggested, but he declined, having lost a leg during the war. However, Nancy had campaigned in the constituency many times on behalf of her husband, and the Astor name carried considerable clout. If she won, she would not be the first woman to be elected (that distinction had already gone to Countess Markievicz, who had won a seat for Sinn Féin but refused to take it up in protest), but Nancy would be the first woman MP actually to sit in Parliament.

Nancy had not supported the women's suffrage movement that had been so active before the Great War, but she refused to be barred from a course of action because of her gender. Her friend J. M. Barrie complained of her 'presumptuous ambitions' in standing for election against a man, but she agreed to contest the seat in Plymouth, planning to retain it until Waldorf could introduce a bill to allow peers to be MPs.

However, she thrived in public life, and as events were to prove, she would not retire from it without a struggle.

It is ironic that in 1919 Lady Astor planned to take on a role unwillingly vacated by her husband, while all over Britain women who had found interesting and challenging war work outside their own homes were forced to relinquish their jobs to the menfolk returning from the conflict. Nevertheless, Nancy was popular with the voters, especially the newly enfranchised women of Plymouth, who numbered 17,000. Her informal, unpredictable style of campaigning charmed the electorate. She advocated temperance – not a vote-winner in Plymouth, with its naval tradition and its famous gin distillery – but remarkably, both her opponents, Labour and Liberal, were also teetotallers. Her stance provoked some wry mirth: 'I would rather commit adultery than have a glass of beer!' she proclaimed. 'Who wouldn't?' came a voice from the crowd.

She was returned on 28 November 1919 with a majority of 5,000 votes. Her eldest Astor boy, Bill, aged twelve, made a speech, surely unique in British political history, thanking the voters of Plymouth for having elected first his father and now his mother as their MP. Nancy took up her seat on 1 December, and nearly forty years later she recalled her first appearance in Parliament, flanked by Arthur Balfour and Lloyd George. She remembered in later years that, although both men had claimed they believed in women becoming MPs, they gave the impression they would have preferred to have a rattlesnake in the House.

One of the many people who wrote to congratulate Lady Astor on her election as an MP was Edith, Lady Londonderry. Nancy's reply was frank and sincere: 'I feel you realise what a great responsibility it is. I shall hope never to let you down.

We may not always agree about politics but we will each know that the other is trying to be honest [...] I cannot express myself in "Parliamentary language", only I do deeply appreciate your letter.'

Waldorf threw himself into other work and led an austere and self-contained life, largely dedicated to philanthropy. The Astors spent £20,000 of their own money to create a model housing estate in Plymouth to replace some of the worst slums, and provided social centres in the city for young and old, especially the demobbed servicemen returning to civilian life. The family ran a combined home and constituency office at 8 Elliott Terrace, a five-storeyed terraced house with views of Plymouth Sound. Waldorf employed the best staff to assist Nancy's career, to research on her behalf and help her compile cogent arguments. By nature she was an instinctive advocate, passionate and compelling, but she had to be better informed and better briefed than her opponents to achieve credibility as the first active female MP.

From the outset, her twin passions were improving the lives of women and children, and combatting the scourge of alcohol. Social welfare was generally considered a noble cause, but it took courage to champion temperance. 'One reason I don't drink is because I want to know when I am having a good time', she declared. However, she frequently clashed with the interests of the powerful brewing lobby, whose fortunes came from supplying the nation with their favourite intoxicants. Many a political family from the 'Beerage' had first made a fortune from brewing or distilling, among them the Guinnesses, the Youngers and Mr McEwan and his ward, Mrs Greville. Even the Astors had traded in alcohol in their early years in New York. Nancy chose the Parliamentary debate about rescinding wartime drinking restrictions on 24 February 1920 to make her maiden speech. Despite concerted opposition, in 1923 she managed to change the law, banning the sale of alcohol to people under eighteen; this was the first bill to be introduced and steered through Parliament by a woman.

Her habit of heckling other speakers did not make her popular with her fellow politicians. Certain MPs ignored her when she attempted to sit on the famous green benches, so athletic Nancy would clamber over their knees as though they were boulders in her path. Ironically, some had been colleagues of her husband, Waldorf, and had received ample hospitality from the Astors in the past. Now their behaviour was overtly or covertly hostile. Nancy tackled Winston Churchill, who had been lent the Astors' seaside house in 1912 so that Clemmie could recuperate after an illness. Why, she wanted to know, was Winston now ignoring her? 'When you took your seat, I felt as if a woman had come into my bathroom and I had only a sponge with which to defend myself,' he growled. 'You are not handsome enough to have worries of that kind,' she retorted.

Nancy avoided the masculine atmosphere in the bars and lobbies of the House of Commons; she could not help being conspicuous, one member likening her presence to that of a butterfly flitting around an old library. In fine weather she would endlessly practise her golf swing on the terrace, over-looking the Thames. Otherwise she would work with her secretary in a small but cosy sitting room. To create the right impression as a female MP she devised a sober but versatile work outfit, variants of which she would wear constantly for the next twenty-six years. It was an early example of 'power dressing': a simple, tailored black coat-dress with a white fichu collar and cuffs, a buttonhole of fresh white flowers and a black tricorne hat. She wore silk stockings in gunmetal grey, and low black shoes with Cuban heels. Her outfit could be seen as 'protective colouring', blending in with her monochrome male counterparts, with their dark tailored suits, flashes of white on the breast and at the cuff, and impressive hats to add height.

One aspect of her new public role particularly troubled Nancy. In April 1920 a new law was proposed to make divorce easier for married couples. After much thought she spoke against the proposal, as she felt it would merely enable dissatisfied men to discard their wives. It was not generally known that Nancy was a divorcée; Waldorf's entries in *Who's Who* and Burke's Peerage erroneously stated that he had married 'the widow of the late Robert Gould Shaw', but in fact her first husband was still alive. Nancy's rival Horatio Bottomley MP launched a poster campaign for his magazine *John Bull*, with the sensational phrase 'Lady Astor's Divorce', implying that she was separating from Waldorf. She was accused of hypocrisy; having obtained a divorce herself in 1903, she now denied other unhappy couples a chance to start again. Nancy was furious, although the Astors had been economical with the truth over her first marriage. But Bottomley had gone too far; Nancy's fellow MPs showed their sympathy at the next Commons session by roundly applauding her, and heckling him.

She admitted later in life that her first two years as an MP were very stressful, until she was joined by another female MP, Margaret Wintringham. Nancy also became friendly with 'Red Ellen' Wilkinson, a former Communist, now a Labour MP. Nancy's trail-blazing path was not rewarded by high office, owing to her occasionally abrasive manner. However, she did provide a valuable figurehead for various female interest groups, organising receptions at her London home, 4 St James's Square, where women could lobby the other guests in support of different causes. Nancy made her receptions effective by introducing name badges for all her guests, with a one-word indication of their interests, a radical innovation; this enabled her guests to dispense with small talk and identify their targets. Her excellent hospitality attracted businessmen and captains of industry, aristocrats and academics, opinion-formers, senior civil servants and judges. Feminist Mary Stocks later recalled it was at Lady Astor's parties that she and her colleagues were first able to mingle with the politically powerful.

Nancy felt that providing a forum for informal contacts was the best use of her time and the family's considerable wealth. She would point out two portraits in her London dining room, one of the first John Jacob Astor, who had established the family's fortune, and the Sargent portrait of herself. She would say, 'That's the man who made the millions, and that's the woman who is spending them.' Nancy also argued persuasively for the employment of women in socially influential public positions, such as in the police force and the civil service. She remarked ruefully: 'Pioneers may be picturesque figures, but they are often rather lonely ones.'

Meanwhile the Astor family had inherited the makings of a media empire from the first Viscount, and this was to prove to be useful in promoting the family fortunes. Waldorf had been given the *Observer* by his father in 1916. His brother, John Jacob Astor, had his sights set on owning *The Times*, and after a tussle with Lord Rothermere, he secured 90 per cent of the ownership, buying the paper from Lord Northcliffe. Geoffrey Dawson was appointed the editor, and under his control the paper supported its proprietor in his second bid to become an MP in 1922 – this time, with the support of The Thunderer, he was successful and was elected as the Tory representative for Dover. John Jacob Astor never fully approved of his sister-in-law's Parliamentary career on principle. But blood was thicker than water, as events were to prove.

Nancy's high-powered life, combining a demanding career with family and social commitments, required the support and co-operation of her staff. She relied on a lady's maid to manage her wardrobe and a secretary to handle her correspondence and social life. On becoming an MP, she also employed a Parliamentary secretary, who managed her constituency correspondence, meetings and diary. Cliveden and St James's Square were the centres of her social life, and for decades she depended on the indefatigable butler Edwin Lee, known to his underlings as 'Skipper' or 'Skip'. Working with Mrs Addison the housekeeper, Arthur Bushell the valet and (from 1928 onwards) Rose Harrison, Lady Astor's personal maid, these four senior servants ensured that both houses were run like clockwork. At 5 a.m. the housemaids began cleaning and laying fires in grates in Cliveden's reception rooms; Rose would help Lady Astor out of her gown and into her nightclothes around midnight. Bobbie Shaw likened his diminutive but energetic mother to the rudder of a huge liner, steering the whole complex enterprise.

The Astors were generous employers, paying decent wages and providing cottages for the estate workers and funding the education of their children. Waldorf adored his own offspring, who were looked after by much-loved Nanny Gibbons. The Astor boys lived at Cliveden until they reached the age of eight, at which point they were sent to Eton. Wissie (Phyllis) was tutored by a governess at home. Nanny Gibbons did not approve of Arthur, the valet, who seized any opportunity to dress up as a woman for staff parties; she did not like his smutty innuendo. When she died, Nanny left £7,500, an impressive sum, of which £2,000 had been given to her by the Astor children in appreciation of her benign presence in their lives. Their restless but well-meaning mother, by contrast, would occasionally descend on the children's nurseries at Cliveden, appropriating toys she decided were no longer wanted and sending them to the poor.

Family life was important to Waldorf and Nancy Astor, though they both had full and busy lives. Michael Astor commented:

> I was vaguely aware that my mother was a famous person. As well as being the first woman to take her seat in Parliament she symbolised throughout the world the new place that women were making for themselves in public life. Inevitably she attracted a great deal of publicity because her like had not before been seen. She was a rebel and a conservative and a feminist, a new kind of firebrand who managed at the same time to conduct a social life at Cliveden on such a grand scale that even that attracted attention. She was as much a household name as later became – though for different reasons – Mrs Roosevelt, Greta Garbo and Marilyn Monroe. I knew that she was famous, although I did not then understand why this should be.

Nancy Astor was even better known in the States than in Britain, owing to her Parliamentary career. Her arrival in New York with Waldorf on the *Olympia* in April 1922 caused a media frenzy. She was invited to address the Pan-American Women's Convention in Baltimore, and the Canadian House of Commons, but she also gave numerous interviews to news-paper and radio journalists. It is an indication of Nancy's international celebrity that the Astors met President Harding and were invited onto the floor of the Senate. The couple acted as unofficial transatlantic ambassadors, advocating friendship between Britain and the United States.

At home at Cliveden during the school holidays the chil-dren joined their parents for afternoon tea, and Nancy was usually on fine form, entertaining guests and family alike. She would act out stories from her childhood in the southern States for their amusement. In fact, mimicry and dressing up were regular pastimes at Cliveden; Nancy had a number of 'comic turns': a Russian *emigrée*, a horsy Englishwoman who hunted in Leicestershire and a vacuous lady who thought Americans vulgar. The children were high-spirited and often witty: discussing a possible biography of Nancy, her youngest son John Jacob Astor VII, known as Jakie, suggested the title 'Guilty but Insane'.

The armistice brought new opportunities for both Edith and Charley Londonderry. They had spent a large part of the war apart, Edith based in London with her Women's Legion work, her involvement with the hospital at Londonderry House and social life with the Ark. Charley was on active service in France till 1917, before being posted to Northern Ireland. Edith's formidable mother-in-law, Theresa, died in March 1919, aged sixty-two, a victim of the Spanish flu epidemic sweeping Europe. She had been the foremost Tory political hostess of her era, and her passing left a huge gap in the social milieu that involved politicians of all parties. After a suitable period of mourning, Theresa's son and daugh-ter-in-law were asked to host a reception for the coalition government on 18 November 1919. After the conflict of the last four years it would be a harmonious gesture to host an event with the Prime Minister, Lloyd George (Liberal), and the Deputy Prime Minister, Andrew Bonar Law (Conservative). Edith stepped into the role as hostess, and the reception was a magnificent success. Many present had thought they would never see a 'pre-war' grand party again, although this time the guest list was more inclusive. As well as the British establishment, there were the doctors and nurses, the VADs (Voluntary Aid Detachments, who worked as field nurses) and the army women, the new Dames of the British Empire and many patients who had been treated at Londonderry House when it was a hospital.

Edith was from the very top ranks of the British elite. She was a grand-daughter of the Duke of Sutherland, and her husband's grandfather was the Earl of Shrewsbury, the premier Earl of England. The holdings of the Londonderry family were enormous; they owned 50,000 acres of land in England, Ireland and Wales, and their coalfields in Durham employed 10,000 miners. Such vast wealth and prestige enabled her to command the highest possible standards in entertaining and fashion. Though not a natural conservative, Edith would willingly play the part of the consummate Tory hostess to support Charley's Parliamentary career. She had inherited all the accoutrements that the role required: the magnificent setting of Londonderry House, the expertise of the servants, the fortune to fund entertaining on this scale, even the magnificent tiara (she looked 'like a Christmas tree', according to one observer). In addition, she had closely observed both her aunt Millicent, Duchess of Sutherland, and her mother-in-law often enough to know how to entertain the royal family and grand relations.

Charles had ambitions to rise within the Conservative

Party. The Londonderrys' Eve of Parliament receptions were glittering, packed events with 2,000 guests climbing the staircase four abreast to the first-floor ballroom. They had important guests to stay at their opulent country houses. In 1919 Charley was appointed to the new Air Council by the post-war coalition government, then in 1920 he became Under-Secretary of State for Air. He also learned to fly, and described how being at the controls of his own aeroplane provided him with an almost other-worldly sense of tranquillity and distance from his worries.

The Londonderrys were much concerned with family matters by the early 1920s. Their eldest daughter, Maureen, now nineteen, was pursued by Prince Albert, second in line to the throne and a regular attendant at the Ark on Wednesday evenings, where he had the nickname of The Unicorn. However, Maureen preferred a young MP, Oliver Stanley, and successfully persuaded her parents that she should marry him instead. While making the arrangements for the wedding, Edith found herself feeling uncharacteristically 'seedy'. Usually in robust good health, she was initially mystified, then startled to discover she was pregnant with her fifth child. When Maureen and Oliver's wedding took place in Durham Cathedral on 4 November 1920, the bride's mother was four and a half months pregnant at the age of forty-one. Mairi Elizabeth was born on 25 March 1921, and Charley was delighted at this unexpected turn of events. However, his possessive mistress, Eloise Ancaster, was less thrilled and spread scurrilous rumours that the new baby must be the result of Edith having had an affair, claiming that Charley would never be unfaithful to her. When her efforts to undermine Edith were unsuccessful, Eloise was furious and sent back all Charley's presents to her in one huge sack. It was at this point that Charley ended his affair with her, choosing to spend much more time at Mount Stewart with his wife and the unexpected but much-loved addition to the family.

In 1921 Charley was made Minister for Education in the first Ulster Parliament, and the family based themselves largely in Northern Ireland. Edith brought a new lease of life to the house and its rather plain grounds. Her childhood home of Dunrobin Castle in Scotland inspired her alterations at Mount Stewart. She redesigned and redecorated much of the interior, including the huge drawing room, the smoking room, the Castlereagh Room and many of the guest bedrooms.

The Londonderrys employed twenty ex-servicemen to supplement their own staff in a major programme to clear and landscape the grounds surrounding the house, which had been rather neglected during the war. The gardens had been rather dull, comprising plain lawns with large decorative pots. Between 1921 and the mid-1930s Edith redesigned the gardens, creating a series of distinct, interconnected 'outdoor rooms'. In addition she laid out walks in the Lily Wood and increased the size of the lake. She excelled at garden design and exploited the mild climate of Strangford Lough to experiment with imaginative planting. The formal gardens recall those of Italy, while the wooded areas boast a wide variety of plants from other countries. The result is one of the most inspiring and unusual gardens in the British Isles. It was a labour of love; Edith used horticulture as a means of expressing stories from Irish folklore and mythology. There is an Irish harp in topiary and a trefoil-shaped hedge representing the shamrock. There were practical measures too. Edith was very fond of dogs and owned a wide variety of them throughout her life, the largest being deerhounds. The ornamental ponds in the gardens were designed with ramps leading from the water so that if one of the Pekingeses (short-legged, short-sighted and very fluffy) accidentally fell in, it could struggle out again.

Four years of rationing, shortages, blackouts and intermittent bombing had taken its toll on the civilian population. There was a desperate pent-up desire to travel. In March 1919 Mrs Greville scooped up her young friend Osbert Sitwell, who had been recuperating from flu and jaundice, and they set off for Monte Carlo. This was his first trip abroad for pleasure since 1914. The war had left him depressed, ill and hard up, so staying as Mrs Greville's guest in the luxurious Hotel de Paris, overlooking the Mediterranean, was bliss. They gambled in the casino, met the celebrated dancer Isadora Duncan and enjoyed the sunshine. Their chauffeured Rolls-Royce took them on to Biarritz, where Osbert met his brother Sachie, and they planned an exhibition of modern French art to be held in a London gallery that summer. The brothers stayed at Polesden Lacey while it was on, commuting daily to London in a heatwave and returning to Surrey at night to face the outrage of their fellow guests, who deplored the French avant-garde art scene. Mrs Greville was not a natural enthusiast of Picasso, Modigliani, Léger and Matisse, but she was fond of Osbert, no doubt partly because he was an ex-Guards officer and the heir to a baronetcy.

Meanwhile Mrs Greville was at last able to return to her regular haunts of Paris and meet her old friend and social rival Grace Vanderbilt, from New York, of similar vintage and even wealthier than she was. The two middle-aged ladies ventured out to a plush restaurant in Fontainebleau for a sumptuous lunch of lobster and Château d'Yquem. During the return journey, while they were driving along a lonely rural road, the back axle of the car broke, the vehicle overturned, and the passengers were deposited into a ditch. Their chauffeur, Pierre, was knocked unconscious in the accident, and they faced a dilemma; Mrs Greville insisted that they must flag down any passing vehicle and persuade the driver to take him to hospital. Grace Vanderbilt asked fearfully, 'But supposing we were to be taken for two cocottes?' Maggie eyed her burly friend, brushed a clump of weeds from her rubies, and answered, 'I think my dear, that we may take that risk.'

Mrs Greville was an observant woman with a strong romantic streak, and she took a keen interest in the affairs of the younger generation, often taking an active role in assisting courtships along. She noticed that one of her housemaids was obviously smitten by a handsome but tongue-tied young gardener at Polesden, but they were both too shy to speak to each other. Mrs Greville told the maid that she must spend the summer looking after one of Madam's lapdogs at Polesden, and that the pet required frequent walks in the grounds. Physical proximity and the introduction of a dim Pekingese as a safe conversational topic had the desired effect: the relationship developed, and the young couple married.

She also assisted her beloved god-daughter Sonia Keppel, whose romance with the Hon. Roland Cubitt had hit the buffers, owing to his parents' disapproval. His father and mother, Lord and Lady Ashcombe, were near neighbours of Mrs Greville. Rollie's three older brothers had been killed in the war; understandably, he was very precious to them. Sonia's older sister Violet had recently eloped to France with Vita Sackville-West, to the titillated horror of polite society. The Cubitts were wary of their son marrying into a family so rife with scandal: Mrs Keppel's well-known affair with Edward VII was safely in the past, but was lesbian adultery acceptable in one's in-laws? In a pincer movement worthy of a brace of formidable aunts in a P. G. Wodehouse novel Mrs Keppel and Mrs Greville bore down on the jeopardised romance. Mrs Greville's chauffeur drove her to the neighbours' country house; while her Rolls idled gently on the gravel, she refused to step inside. When a puzzled Lord Ashcombe came out to greet his unexpected visitor, she told him plainly that she did not consider his family good enough for her god-daughter and swept off. Meanwhile, with a professional poker player's skill, Mrs Keppel trapped Lord Ashcombe into settling a huge financial sum on the young couple, in order to match the Keppels' dowry. The wedding went ahead on 17 November 1920, and Mrs Greville was lavish with gifts for the young couple.

Mrs Greville's Edwardian glory days left many a legacy. Both she and Alice Keppel had been friendly with Sir Ernest Cassel, Edward VII's financial adviser of genius, and they benefitted from his advice. Sir Ernest was very fond of his two grand-daughters, Edwina and Mary Ashley, especially as their mother, Sir Ernest's only child, had died in 1911, when they were very young. The girls had a stepmother, with whom relations were strained, and so Edwina went to live with her grandfather in London. Mrs Greville particularly liked young Edwina, who joined a Polesden house party in July 1920. Fellow guests that weekend included Prince Bertie and Grace Vanderbilt, the American millionairess. Through Grace, Edwina met Louis Mountbatten, known as Dickie, in the summer of 1921, and the young couple were instantly attracted to each other.

However, Dickie was just about to set out on a nine-month tour of India and Japan with his cousin the Prince of Wales. He knew that Mrs Greville was planning a lengthy trip to

India to coincide with the royal visit. Like them, she would be a guest of her old friend Lord Reading, the Viceroy of India. Dickie was sure Mrs Greville would be willing to act as chaperone if Edwina's grandfather, Sir Ernest, approved, and then Edwina could join him in India.

The lovers' plans were overturned by the sudden and unexpected deaths of first Dickie's father, Lord Mountbatten, and then, just ten days later, of Sir Ernest Cassel. Both Dickie and Edwina were grief-stricken. Under the provisions of Sir Ernest's will Edwina stood to inherit £7 million, but not until she was twenty-eight or married, whichever came sooner. Meanwhile, she was very short of cash, while Dickie worried that his motives for wanting to marry her might now be misconstrued as fortune-hunting.

Resourceful Edwina went to see Mrs Greville and mentioned the attractive young ADC who would be in India with the Prince of Wales at the same time as her friend. A practised matchmaker, Mrs Greville took her cue and asked Edwina's father, Colonel Ashley, if his daughter could stay at Polesden after Sir Ernest's funeral; having obtained his approval, she invited Dickie Mountbatten too. Their romance was supposed to be secret, but it was evident that they adored each other.

Nevertheless Dickie set off for India on 26 October with the Prince of Wales, leaving Edwina behind, still in full mourning, and Mrs Greville had to sail to Bombay without her on the SS *Morea*. But on her arrival Mrs Ronnie prompted the Viceroy to write and invite Edwina to come and stay in the middle of January, when she would be in half-mourning; with the letter Edwina was able to get her father's grudging agreement, and she finally arrived at the palatial Viceregal Lodge in Delhi in the early hours of 12 February 1922.

The setting was extremely formal, and etiquette rigidly

observed: maharajahs and princes came to meet the Prince of Wales, uniforms and decorations were worn at a succession of state banquets, garden parties and fancy-dress parties. Mrs Greville sported her famous emeralds. There were trips to tombs and forts, hunting and parties, but there was also a rather fraught atmosphere. The Prince was not an easy guest: he was petulant at being separated from his mistress, Mrs Dudley Ward; he resented the business of 'kinging' as he called it; and he smoked and drank too much. His only consolation was the company of his companions, his cousin Louis Mountbatten and an officer in the British Indian Army, 'Fruity' Metcalfe, who was to become his equerry and loyal friend. The Prince appreciated the company of pretty, compliant women, and consequently he resented having the fifty-eight-year-old Mrs Greville, his mother's great friend, keeping a beady eye on him at banquets and garden parties, tiger shoots and cocktail evenings. She even managed to rearrange the seating at a dinner party for 220 people so that the Prince, the guest of honour, was forced to sit facing her across the table.

Meanwhile Dickie and Edwina's romance flourished, and Mrs Greville lent them her vast drawing room so that they could have somewhere private to meet. They believed that only the Prince and Mrs Greville knew that they were in love, but when Dickie found his valet, Hiscock, unexpectedly cleaning Edwina's riding boots, and Edwina's maid, Weller, carefully ironing his ties, he realised the secret was out. Dickie proposed to Edwina on 14 February, and she accepted. They decided to keep the engagement secret, but by 20 February they had confided in Mrs Ronnie, as she had been Edwina's chaperone, and then broke the news to Lord and Lady Reading, their hosts.

The announcement alarmed the lackadaisical chaperones. A budding *tendresse* between two young people in a romantic, exotic setting was one thing; an engagement between a member of the royal family and a juvenile multi-millionairess with whose care they had all been entrusted while she was more than 4,000 miles from home was quite another. Somewhat belatedly, doubts crept in. Mrs Greville seems, rather late in the day, to have questioned Lord Mountbatten's true motives and worried that perhaps he was only after Edwina for the vast fortune that she would inherit on marriage; and what would Edwina's family say to the whirlwind romance that had swept through Viceregal Lodge? Could they at least dissuade Edwina and Dickie from making any formal announcement until their respective families had given permission? Mrs Greville wrote a distraught note to Lord Reading:

My dear Viceroy

I am absolutely wretched about that child – I couldn't sleep a wink, I have grave misgivings. They were both at me last night – & she will not be reasonable, all I begged for was that no engagement should take place now, in a year she will be sick of him.

She has promised me that she will not write home till she has seen you, but she promised me she would do nothing here – I want time – this is absolutely confidential only I feel she is being thrown to the wolves so although it is mean of one to betray her confidence I feel you are the only pillar of strength [...] I don't dislike him but he is wily and I am really wretched and very sore at her for breaking her word

*to me. And she looked so white-faced and mother-
less last night. Dear Viceroy please insist on no
engagement – I have failed ignominiously but you
are so strong. Bless you and forgive me.*

Lady Reading wrote somewhat apologetically to Edwina's
father, Colonel Ashley, expressing the view that she had hoped
Edwina would have fallen for someone more mature and
established. Edwina's father was offended that King George
V heard about her engagement before he did, because Louis
Mountbatten sought his approval, and he dragged his feet in
giving permission for months, but eventually at the beginning
of May 1922 all was resolved and the engagement was offi-
cially announced to general relief, with the wedding planned
for 18 July 1922.

Back in Britain, Edwina's supposed chaperone recovered
her equilibrium and promptly claimed credit for the match.
Mrs Greville held a congratulatory dinner party for the
Mountbattens and some fifty guests, including Prince Bertie,
her heir, at Charles Street, and a ball for 300. She also had
the Mountbattens to stay at Polesden Lacey. London society
could not get enough of the glamorous young couple; a potent
combination of good looks, fabulous wealth and royal
connections made them a magnet for the hostesses. Lady
Cunard gave them a luncheon party, a dinner party and two
dances, and Mrs Corrigan threw a party for them.

It was the society wedding of 1922, with 800 guests,
including numerous royals. Dickie Mountbatten's best man
was the Prince of Wales. Lady Cunard gave Dickie a set of
onyx and diamond waistcoat buttons, but unfortunately he
thanked Mrs Vanderbilt for them by mistake. Mrs Greville
gave diamond hairclips for Edwina, cufflinks for Dickie and

a silver inkstand and bellpush. Mrs Greville attended the wedding, and she remained on good terms with the couple for many years to come.

While lavish party-throwing and sumptuous gifts were the preserve of the truly wealthy, lower down the social scale money was hard to come by in the years immediately after the war. The Colefaxes were forced to face some hard realities. Arthur's worthy but unpaid wartime role at the Ministry of Munitions had resulted in a knighthood in 1920, but Lord and Lady Colefax's financial situation, like that of many others immediately after the Great War, was uncertain. They decided to sell both Old Buckhurst, where they had entertained more than 800 guests between 1914 and 1921, and their house in Onslow Square, to buy a single house in London as both a family home and a forum for Sibyl's entertaining. In 1921 they found Argyll House, at 211 King's Road in Chelsea. It had been designed by the Venetian architect Giacomo Leoni around 1720 as a 'small country house' in the neo-classical style, with a high-walled garden on the south side, iris beds and an ancient grapevine that rambled up to the roof.

The Colefaxes fell in love with it instantly. The house needed considerable amendments to make it suitable for modern life; the stable was demolished and an extension added in matching yellow brick, which was then 'treated' with a mixture of water and soot to match the original structure. Servants' quarters were created, including a pleasant sitting room for staff. The cellar was turned into a large kitchen with a garden window, and a luggage lift was installed.

Sibyl tackled the interior, removing Victorian additions. The rooms were repanelled and painted the colour of old ivory. A fine Georgian staircase was added, and Sibyl introduced antique walnut or lacquered Chinese furniture and colourful antique rugs. The dining room was rather small, but seemed larger because of the antique mirrors, which reflected the wall-sconces, and the central chandelier made of assorted crystals collected by Sibyl. She liked symmetry, with matching pairs of chairs, vases and flower arrangements. She also favoured the type of colourful floral chintz that had been brought to Britain from India by the East India Company in the seventeenth and eighteenth centuries, which still tended to be found in the bedrooms of English country houses; now it livened up convivial groups of upholstered chairs and sofas, encouraging her guests to sit and talk. Sibyl's gift was in identifying the essential character of the organically grown English country house, but making it cleaner, tidier, more comfortable and better lit. Her genius was in distilling these traditional features to make homes that looked historic, but subtly better. She recognised precisely what the newly wealthy required, a ready-made heritage, because she came from exactly the same background. For the next fifteen years Argyll House was to be her beloved family home, a showcase for her decorating talents and the stage on which she performed.

Unlike the other hostesses, Sibyl was keen to cultivate the Bloomsbury group, a loose agglomeration of Modernist writers, artists and intellectuals. Two talented sisters, Virginia and Vanessa Stephen, lived at 46 Gordon Square in Bloomsbury, the leafy residential area near the British Museum, until their marriages, and their location gave the movement its name. Their social circle included their husbands, Leonard Woolf and Clive Bell, and Duncan Grant, Virginia's lover Vita

Sackville-West, the economist John Maynard Keynes, the critic Roger Fry and the painter Walter Sickert. Their personal relationships were closely intertwined. Their somewhat louche lifestyles and ill-defined romances raised eyebrows. It was said that the Bloomsbury group 'lived in squares, but loved in triangles'.

'The Bloomsburies' were championed and cultivated by Lady Ottoline Morrell, who was related to the first Duke of Wellington: her half-brother was the Duke of Portland. She was married to the Liberal MP Philip Morrell, was six feet tall, had flaming red hair and dressed eccentrically in brilliant colours. The Morrells had bought a Tudor mansion called Garsington in Oxfordshire in 1914 and restored it, and they also had an impressive London house, 44 Bedford Square. Both houses were to become regular haunts for the Bloomsbury group, who appreciated the better things in life, especially if someone else was paying. In 1916 Lady Ottoline offered a refuge to Clive Bell and other conscientious objectors by inviting them to stay at Garsington and work on the home farm so that they could avoid conscription. She was a resolute friend to avant-garde writers such as Virginia Woolf, Siegfried Sassoon and T. S. Eliot.

The Morrells maintained what would now be called an 'open marriage'; Lady Ottoline's lovers included Bertrand Russell, Dora Carrington and Roger Fry, as well as a stone-mason employed at Garsington. Her unorthodox lifestyle prompted D. H. Lawrence to make her the central character of his book *Lady Chatterley's Lover*, and he also pilloried her as Hermione Roddice in *Women in Love*. Aldous Huxley mocked the free-thinking atmosphere to be found at Garsington, where the Morrells entertained weekend house parties in style, in his 1921 novel *Crome Yellow*.

Lady Ottoline was an aristocratic woman who acted as patron for a particular set within the creative avant-garde. By contrast, Sibyl Colefax rose from unremarkable beginnings to collect the celebrated from all fields – the well born and wealthy as much as the *literati* and the avant-garde. In most aspects of her life Sibyl was more conventional, and therefore less vulnerable to sniping and ridicule. She too cultivated Bloomsbury, despite their vinegary disparagement of her and the other 'celebrity' hostesses. Sibyl first began to pursue Virginia Woolf in 1922, bombarding her with invitations, which irritated the irascible novelist. Woolf claimed she refused Sibyl's initial overtures not only because they had not met but also because she was aware that her suspenders and stockings were shabby, and she loathed shopping for new clothes in order to appear respectable. In time the two women became oddly friendly, though Virginia Woolf remarked that Sibyl liked 'to listen to clever talk, and to buy it with a lunch of four courses and good wine'. Woolf preferred to see Sibyl alone, avoiding other writers, especially those she called 'great men', and resisted having to sing for her supper in a cluster of other guests. Virginia Woolf termed gossip about Sibyl as 'Colefaxiana' and coined the term 'Colefaxismus' to denote a casual remark intended to imply privileged knowledge of the subject.

Sibyl made a speciality of collecting literary lions: at Argyll House one might encounter Arnold Bennett, H. G. Wells or Max Beerbohm. Grand Irish writers appreciated her hospitality too; George Bernard Shaw would grace her table as well as that of Lady Astor, and the poet W. B. Yeats was an occasional fellow diner as well as being a regular guest of Lady Londonderry at Mount Stewart. Perhaps Sibyl's most satisfying literary scalp was that of George Moore, who, although he adored Lady Cunard for decades, still loathed sitting at her dining table with his rival Sir Thomas Beecham, and preferred the deference given to him by Sibyl. She also cultivated Harold Nicolson and Vita Sackville-West, and there was a nearly an unfortunate encounter at a party at Argyll House on 7 April 1921, when Denys Trefusis, unhappily married to Violet, spotted Vita across the room and left immediately; Violet and Vita had recently had a passionate affair and eloped together to France, leaving their respective, unfortunate husbands behind.

Like many in society, the Colefaxes returned to Europe at the first opportunity. It was in Italy that Sibyl was able to add to her collection of artists and aristocrats. The journalist Beverley Nichols recalled meeting Sibyl in Venice in 1920, and being amused by her cavalier use of the first name of people she had only just met. 'Dear Gerald [Lord] Berners – so many talents! Serge [Diaghilev] tells me he is going to commission him to write a ballet.' He continues:

> I remember her standing at the window of some palazzo or other – (I don't remember which one but I vaguely recall that our hostess had been the mistress of the Kaiser) – and I was much impressed by the way in which her beady eye swept the Grand Canal, seeking whom she might devour. 'Surely', she murmured, leaning over the balcony, 'surely that is dear Jane [Princess Faustino] in the white gondola below?' It was not, in fact, dear Jane; it was a drunken woman from Minnesota who was to give us all a lot of trouble; but Sibyl had made her point, she had created the atmosphere.

In 1922, 1923 and 1924 Sibyl spent the summer months with her two sons, Peter and Michael, touring Italy and

France. She frequently took them to Florence to stay with Bernard Berenson and Harold Acton, and they attended the Palio, the historic horse race in the square in Siena. Arthur and Sibyl were very close, and when separated by the necessity of his work, as she travelled in Europe, they wrote affectionately to each other – she signing herself 'Billie' and calling him 'My darling Gogo'. By travelling extensively, she was echoing the restless habits of her mother, but in Sibyl's case it was in order to experience the best that life had to offer, to see as much of beauty and culture as she could manage to absorb. She was driven by an ambition to mix with the creative elite, and to experience avidly whatever she found absorbing and moving, as though to make up for her early years of colourless repression.

While literature and art provided Sibyl Colefax with the stimulus she craved, for Lady Cunard it was music in all its diverse forms, a genuine passion that was inextricably linked to her devotion to the interests of her lover, Sir Thomas Beecham. As Osbert Sitwell wrote:

> In the world of opera and ballet, Lady Cunard reigned alone. Her boundless and enthusiastic love of music places all those who enjoy opera in her debt: for it was largely her support, and the way she marshalled her forces, that enabled the wonderful seasons of opera and ballet in these years to materialise [...] she had grasped the fact that in the London of that time, in order to ensure the success of such an art-luxury of Grand Opera, it was absolutely necessary to be able to rely on a regular attendance by

numskulls, nitwits and morons addicted to the mode even
if they did not care in the least for music.

There was a pent-up demand for dancing, music and entertainment in the aftermath of the war, and Lady Cunard
championed the cause of the Ballets Russes. Maud organised
a fundraising ball on their behalf on 4 December 1919 at
Covent Garden. Diaghilev was constantly seeking funds, and
he approached Mrs Greville about becoming a theatrical
'angel', investing in his company. She gave him dinner but
declined to invest in entertainment. Even Lady Cunard struggled to raise enough money to put on *Pulcinella* at Covent
Garden, because it was an unknown quantity, a new ballet
with music by Stravinsky and sets designed by Picasso.
However, the less expensive venue of the Coliseum proved
suitable, and the production went ahead to great acclaim in
the summer of 1919.

With his passion for music and his friendship with
Stravinsky and Diaghilev, it is not surprising that gifted but
eccentric Lord Gerald Berners became friendly with Lady
Cunard. They were both knowledgeable about ballet and
opera, and once he had acquired an apartment in Half Moon
Street he was able to entertain Maud with cosy post-opera
suppers, a short taxi ride from the theatres and concert-halls
of the West End. He was a great practical joker, and at
open-air summer parties he would pretend he'd just been
stung by a wasp, a prospect that petrified Lady Cunard. It
was Lord Berners who reflected that Lady Colefax's parties
were like a gathering of lunatics presided over by an efficient,
trained hospital nurse, while Lady Cunard's were like a party
of lunatics presided over by a lunatic.

Maud Cunard was much involved in fundraising to support

a new venture, raising more than £70,000 for the Sir Thomas Beecham Opera Company Limited. Maud, the Aga Khan and Lord Howard de Walden each invested £5,000, and the company was incorporated on 1 April 1919. But it was an uphill struggle to make the company pay – there was a post-war slump, money was tight, and the repertoire patriotically avoided the works of German composers, which limited its appeal for music lovers.

Maud gained the patronage of prestigious guests by inviting them to gala performances and opening nights when Sir Thomas was conducting. She chose to overlook his frequent absences, and the rumours of his numerous affairs with singers and performers. In 1920 she was forty-eight, but she boasted of her younger lover, 'Sir Thomas is quite a Don Juan'. Beecham was still married to Utica, who would not agree to a divorce, but he was also frank about the true nature of his relationship with Lady Cunard, on one occasion allegedly remarking to his musicians, 'Gentlemen, you will be pleased to know that the future of the orchestra is assured, thanks to the virility of your conductor.' Meanwhile, faithful George Moore still adored Maud and occasionally dined with her; on 7 December 1920 he wrote to her:

> You brought into the world a hard heart as well as much beauty, grace and charm, and it is small wonder I fell in love with you, and shall always love you. Your party last night was animated with your personality and everybody was inspired with an unwonted happiness [...] all were smiling and agreeable, magnetised by you, for you charm even the morose.

Family matters were still a cause of concern to Maud Cunard, in particular the state of mind of her only child.

Nancy Cunard's lover Peter had been killed less than a month before the end of the Great War, but her husband, Sydney Fairbairn, had survived, being awarded the Military Cross for conspicuous gallantry for his actions in the last week of the war. Nancy became increasingly bitter about her marriage. She contracted Spanish flu in January 1919, then pneumonia, and had to recuperate at her mother's new house at 44 Grosvenor Square. Sydney was finally demobbed from serving in France and returned to London only to be told by Nancy that she could no longer bear being married. Duff Cooper, Nancy's friend, commiserated with him over two bottles of champagne; Sydney confided that he still loved her and believed her to be faithful to him, and Duff Cooper chose not to disillusion him. Nancy convalesced in the south of France, and in January 1920 she moved permanently to Paris and threw herself into writing. Striking-looking, reed-thin and elegantly dressed, with pale, glittering eyes and an unusually husky voice, she quickly attracted attention, and became the toast of the French avant-garde. Brancusi sculpted her, Man Ray photographed her and Oskar Kokoschka painted her. She was a literary and artistic muse in London too; Aldous Huxley's character Lucy Tantamount in *Point Counter Point* is based on her, and in Michael Arlen's *The Green Hat*, Iris March is unmistakable as Nancy. The portraitist Augustus John and the Vorticist Wyndham Lewis were also captivated by her.

Nancy fell seriously ill in Paris in the winter of 1920–21 and underwent a hysterectomy, followed by peritonitis. Her mother and father were constant visitors while her life was in peril. While she recovered in Paris, her first solo book of poetry, *Outlaws,* was published in London, to good reviews. Lady Cunard notified the press and both the *Nation* and the

Observer featured Nancy's poems. In March 1922 mother and daughter holidayed together in Monte Carlo, but the relationship between them was always uneasy. When in London, Nancy tended to stay in rooms above her favourite restaurant, the Eiffel Tower, but would join her mother for lunch or dinner at Maud's new house, 5 Carlton House Terrace. Maud was also determined to resolve Nancy's unhappy marriage, and in November 1922 she persuaded Duff Cooper to lunch with Nancy's husband, Sydney, to induce him to agree to a divorce. Meanwhile Maud was conquering London society; in later years Nancy remembered meeting T. S. Eliot at a ball given by her mother in 1922, and dancing with the Prince of Wales. She observed how ably her mother orchestrated these formal occasions.

Maud Cunard used considerable personal charm to infiltrate the circles she most admired, adroitly slipping through the increasingly permeable class boundaries. As the traditional aristocratic hostesses retreated to their country estates in the early 1920s, their places were quickly filled by new arrivals, who deployed intelligence and bottomless bank balances. Mrs Laura Mae Corrigan arrived in London on 1 April 1922. She had been rebuffed by Euclid Avenue, the Millionaires' Row in her second husband's home town of Cleveland, because the inhabitants resented the former waitress and divorcée who had acquired such a wealthy rough diamond, James Corrigan. The couple had lived in a New York hotel, which they thought would garner them opportunities to mingle with the wealthy, but despite having hired an 'aristocratic lady' to provide them with introductions, the grand Fifth Avenue families, the Rockefellers and Vanderbilts, simply ignored those so far below their own social circle. Magnificent wealth was not enough to gain access to the

'Four Hundred', New York's elite. One of Laura's targets even had a stock of RSVP cards specially printed by Tiffany & Co., declining Mrs Corrigan's kind invitation (with a gap so that the appropriate date could be added by hand), to despatch as his standard response to any overture from her.

The fictional American Mrs Whitehand in E. F. Benson's *Freaks of Mayfair* bears an uncanny resemblance to social mountaineers like Laura Corrigan. Having failed to achieve acceptance on the east coast, Benson's millionairess heroine decides to conquer London society after 'Nittie Vandercrump, the acknowledged queen of Newport, cut her dead for the seventeenth time, and with her famous scream asked her friend, Nancy Costersnatch, who all these strange faces belonged to'.

Arriving in London, Mrs Corrigan recognised that one needed a leg-up to get on the social ladder, and she contacted a fellow American, the thrice-married Lady Cora Strafford. Cora's first husband had been Mr Samuel J. Colgate, the toothpaste millionaire, who was thirty-nine years her senior, and Cora had no qualms about fortunes derived from trade. She invited Laura to an intimate little dinner party, where the newcomer learned from a fellow guest, the Duke of Portland, brother of Lady Ottoline Morrell, that the famous Mrs Alice Keppel might be willing to rent out her vast Georgian mansion at 16 Grosvenor Street in Mayfair.

A meeting was arranged, and within a month of her arrival Laura had leased Mrs Keppel's town house, complete with its exquisite ceramics, red lacquer furniture, grey walls, magnificent paintings and glittering chandeliers. George and Alice Keppel had maintained the original layout of the building as apartments, so that each had their own suite of rooms; Laura initially objected to this arrangement, pointing out that 'Mr Corrigan and I live intimate', but Edward VII's former mistress suavely pointed out a discreet private staircase linking the two suites. Despite her misgivings about the exquisite Persian rugs ('Why, they're not even new!') and the Chippendale chairs (which Laura felt were slightly marred by the 'petits pois' covers), the outgoing and incoming society hostesses reached an agreement that suited them both. For £500 a week Laura would lease the house and contents, keeping on Mr and Mrs Rolfe, Alice's exceptional butler and cook, and the twenty household staff. In a master-stroke, she also bought a copy of Alice's address book, so that she had the names and addresses of everyone worth knowing in London. The Keppels decamped, and Laura moved in.

Mrs Corrigan's entrée to London society was facilitated by Mr Rolfe, who lured into the house the friends of his previous mistress, to meet her mysterious successor. She was a curiosity, and phenomenally wealthy; the antennae of high-class ladies who devoted themselves to good works twitched at the prospect of the sums that might be diverted to benefit their Dumb Chums or Distressed Gentlefolk. As an American, of course, she was classless – but was she quite *acceptable* in polite society? To ensure that she was, Mr Rolfe recommended the services of Charlie Stirling. He was the nephew of Lord Rossmore and well-connected in aristocratic circles; he was young, witty and popular. Significantly, he was already social secretary to Edith, Lady Londonderry, one of London's most influential hostesses.

Charlie Stirling launched Laura Corrigan on the London scene. First he arranged for her to dine at Londonderry House, as Lord and Lady Londonderry's son Robin, who had been visiting the States, had already met hospitable James Corrigan. Edith took to Laura at once; she appreciated the liberal donation to one of her favourite charities, as suggested by

Charlie, and the two women became and remained unlikely friends. In return, the Londonderrys were among the guests at Laura's first dinner party in her new home, which was reported in *The Times*. Their attendance was an endorsement from the aristocratic and political elite. A few weeks later, *The Times* stated that Princess Marie-Louise, a cousin of George V, was the guest of honour at another dinner party *chez* Corrigan. The hostess's outfit was described as a gown of white crêpe embroidered with opalescent pearls; she was evidently a woman of substance. Court circles also noted that she had been a guest of the Duchess of Rutland, and through the wife of the American Ambassador, Mrs George Harvey, Laura Corrigan was presented at court. Thanks to the connections of Mr Rolfe, Charlie Stirling, the goodwill of a few establishment ladies and her own determination, Laura was launched on London society.

Mrs Corrigan courted a fun-loving bunch of younger aristocrats and socialites, having no interest in cultivating intellectuals, the artistic or the serious. She preferred display and luxury, and her husband, James, who would visit London for stints of ten days or so, was happy to provide ample funds to obtain it. One of her earliest social successes was a fluke: the handsome and highly eligible Duke of Kent, younger brother of the Prince of Wales, was rumoured to be the guest of honour at one of her parties. The Duke heard the gossip, and was amused enough to present himself on the appropriate night. Laura's reputation as a hostess of note was instantly established, and she was so excited that she stood on her head, having first secured her skirts around her knees to protect her modesty. The headstand habit, accompanied always by a drum-roll from the band, was immortalised in Noel Coward's comic song 'I've Been to a Marvellous Party'.

One could not imagine Mrs Greville performing such a trick.

Laura Corrigan responded to the slightly febrile mood of the 1920s by providing sumptuous venues with ample entertainment for her curious guests. As well as targeting aristocrats, she consciously cultivated the Bright Young People, those who were too young to have served in the forces during the Great War, but who were reacting against its legacy with a defiant superficiality, with parties and dances, madcap bets and gambles. The decorative guests of Mrs Corrigan were rather like the party-goers in F. Scott Fitzgerald's *The Great Gatsby*. They knew little of the personality who had invited them, or the origins of the industrial fortune that enabled such prodigality, but they enjoyed her lavish hospitality. As Barbara Cartland wrote:

> Acrobats, jugglers, knockabout comedians, and on one occasion, performing seals appeared in Mayfair drawing rooms in a search for the sensational. Few British hostesses, however, could compete with the standard set by wealthy Mrs James Corrigan [… who] settled down to startling London with her sensational parties. Amazing, costly settings, gold tombola prizes, and the best theatrical turns procurable made her at least the most-talked of hostess of the period. Such parties always seemed to me to be filled with people who were afraid they were missing something or someone in the next room.

At any one of Laura's dinner-dances there might be fancy dress competitions, games of chance, including lotteries and tombolas (pronounced as two disparate words by the hostess as 'Tom Bowlers', as though enunciating a person's name.) The prizes were highly desirable and expensive little gewgaws from Cartier. Each lucky party-goer would win a pair of braces with gold buckles, or a pretty little diamond hairclip. Mr Rolfe was careful to ensure that everyone went home with something, in the manner of participants at a child's birthday party. These were valuable prizes, and while none of her guests was exactly impoverished, it is human nature to be both acquisitive and competitive. Conspicuous consumption was the theme, and Laura planned her parties with precision and an eye to an overall budget of around £6,000 per occasion, the equivalent of more than £100,000 today. By 1923, her second season, she was able to give a wildly successful party for 140 people, including a number of overseas guests who were in London to attend the marriage of the Duke and Duchess of York. As her friend Elsa Maxwell wrote: 'Europe in the 1920s was awash with rich Americans who used money as a springboard for high dives into society, and no one made a bigger, cruder splash than Laura.'

So rapid was her ascent up the social scale that in 1923 Laura and James Corrigan were invited into the Royal Enclosure to watch the Epsom Derby, in the august presence of Queen Mary. Through her own ingenuity and determination Laura had achieved in Britain what had been denied to her in her own country; acceptance at face value. She was keen to ensure that those who had snubbed her in Cleveland or New York were left in no doubt about her social successes.

Mrs Corrigan often gave interviews to the press, and her *bons mots* and frequent malapropisms were widely reported in print. It was through the gossip columns of newspapers that the new London hostesses were able to advertise their social triumphs in the 1920s. There was an avid appetite among the readership for humorous stories, amusing features or tales of misdeeds among the aristocracy. The Bright Young Things were always good copy, with their themed fancy dress parties and treasure hunts. After the war many newspapers employed well-connected correspondents to write their social news, and gossip became more alive and better informed. Some hostesses even invited gossip columnists to their parties for the purposes of advertisement, though they had to be prepared for the occasional bad review, in the manner of theatrical impresarios, if an evening did not go as planned. Other hostesses continued to use the papers as a means of recording their social triumphs, supplying all the details of an event through their social secretary; *The Times* would dutifully run two whole columns of the names of guests the morning after a Londonderry House political reception. Some hostesses were astute enough to cultivate the press so as to 'plant' unattributable stories that served their own purposes. One of those was Mrs Margaret Greville, in her determination to advance the courtship of Prince Bertie.

She had failed utterly to charm the Prince of Wales while they were in India; he resented the constant scrutiny of one of his mother's close friends. Undaunted, Mrs Greville nurtured his younger brother, taking a keen interest in every aspect of Bertie's life; after all, she was planning to leave him a substantial sum and her home after she was gone. It was generally believed that Bertie was unsuited to any public role, as he was incapacitated by his stutter. However, he was much liked by his family, and he inspired strong friendships. In the summer of 1920 Bertie was smitten by a young Scottish lady called Lady Elizabeth Bowes-Lyon. She was small and pretty, with a radiant smile and fluffy hair, and was much in demand in London society. As a daughter of the fourteenth Earl of Strathmore, brought up at Glamis Castle, she could have her pick of suitors. They met at a dinner-dance in Grosvenor Square on 10 June 1920, and were introduced by Bertie's equerry, James Stuart. James's family, the Earls of Moray, were near neighbours of the Strathmores, so he and Elizabeth knew each other well, and there had been speculation that they might marry.

Bertie enlisted the help of his fairy godmother, Mrs Ronnie, to court Elizabeth. The first letter in the Royal Archives from Elizabeth to Bertie dates from December 1920; she says she is looking forward to Mrs Greville's forthcoming dinner party in honour of his twenty-fifth birthday. Mrs Greville often invited Elizabeth to her parties, but still she seemed to prefer James Stuart. She turned down Bertie's offer of marriage in the spring of 1921, so Sir Sidney Greville, consummate court fixer and old friend of Mrs Ronnie, made James Stuart an offer he couldn't refuse: a lucrative posting to learn the oil industry in distant Oklahoma. The field was now clear for Bertie, but Elizabeth still said no. She was fond of him, but had no wish to marry into the royal family. King George remarked, 'You'll be a lucky man if she accepts you.'

On 13 December 1922 Mrs Greville held yet another dinner-dance at Charles Street for the couple, an event also attended by the Prince of Wales, and subsequently leaked a suggestion to the *Daily Star* that an engagement was imminent between Bertie and Elizabeth, claiming the credit for yet another 'royal engagement' along the lines of the Mountbattens' nuptials. However, a further three weeks went by without a break-through. Desperate measures were now called for.

On 5 January 1923 the *Daily News* gossip column carried a startling headline: 'Scottish Bride for Prince of Wales'. The article suggested that the heir to the throne was engaged to the daughter of an (unnamed) Scottish peer, who owned castles both north and south of the border. Elizabeth Bowes-Lyon was the obvious candidate, and the story's source was unattributed. Bertie was unnerved – Elizabeth would make a very suitable wife for the Prince of Wales, his older brother, and he had seen them dancing together. Elizabeth had twice refused Bertie; did she secretly hope to marry his older brother, the future king? The marriage of Bertie's own parents had only occurred because of the unexpected death of his uncle the Duke of Clarence, to whom the future Queen Mary had been engaged. A bride deemed suitable for one prince might well marry another if circumstances changed. There was a shortage of suitable candidates as a potential match for the Prince of Wales, and it was imperative in the minds of King George and Queen Mary that their eldest son should marry to ensure the royal line of succession. Faced with the appalling thought that his more glamorous elder brother might marry the love of his life, Bertie proposed to Elizabeth for the third time. She too had been unnerved by the erroneous press speculation, and on 13 January 1923 she finally said yes.

Their wedding took place on 26 April 1923 in Westminster Abbey, and the young couple went to stay at Polesden Lacey for the first part of their honeymoon. Only five years after the end of the Great War, many Britons were relieved that a royal prince was marrying a resoundingly Scottish aristocrat, rather than a German bride, as in the past. That arch matchmaker, Mrs Greville, was delighted. Elizabeth was Scottish, she was charming, and of course she would be the doyenne of Polesden in time, once Bertie had inherited the estate. The Duke and Duchess of York became frequent visitors both at Polesden and at her London house. In return Mrs Greville was invited to receptions and dinner parties at Buckingham Palace. She was now the 'favourite aunt' of virtually the whole royal family. It was all a very long way from helping to run a lodging house in Edinburgh.

5

The Roaring Twenties

Politics were on the minds of many in the 1920s. One particular hostess, the Tory *grande dame* Lady Londonderry, found a new friend from the other side of the political divide. She had the magnificent setting of Park Lane, the highly experienced staff and the jewellery. All Edith's efforts were in support of her husband, Charley, who viewed himself as destined for high political influence. She chose to deal with his philandering by excusing him on the grounds that other women found him as devastatingly attractive as she did, but, socially successful, intelligent and very good-looking, it was perhaps inevitable that eventually Edith would look outside her marriage for emotional involvement. She found it in the unlikely and substantially older figure of Ramsay MacDonald, the first Labour Prime Minister.

Ramsay MacDonald's story would be remarkable in any age. He had been born in Lossiemouth in 1866, the illegitimate son of a Scottish crofter. An early career as a teacher led him into politics, and by 1911 he was the leader of the Parliamentary Labour Party. He resigned in 1914 in protest against Britain's involvement in the Great War, and attracted opprobrium for his stance as a pacifist, but by 1922 he was leader of his party again, and in January 1924 he was elected the first Labour Prime Minister, with support from the Liberals. This came as a profound shock to the Conservative elite. Mrs Ronnie Greville (very much a Scottish snob, though with plenty of skeletons in her own family's closet) remarked, 'My dear, one couldn't be *seen* with Ramsay MacDonald!' However, he was the Prime Minister, and the proprieties needed to be maintained.

King George V was determined to support MacDonald, and in an unprecedented move he invited the entire Cabinet to dine at Buckingham Palace. Lady Londonderry and Ramsay MacDonald were among the guests; she was asked whether she was willing to be 'taken in' to dine by the new premier, even though he was a member of the Labour Party. She replied that of course his position trumped any party loyalties. She was impressed by the personable gentleman who offered her his arm. He had been a widower since 1911; he was intelligent, courtly and excellent company; and they shared a love for Scotland, where both had been brought up. Their friendship started that night and lasted for more than a decade, despite political vicissitudes. The Londonderrys were the first guests he invited to stay with him at Chequers, the Prime Minister's official weekend residence, and he was to become a frequent visitor at Edith and Charley's magnificent homes. It is uncertain whether the pair were ever lovers in the physical sense, but their surviving letters are evidence of the ardent nature of their feelings for each other.

Mrs Greville also had an admirer in high-ranking political circles. For many years Sir John Simon was romantically interested in her. A barrister and career politician, he was widowed with three children, and was a frequent visitor to both Polesden Lacey and Charles Street. Sibyl Colefax claimed that Margaret was far too outspoken to make a politician's wife. However, Mrs Greville insisted that in 1917 he had proposed to her, dropping to his knees on her drawing-room carpet to do so, but that she had refused because of his children. Leo Amery MP heard that after her refusal Sir John wrote to Mrs Greville saying he would now propose to the first woman who would accept him, and promptly married his children's governess. Nevertheless, Sir John and Mrs Greville were great friends, and she wielded considerable influence over him as he held high office as, variously, the Attorney-General, Foreign Secretary, Home Secretary and Chancellor of the Exchequer. Years after Mrs Ronnie's death, Osbert Sitwell discovered by chance that Sir John still visited her grave.

Sir John was instrumental in bringing about a peaceful conclusion to the General Strike of May 1926. There was genuine fear of a Bolshevik-style revolution. Prime Minister Stanley Baldwin warned that the strike placed Britain closer to civil war than it had been in centuries, and he was concerned that it might end in carnage. Five days into the General Strike, with public transport at a standstill and an ugly mood abroad, Sir John Simon, the former Attorney-General, drew on his knowledge of the law to point out that the strike was illegal on the grounds that it did not comply with an act of twenty years previously, which allowed trade union funds to be immune from claims of damages caused by industrial disputes. Consequently, he stated, every trade union leader was 'liable in damages to the uttermost farthing of his personal possessions'. It was a very British end to a political crisis. Relief at the end of the strike was palpable. As the Duchess of Westminster later breezily recalled:

> The dark shadows were caused by labour problems, strikes and unemployment. From time to time I wrote cheerfully in my diary that we seemed to be on the brink of a bloody revolution, but it was a possibility which had been at the

back of the minds of the upper classes since the days of Marie Antoinette and which they had got quite used to, so in the next sentence I went on to describe how I was trimming a hat or arranging a dinner party.

While labour relations remained stormy and unemployment rose in manufacturing cities and provincial industries, the very wealthy were cocooned from the harsh realities of everyday life for many Britons. The upper classes were reliant on the dedication of their expert servants to provide everything they needed. The collapse of the General Strike reassured the elite that a British Bolshevik-style revolution had been averted, though the more politically astute were aware of the yawning divide between rich and poor. As the cynical MP Bob Boothby observed: 'Those were the days of large houses in London and the country, butlers and footmen galore, gleaming silver, superlative food and drink, and the Embassy Club. Fortunately the unemployed were out of sight; and, I am afraid, out of mind.'

Each of the Queen Bees was tended by people who ran her household, managed her social life, organised her estate, drove her to parties, helped her dress and undress and ministered to her guests. Servants were crucial to the career of any aspirational hostess because they ensured the smooth running of the household. By the late 1920s reliable staff were becoming hard to recruit and retain. Domestic service had lost much of its appeal since the turn of the century, and only the wealthier establishments could afford to maintain their workforce at the same level as when Edward VII was on the throne.

The best servants were dependable and loyal, but occasionally human foibles crept in. The imperturbable Bole was

Mrs Greville's butler for four decades, and he exuded Jeeves-like competency and discretion. His second-in-command, however, Bacon, was short, stout, red-faced and claimed to be a Communist. He also had a habit of shamelessly consuming food and drink intended for the guests. It was Bacon who, while bending low over his hostess with a serving dish of *pommes gaufrettes*, unexpectedly belched and liberally sprayed the hair of Mrs Ronnie and the lap of Princess Juliana of the Netherlands with pulverised potato. Mrs Greville was surprisingly tolerant of such personal lapses, but she was outraged when one of her American friends, Mrs Grace Vanderbilt, attempted to lure away her personal maid, Mademoiselle Liron. However, she was not above a spot of poaching herself; it is likely that she acquired her pretty and popular lady's maid Gertie Hulton from her Charles Street neighbour the Countess of Waterford. As Beverley Nichols wrote:

> The hostesses of the twenties were like great galleons, sailing the social seas with all flags flying and all guns manned, relentlessly pursuing their charted course – and not above indulging in a little piracy if the occasion demanded it. Those were days when women really did ensnare each other's chefs and kidnap each other's head gardeners, and offer the most shameless bribes to each other's 'treasures'.

Nancy Astor was particularly ruthless in acquiring staff; in 1928 she shamelessly poached one of her friends' maids, Rose Harrison, when she was staying at Cliveden and, having employed her to look after her daughter Wissie, coerced her into being her own lady's maid, a role Rose fulfilled for more than three decades. The relationship was stormy; they even came to blows on one occasion, with Lady Astor lashing out at Rose with her foot, and Rose catching it to tip her over (Rose had been a keen footballer as a girl, and an impressive goalkeeper). Their rows became famous throughout the household; Waldorf Astor would eavesdrop from his dressing room, amused by the waspish exchanges. His valet offered the opinion that Waldorf was glad that Nancy was taking out her venom on someone other than him. Nevertheless, Rose and Nancy were good friends; Rose wrote admiringly of her employer that she was

> short, five foot two, but slim. She had a good figure and carried herself well, though often she moved too fast for my liking. She was strong and had no time for illness or feminine weakness. She had adopted the faith of Christian Science at the beginning of the First World War. Before her conversion she had been a semi-invalid and spent a lot of time in bed, but while I was with her she was as strong as a horse. Although she was small she made no attempt to increase her height by wearing high heels [...] either she was very fond of games or she believed in keeping fit, probably a bit of both, for she was always taking exercise. She swam nearly every day in the river at Cliveden, or the sea at Sandwich; she played squash at St James's Square. She got His Lordship to build her a court for her own personal use. She played tennis and golf; there was a practice course at Cliveden. And she rode regularly until her later years. In the winter we always went abroad for sports; skiing and skating. It seemed there was nothing she couldn't do, and do well.

In later years, the formidable Lady Astor also took a shine to Charles Dean, who was butler to her niece Nancy Lancaster.

She needed a butler for her London flat and offered him a job, but he politely declined; she drove over to see Charles's octogenarian mother, taking with her a beautiful shawl as a gift for the old lady, and talked Mrs Dean round. Still Charles resisted; then he was phoned by Edwin Lee, the Cliveden butler, and talked into accepting the post.

The Astors were notoriously careless with valuables. In the 1920s Lady Astor lent the famous Sancy diamond to her sister Mrs Nora Phipps, who was attending a ball at St James's Square. In the early hours of the morning Lady Astor told Mr Lee that the diamond was missing and suspected it had been stolen by one of the staff or the orchestra who had played that evening. Fortunately one of the under-housemaids spotted a lump under a carpet the following morning, and the diamond was returned. On a previous occasion, in 1919, Lady Astor was sure that her new lady's maid, a Miss Samson, had stolen the pearls she had worn the night before, during a party at Elliott Terrace in Plymouth. The police were summoned, and the unfortunate maid was interrogated in the library by an officer who tried to make her sign a pre-prepared confession. When she refused, he forcibly searched her. Meanwhile, Lady Astor's pearls were spotted in a waste-paper basket in the drawing room – she had forgotten she had taken them off there the previous night, and they had slipped from view.

But if Nancy's treatment of her staff was occasionally cavalier, they were capable of repaying her in kind. Gordon Grimmett, the footman, was adept at 'acquiring' clothing from the guests for whom he was valeting. Edwin Lee, seeing Gordon's personal laundry hanging on a line to dry when he paid an unexpected visit to Gordon's bedroom, wryly observed that if the footman ever ended up unconscious in hospital, those responsible for his care would have to refer to a copy of Debrett's to try to identify the patient by the many coronets and high-ranking coats of arms to be found on his underwear.

Butler Lee sagely remarked, 'Never judge a sausage by its skin'. He was courteous to the numerous beggars who called at the London house, and Nancy would often give them a sizeable sum, on one occasion handing over £5 to a tramp who turned up at the door, infuriating Rose, who had fought long and hard for an annual pay rise of the same amount. But her employer's generosity was quixotic. Nancy once bought a large number of hats as Christmas presents for all her maids – they were identical in shape, but in different sizes and colours. They were also extremely cheap, each one costing a modest 2 shillings and 11 pence, as was discovered from the labels. Underwhelmed by their extremely wealthy mistress's generosity, the maids customised their hats, the footmen tried them on, and theatrical Arthur Bushell, Lord Astor's valet, donned one and imitated Lady Astor to great effect. Amid general hilarity, a free-for-all broke out, the hats came to grief and they were all incinerated in the stove.

Between the hostesses there was often intense rivalry. They were aware of each other's activities through stories in the press. There were also personality clashes; Mrs Greville resolutely ignored Laura Corrigan's invitations, announcing loftily, 'I am never hungry enough.' When asked why, she replied: 'To be known in the States as an English woman who doesn't go to Mrs Corrigan's parties is to be placed on a pedestal', adding after a pause, 'I like pedestals'. Eventually their paths crossed in Paris, when both ladies were the dinner guests of society hostess Lady Mendl (formerly Elsie de Wolfe), the American-born interior decorator. Laura Corrigan attempted to 'cut' Mrs Greville, who subsequently crowed about it all over London. Mrs Greville resented competition; on one occasion she and Mrs Arthur James, another wealthy hostess, attended the same ball, both wearing lovely sets of pearls. When Mrs Greville realised that Mrs James was showing four rows of pearls, compared with her own three, she reached under the neckline of her own dress and revealed another three rows of pearls, making six altogether.

Hostesses sometimes clashed because they pursued the same quarry. Virginia Woolf recalled one occasion when Sibyl Colefax was visiting her, and a message arrived from Lady Cunard inviting the writer to dinner, despite the two women never having met. Virginia was amused at Sibyl's outrage, because Lady Colefax had bombarded the writer with unsolicited invitations for months in order to scrape acquaintance. '"I've never heard of such insolence!" she exclaimed. Her face was contorted with a look that reminded me of the look on a tigress's face when someone snatches a bone from its paws. She abused Lady Cunard. Nothing she could say was bad enough for her.'

Oswald Mosley was much in demand with a number of the Queen Bee hostesses; he had served with distinction in the Royal Flying Corps in the Great War, had been injured and was a wealthy young man with flashing eyes, a slight limp and a rented flat in Grosvenor Square. He was elected the Conservative member for Harrow in the 'Khaki Election' of 1918. Nancy Astor, Lady Colefax, Lady Cunard, Lady Londonderry and Mrs Greville vied to attract him to their receptions and dinner parties. Lady Cunard, in his opinion, was the most effective of the hostesses; as Oswald Mosley said, she understood that society should consist of 'conversation by brilliant men against a background of lovely and appreciative women, a process well calculated continually to increase the supply of such men'. Naturally, he saw himself as one of the brilliant men. Another young would-be politician who benefitted from the hostesses' benign influence was Bob Boothby MP. He was taken up by all the hostesses, but his particular favourite was Mrs Ronnie Greville. He described her as 'a bit of an old bag, but very good to me [...] she regarded me as a boy from her native city who was making good; and we had an agreeable relationship on this basis. She had the shrewdness of a typical lowland Scot, and as far as patronage was concerned, she was extremely powerful.'

The hostesses used their desks like those of captains of industry, planning and working. Sibyl Colefax had a fold-down writing flap installed in the back of her chauffeur-driven Rolls so that she could deal with her correspondence between appointments. Securing guests required organisation and planning. Weekend parties and formal dinners were arranged well in advance. The Big Six hostesses would pore over their lists of names to achieve the right mix; they were aided in this organisational task by filing systems and planners, often devised for them by their personal secretaries. Some devised helpful systems allowing the dedicated hostess to compile categories of guests according to their status and interests. Margot Asquith maintained a mysterious code, which was eventually cracked by Consuelo Vanderbilt Balsan, who found herself described on Margot's list as 'B.T. and G.', which it turned out meant bridge, tennis and golf.

Having drawn up a shortlist of targets, they would write to them with an invitation and an instruction to RSVP, and a prompt acceptance or a swift 'with regrets' note was expected by return. Having secured their quarry, they would expect the guest to keep the date; 'Put it in your book' was the command from formidable society mavens such as Mrs Greville, Lady Cunard and Mrs Vanderbilt. A last-minute cancellation was, of course, always a possibility, and a presentable substitute was often scrambled for at the last minute.

There were fixed events: Mrs Corrigan gave an annual cabaret party, and by the late 1920s Lady Cunard was regularly arranging suppers for the Prince of Wales and his latest mistress. There were frequent and lavish house parties and dinner parties all over Mayfair and Belgravia, and royal visitors were welcomed with red carpets on the pavements outside the houses. 'One uses up so many red carpets in a season', sighed that veteran hostess Mrs Greville. The prospect of famous faces and glamorous gowns always attracted crowds of bystanders, the public and journalists, who were marshalled by police. Typical of the excitement was the ball in aid of the Italian hospital held at Mrs Ronnie's house, 16 Charles Street, in May 1924. So well attended was the event and so immense the crush that many lovely evening frocks were damaged. The hostess herself, who had been dining elsewhere, had to convince the police of her identity before she was allowed to drive up to her own front door. Even the guests of honour, the King and Queen of Italy, had to sit waiting in their car while their footmen cleared a path through the throng. Inside the house, the Prince of Wales, unnoticed in the crowd, tried for ten minutes to climb the wide staircase to the first-floor ballroom, but was wedged half-way. A commanding voice behind him boomed, 'Make way for the Duke and Duchess of York'. The heir to the British throne complained huffily, in the manner of Eeyore, 'Don't bother about me.'

Mrs Greville specialised in attracting the grand, the

powerful and the well-connected; when Lady Strathmore, mother of the Duchess of York, remarked that 'Some people need to be fed with royalty on a frequent basis, like sea-lions with fish', she may well have been thinking of Mrs Greville. She certainly had few aspirations to cultivating the creative or artistic types favoured by other hostesses, and tended to view a grand piano as a suitable surface on which to display signed silver-framed photos of European nobility, rather than as a musical instrument. However, she encouraged some of her younger friends, such as the Sitwells, in their various literary and theatrical ventures, and proved to be a particularly loyal friend to Osbert. Beverley Nichols waspishly remarked that this was because the aristocratic Sitwells were 'Chelsea de luxe' rather than genuinely creative.

By contrast, dark-haired, sharp-featured and relentless Sybil Colefax was known to be a 'snob for brains', and her exquisite eighteenth-century home on the King's Road was known as the 'Lions Corner House', a pun on the name of a chain of tea-shops run by the firm of Lyons, because of her hunting abilities. By the late 1920s she had really hit her stride; she was so widely known for her insatiable desire to attract the most prominent guests that she was cruelly satirised in a short story written by Mary Borden, published in *Four O'Clock and Other Stories* in 1926. 'To Meet Jesus Christ' is an account of a desperately ambitious society hostess who cracks under the strain and invites her guests to meet Christ, talking animatedly to an empty chair.

Sibyl was hurt by such mockery; she did hunt celebrities and royals, but she also cultivated genuine artistic or creative talent, whether musical, theatrical or literary. She was very loyal and did not drop any friend whose star was on the wane. However, she was the butt of many a joke: Lord Berners sent her a card inviting her to dinner 'to meet the P of W'; she was disappointed when his guest turned out to be the Provost of Worcester, rather than the Prince of Wales. On another occasion he complained of insomnia, claiming that Sibyl had been staying in the room next to his 'and she hadn't stopped climbing all night'.

Sibyl continued to travel in Europe, but after her son Peter went to work in New York, she was increasingly drawn to America and Americans. In France in 1926 Sibyl stayed in a château at Gourdon that belonged to an American interior designer, Miss Norris, a friend of Cole Porter. Sibyl was fascinated to learn that her hostess had earned the money to transform the château through her career in interior design, and this was a valuable object lesson to her. There were also a number of interesting expat Americans enjoying life in 1920s France; Elsie de Wolfe and the Cole Porters, and Edith Wharton at Hyères. America began to seem very appealing to Sibyl and her contemporaries.

The 1920s and '30s were particularly fruitful decades for the relationship between Britain and America, who had been allies during the First World War. Elite citizens – as well as young hopefuls – from both countries crossed the Atlantic on the new luxury liners: everyone from Charlie Chaplin, Gloria Vanderbilt and Charles Lindbergh to Randolph Hearst, Douglas Fairbanks and Noel Coward.

Although principally based in London, all six hostesses were inveterate travellers, combining extensive knowledge of Europe with frequent visits to the USA. They deliberately cultivated the 'great and good' of American society between the wars, from the established families of Fifth Avenue and Long Island to the industrial entrepreneurs, philanthropists and Hollywood stars. In their salons they skilfully blended visiting American actors and actresses, songwriters and composers, millionaires and art collectors with European aristocrats, international royalty and creative mavens. The cultural influence of the USA on British society in this era was immense – from musical theatre and popular song to the appeal of Hollywood films, the British public took to its heart the American-inspired cult of celebrity. The Americans also liked the Prince of Wales, who had visited the States in 1919 and 1924 and irritated his father by adopting a faintly transatlantic mode of speech. On his first trip he met President Wilson in Washington; on the second he travelled largely incognito, remaining on Long Island. However, the American public were wildly enthusiastic. As Sir John Foster Fraser wrote in 1926, 'the Americans really must get a King and Queen of their own. They will never be happy until they do.'

Sibyl Colefax's first visit to the States was in November 1926, when she was fifty-two, and she went primed with letters of introduction and a list of contacts provided by Walter Page, the former American Ambassador. She was struck by the vibrancy and frenetic commerce of New York, where even grand nineteenth-century mansions were being replaced by soaring modern apartment blocks. The crazy pace, the booming property market and the constant talk of money were stimulating, but she had a feeling that this hyper-consumption couldn't last. She met the millionaire owners of private art collections such as Mrs Otto Kahn and Miss Frick. She socialised extensively, visited the opera and theatre and lunched with Noel Coward. Sibyl and her son Peter spent Thanksgiving with the Cole Porters, and Sibyl renewed her acquaintance with Elsie de Wolfe, society decorator, now in her sixties. The two women had met in the summer in Paris. Sibyl admired Elsie's taste, her 'wonderful shop full of beautiful things' and the way she had transformed her clients' houses. Elsie was a woman running a successful, creative business within the upper echelons of society, by exercising her own aesthetic judgement and style.

Sibyl made new friends in the booming film industry, from Gloria Swanson to Mary Pickford and Douglas Fairbanks. She was very taken with British-born Charlie Chaplin, and the two expats seemed to find a great deal to talk about. 'He is a wonder – there is no doubt about it,' she wrote. The Chaplins gave a private dinner party for Sibyl, which thrilled her, and she was also taken to the film première of *Don Juan*, a star-studded evening where immense crowds of fans were controlled by police.

Sibyl returned to a snowbound New York with some relief, and embarked on a programme of visiting private collectors' art treasures, which had been arranged for her by Joseph Duveen, an associate of Bernard Berenson, her old friend from her first visit to Florence. Duveen was an exceptional art dealer and consummate salesman specialising in Old Masters (paintings created before 1800). He was adept at brokering art sales from Europe to American collectors, a lucrative but sensitive business. Joe Duveen helped the very wealthy of the New World augment their collections of art from the Old World, relying on authoritative attributions from the respected art historian Berenson, and he profited enormously from their enthusiasm. Duveen respected Sibyl's genuine interest in fine art. Every summer he took a suite at Claridge's in order to court millionaires and to visit the London galleries, and she would hold a dinner for him at

Argyll House, where he could meet interesting people and expand his range of contacts. She admired his business acumen, and he liked her ability to charm his clients.

In 1928, as Sibyl was planning another trip to the States, the Royal Academy was preparing a major exhibition on the great Italian master painters, including loans from big American collectors. Major Longden of the RA asked Sibyl if she could approach any of the American owners on the curators' wish list whom she knew, and persuade them to lend their precious paintings. She had made a number of friends among museum curators and private collectors in the States, from the East Coast to Chicago, from Long Island to Hearst's castle.

In New York, Sibyl's personality and charm secured the required paintings, and she also suggested other art works she had seen in the States of which the curators were previously unaware. Her knowledge of this field was impressive; by December 1929 the 'American contribution' was being hailed by Major Longden as 'splendid'. Sibyl was beginning to think she could make a career in the American manner, using her taste, her knowledge and her contacts.

> In 1926 Lady Cunard, sensing the altered atmosphere, changed her name to Emerald. Soon she will have few guests old enough to remember her as Maud. This transition to the Emerald Age was an event of profound significance.   (Patrick Balfour, *Society Racket*)

In 1926 Lady Cunard's life changed completely. After living alone since 1914, Sir Bache Cunard fell ill. His daughter visited him in his final weeks. He died on 4 November 1925 with Nancy at his bedside, and was buried, in line with his wishes, with minimal ceremony. Sir Bache was seventy-four and had always hoped that his wife would return to him in the end, but he was disappointed. Maud was not mentioned in his will, and he left most of his estate to Nancy, who spent some of the £14,408 bequest on a house in the Normandy countryside. He also left her a life-size statue of a fox in silver, a token of the other two passions that had dominated his life, metalwork and hunting.

Maud was finally free of the husband who had provided her with a prestigious title and status, a daughter, a substantial fortune, which she spent on supporting her lover and entertaining her social circle, and a position in British society. After a period of mourning, as was expected of a widow, even a semi-detached one, she moved from Carlton House Terrace to 7 Grosvenor Square and resumed her life as one of London's most active hostesses.

Her old admirer George Moore wrote to her just after the death of her husband in November 1925; his brief note reads, 'I loved you in the beginning and shall love you to the end.' The following year he told her he was planning to sell some valuable paintings (two Manets, two Morisots, one Monet and a Degas pastel) to invest in American government securities known as Liberty Bonds, for her to inherit on his death. He also begged her not to travel to Venice, as she was planning that summer, because if anything happened to her he would die of grief. Needless to say, she took no notice; Sir Thomas Beecham and Lady Cunard spent a large part of the summer of 1926 travelling round the Continent together. When Cole Porter installed a floating night club complete with jazz band under their windows, they left Venice and travelled to Switzerland. It was from here that Lady Cunard sent a letter to George Moore, signing it, 'Maud Emerald (a new name)'. She had decided to adopt the more glamorous alternative name, to mark her emancipation. The elderly writer assumed she had married a Mr Emerald; the only person he could find in the London telephone directory with that surname was a paint manufacturer, but anything was possible with Maud. Distraught, he sent her a telegram: 'Who is Emerald are you married? GM'. He followed it up with a letter: 'You cannot fail to understand that it is unfair to leave a man who has loved you dearly for more than thirty years in doubt.' Her blithe response was that she had adopted her nickname because of her fondness for the gem. Certainly it was an appropriate name; emeralds were very much in vogue in the 1920s, admired for their multi-faceted, polished and glittering charms, though they were known to be brittle and full of flaws.

In fact, she had always disliked her first name. She resented the associations with the famous poem 'Come into the Garden, Maud', which Alfred, Lord Tennyson had written in 1857, and which was a somewhat hackneyed favourite of Edwardian singers. However, there may have been another reason. Sir Bache had had an eccentric streak; he had an absorbing passion for creating decorative metalwork, for which he had genuine talent. It was perhaps unfortunate that he had made his wife shudder by surprising her on her return from London with an extravagant piece of ornamental metalwork bearing the legend 'Come into the garden, Maud'. It was made from welded horseshoes, and he had placed it over the entrance to the topiary garden. Literary Lady Cunard probably knew this romantic poem in its entirety, and perhaps her conscience was piqued by the last verse. The poet eagerly anticipates the return of his love, and declares he would respond even if he was in his grave:

> *She is coming, my own, my sweet,*
> *Were it ever so airy a tread,*
> *My heart would hear her and beat,*
> *Were it earth in an earthy bed;*
> *My dust would hear her and beat,*
> *Had I lain for a century dead;*
> *Would start and tremble under her feet,*
> *And blossom in purple and red.*

Sir Bache, cuckolded, neglected and left behind long ago in Leicestershire, had chosen the opening line of this poem to recreate in wrought metalwork, a misguided attempt to surprise and delight his much younger wife when she returned to Nevill Holt from one of her many absences. Decades later, now that he was dead, it is perhaps understandable that Maud wished to discard the first name, which had such resonant associations. As Emerald, she was now free of her marital bonds, but what she did not know was that Beecham had fallen in love yet again. This time the object of his affections was a talented brunette soprano called Dora Labbette, the daughter of a railway porter. When they met, Dora was twenty-eight, Thomas Beecham was forty-seven and Lady Cunard was fifty-three. When she found out, Emerald boycotted any performance that featured Dora Labbette. Bob Boothby, who was a friend of both Lady Cunard and Sir Thomas and socialised with them in Venice that summer, recalled: 'He was generally accepted as Emerald Cunard's lover; but if so he was certainly not a faithful one.'

Emerald Cunard's world was now focused entirely on the cultivated conversation of intelligent and well-connected people in the theatre and, above all, in opera. With Sir Thomas Beecham she managed to finance seasons of opera at Covent Garden in the days before state subsidies; Beecham used his family's fortune, while Emerald was adept at tickling large donations from the wealthy, who she would then include in her glittering first nights at the opera. Such encounters were not always smooth. On one occasion Sir Thomas, who was conducting the overture to *Fidelio*, yelled 'Shut up!' at the well-heeled occupants chattering in Lady Cunard's box.

Her own knowledge of music was considerable, and she would on occasion launch into surprisingly accurate renditions of arias by Verdi, Puccini or even Wagner. By making opera attendance fashionable among a certain moneyed section of society, Emerald Cunard enabled some of the best orchestras and singers to come to London to perform, thus giving music-lovers of all classes unprecedented opportunities to hear the best classical music in the world.

In November 1927 Sir Thomas Beecham founded the Imperial League of Opera, an organisation to mobilise opera lovers throughout Britain to support their favourite art form. Membership cost 10 shillings per annum, and the League was aided by a generous donation from Laura Corrigan, who also took a large and prestigious box for the season at Covent Garden. The League was intended to promote the performance of live opera, not only at Covent Garden, but also in six regional cities in Britain. Sir Thomas now concentrated on building up new British audiences for opera and was disillusioned with performing only for the wealthy. The initiative was taken further by the formation of the Covent Garden Opera Syndicate Limited, which reached an agreement with the BBC in 1930 to broadcast the operas on the wireless.

Throughout her life there were whispers that Emerald had

lovers, and certainly she was an experienced flirt and manipulator of men; she had persuaded George Moore that they should, in his phrase, 'stint their desires to blessed adultery' so that she could make an advantageous marriage, but he remained devoted to her for nearly four decades, despite her passion for Thomas Beecham. This was a constant thorn in his flesh; in 1927 he wrote to her, 'It is impossible for me to allow my name to appear along with those who favour Sir Thomas Beecham's operatic scheme. You will know why.' Moore's letters exemplify the full gamut of human emotions, from missives seething with panting desire to brief notes of sulky, terse sentences, which reveal his hatred of his usurper in Emerald's affections.

Meanwhile, Emerald continued to entertain in her unique style. She was famous for introducing people to one another with riveting and sometimes ill-chosen descriptions. On introducing a young author, she trilled, 'This is Michael Arlen – the only Armenian who has not been massacred!' On another occasion an exiled aristocratic Russian was described as 'Grand Duke Dmitri, the murderer of Rasputin'. He walked out in protest.

Her lunch parties were justifiably famous, and few refused an invitation to her lapis lazuli-topped circular table. Lunches tended to be relatively intimate in scale, rarely numbering more than ten diners, because Emerald preferred conversation to be general. Her speciality was the 'throwaway shocker', a statement or question that was uttered to startle the company into a response, and which she probably rehearsed in advance. Typical remarks included 'Christ had a very unpleasant face, and John the Baptist's was little better', or 'Christmas is only for servants'. She defied the convention of having equal numbers of men and women at her table, because 'I invite my friends for conversation, not for mating'. She was described by an unnamed contemporary as having 'a whim of steel'.

Lady Cunard's guests often remarked on her bird-like appearance. She had a slightly beaky nose, a receding chin and fluffy blonde hair. Lord Drogheda described her as a 'canary of prey'. Cecil Beaton thought she looked like 'an amusing-looking little parakeet in her pastel-coloured plumage'. Oswald Mosley called her 'a bright little bird of paradise'. The avian impression was heightened by her habit of flitting from subject to subject. Beverley Nichols said, 'her natural milieu was a gilded cage. At her best she was one of the most brilliant conversationalists I have ever known – and again the bird-like simile is apposite, for her talk was a series of delicious trills and roulades, with sudden quite irrelevant cadenzas.' This impression was enhanced by her face in profile; she had a receding chin, about which she was extremely self-conscious, and avoided being photographed from the side. Lady Cunard tried massage and some form of electrical therapy to correct her profile, but she was afraid to try plastic surgery. She used a beauty cream marketed by Helena Rubinstein that apparently imparted a temporary scorching sensation when applied to the face, which was thought to be beneficial. Emerald sported extremely heavy make-up in an era when this was uncommon for women unless they were appearing on stage or in films. The art historian Kenneth Clark, who came to know her in the early 1930s, noticed that from a distance one could only see paint and wrinkles; as one got closer, she actually appeared far younger. Mrs Greville, more of a soap-and-water *aficionado*, heartily disapproved. 'You must not think that I dislike poor dear Emerald', she would purr to her friends; 'I am always telling Queen Mary that she isn't half as bad as she's painted.' Emerald was extremely fashionable and *soignée;* she had an exquisite figure and legs, according to the writer and publisher John Lehmann, and always dressed in the height of fashion, adorned with ropes of pearls, diamonds and the famous emerald rings on her small, claw-like hands.

She was charming to her guests but was always late arriving at her own luncheons, which meant they had to make small talk until she appeared among them. Over the dining table she also demanded that they demonstrate their 'party pieces'. Cecil Beaton was critical of her clothes; they were in the vanguard of fashion, but she was too impatient to put up with lengthy fittings so that, in his opinion, the finished garment was often a failure.

She could pounce on a guest with a startling question, such as 'Mr Churchill has just been telling me the most dreadful things about Signor Mussolini. What do *you* think of Signor Mussolini?' A fellow American, Consuelo Vanderbilt Balsan, former Duchess of Marlborough, astutely summed up Emerald's *modus operandi*: 'She appeared to dispense a tremendous energy, but her enthusiasm cloaked an ingrained pessimism. As I grew to know her I realised that it was her need for friendship that caused her to indulge in absurd superlatives. I used to wonder why she did not herself realise that it was the wrong approach, especially in England.'

Laura Corrigan was also primarily driven by a need for friendship, and by the mid-1920s she was well established in London society. Her dinner-dances regularly attracted between 120 and 150 guests, many of whom already knew each other, and she put a great deal of effort into entertaining with an eye to novelty by throwing 'surprise' parties, engaging cabaret artistes and providing a distinctly 'night-club' atmosphere.

Cecil Beaton thought that she relied on 'calculated spontaneity' to charm at her parties, but she was generous; when she hired a cabaret act to entertain her guests, she would willingly pay a week's fees for a single night's appearance.

The food and drink were excellent, and with the avuncular assistance of Mr Rolfe, the butler, the guests were provided with tombola prizes that strangely matched their status. The theme of the 1924 party for 104 guests was the Jardin des Perroquets Verts, and the house was transformed like a set for an exotic, brilliantly coloured ballet. For one evening, the drawing room curtains were covered with powdered glass, which glittered enticingly, while on a further occasion she had a temporary ballroom constructed in the garden, peopled with actors disguised as trees, be-smocked yokels and rustic gardeners. But part of Laura's charm, so far as her guests were concerned, was her happy knack for malapropisms, which were pounced on with glee and repeated all over town. Shown a Gothic cathedral, she made a polite enquiry about the 'flying buttocks'; admiring a Modernist sitting room, she enthused about the 'confused lighting'.

The French language seems to have been one of her Achilles heels; during the Great War she had financed a hospital for soldiers in France, and when she attended the official opening she greeted each inmate with the unfortunate phrase 'Dieu te blesse', which means 'God wounds you', rather than 'God bless you', as she had intended. In London in the 1920s, when offered a ballet act based on *L'Après-midi d'un Faune* for one of her parties, Laura turned it down immediately, saying, 'What do I want with a ballet about a telephone?' British history was similarly a minefield to Laura; an English king was 'Richard Gare de Lyon'. While visiting the Duke of Marlborough at his country house, she asked where his illustrious ancestor had won the Battle of Blenheim. He pointed at the statue of the first Duke on its column at the centre of the park and said 'There'. She believed him. She was also asked if she knew the Dardanelles; no, she said, but she had a letter of introduction to them, and she had heard they were very nice. In another case of mistaken identity, when introduced to the Aga Khan, she ventured that she had met his brother Otto Kahn the German-born banker, philanthropist and patron of the arts, in Hollywood. She was also uncertain how to respond when lunching at Lady Cunard's with George Moore, who declared, 'I always think, Mrs Corrigan, that of all sexual perversions, chastity is the most incomprehensible.' 'Wal,' she drawled diplomatically, 'I guess I shall have to think over that, Mr Moore.'

Laura Corrigan's gaffes made society snigger, and she was a further figure of ridicule because of her appearance. She was small, slim, fashionably and expensively dressed, but the fact that she had been bald since the age of around forty was the worst-kept secret in London. Laura suffered from alopecia, which caused most of her hair to fall out, but she had an assortment of auburn wigs made for her to cover all social eventualities. There was an artfully tousled one to be worn in bed, an informal daytime one and an immaculate coiffure for evening – there was even a rubber bathing cap, around the edges of which peeped curls. On one famous occasion she dived off a yacht into the sea, and the bathing cap accidentally came off, floating on the water, to the collective gasps of onlookers. Without surfacing, Laura managed to grab the cap from below, reattach it under water and surface triumphantly with her coiffure only a little askew. The *Sunday Express* referred to her as 'The Big-Wig of London', and the compact travelling trunk in which her hairpieces were transported was known quite openly by her friends as 'Laura's Wig-Wam', but only Emerald Cunard was cruel enough to mention Laura's baldness to her face. The two women were talking at the dinner table about what they planned to wear to a forthcoming gala night at the opera, and Lady Cunard announced that she would be wearing 'just a small emerald bandeau, *and my own hair*'.

Laura Corrigan may have been the butt of jokes and disparaging remarks – Duff Cooper described her simply as 'atrocious' – but she could also be astute and ruthless, as she proved in 1925. James Corrigan's inheritance had been in the hands of the firm's former book-keeper, Price McKinney, since his father's death in 1908. Price owned 30 per cent of the company stock outright and he also managed James's share of 40 per cent. Laura and James wanted to oust McKinney, and to do that they needed an overall majority. Laura contacted the family of the third original partner in the firm, Stevenson Burke, and secretly persuaded them to sell her some of their stakeholding for $5 million. James had difficulty raising that sum, so Laura pawned her jewellery and arranged bank loans. In 1925 James Corrigan brought off a spectacular boardroom coup, dramatically ousting Price McKinney at a stakeholders meeting by announcing that he now owned 53.5 per cent of the company, and therefore was taking control of the company as President. Within a year Price McKinney had shot himself in the bathroom of his mansion on Euclid Avenue; after this, Cleveland polite society turned completely against the Corrigans. They closed up their mansion, Nagirroc, and Laura returned to her social life in London, with occasional forays to Paris, Venice and New York, where she preferred to live in a hotel.

1926 was the apotheosis of both the Corrigans; even though they were 3,000 miles apart, they were now worth about $60 million as a result of having regained control of James's inheritance. Always a fan of horse-racing, James had established the Wickliffe Stables with Price McKinney in happier days. When McKinney was ousted, James took over the entire venture, including the highly lucrative and successful Kingston stud, and pursued his love of racing.

Meanwhile, Laura Corrigan pulled off another social triumph. On 21 July 1926 she threw a lavish party, hiring an unoccupied house in Grosvenor Street, but instead of engaging professional performers, she persuaded her aristocratic guests to provide their own acts. It was Amateur Night in Mayfair. Lady Louis Mountbatten, Lady Brecknock, Mrs Richard Norton and Lord Ashley warbled their way uncertainly through a 'plantation number'. Lord Weymouth and Daphne Vivian, Lady Lettice Lygon and Lord Brecknock cycled round the ballroom on a pair of tandems, simultaneously singing 'Daisy, Daisy, Give Me Your Answer, Do'. Others played the ukulele, while gifted Dorothé Plunket, the illegitimate daughter of Lord Londonderry, executed an exhibition dance. Lady Maud Warrender, daughter of the Earl of Shaftesbury, was only deterred from a plate-smashing act by a timely intervention from the butler, Mr Rolfe, who was anxious to protect the parquet floor. But the hit of the evening was the hostess, who in the manner of a circus ringmaster insisted that her guests try out the latest dance craze, the Charleston, while the band played. Laura watched, then slipped on a top hat and red shoes to dance in the centre of the syncopated throng; she had been practising the dance secretly for weeks with professional tuition. Laura Corrigan always wanted to be the high-stepping star of her very own Busby Berkeley musical, and by the time her party ended at 4 a.m. she had achieved her dream.

Mr and Mrs Corrigan seemed happy enough living on either side of the Atlantic, each pursuing their own pleasures. But their triumph was short-lived; on 23 January 1928, while Laura was entertaining in London, James Corrigan suffered a heart attack and dropped dead outside the Cleveland Athletic Club. He was forty-seven years old. Laura took a year's sabbatical from London society to make a cultural trip around Europe and then returned, as industrious as ever. She also adopted a philosophical attitude when Jimmy's trans-atlantic leisure activities came to light. As Stanley Walker wrote: 'When her husband died she presented identical souvenirs from his personal belongings to a dozen women of society with the explanation that Jim had wanted them to have something to remember him by.'

Laura now needed to make some serious financial deci-sions. Under the terms of Jimmy's will she had the power to sell her shares, but the votes that went with them were vested in the new President, John H. Watson. So she sold her entire holding to William Mather, and Corrigan-McKinney was swallowed up by the Republic Steel Corporation. Laura now had an income of $800,000 a year for life, enough for any hostess to entertain freely.

By 1929 she was back in London and resuming her old life, but no longer the doyenne of 16 Grosvenor Street. The Keppels had now bought a glorious house and estate on a hillside overlooking Florence, the Villa dell'Ombrellino, and so had sold their Mayfair home and shipped their treasures to Italy. Laura rented a succession of grand London houses from their owners as the mood took her, from Crewe House in Curzon Street to the Dowager Duchess of Rutland's home in Arlington Street. She would book a vast first-floor suite at the Ritz Hotel whenever she was in Paris, where she was a keen customer of Cartier's, and she held open house at the Palazzo Mocenigo when she summered in Venice. She did not confine her holidays to Europe; one year she chartered a yacht, filled it with her friends and cruised the Caribbean. At every port where they put in, each passenger was given $200 dollars as 'pocket money' to spend ashore.

Laura Mae Corrigan now had aristocratic friends of her own in British society; she became a welcome and popular country house guest. When staying in castles and mansions, she took a particular delight in using the headed notepaper provided for guests to send brief missives to those snooty matrons who had spurned her back in Cleveland and New York. 'Wish you were here!' she would hand-write below the restrained heading of 'Blenheim' or 'Mount Stewart', adding a careful signature and printing her name, just to rub it in. 'She was once rebuffed at Newport. Later she was accepted by the British royal family, and now she takes great pleasure in snubbing Newport. She has made good' was the approving verdict. Those Americans who had ignored her in the past and now visited London were not invited to any of her events.

But some fellow hostesses in London could be sniffy about her too; living just around the corner in Grosvenor Square was another American who had 'married up'. Initially Lady Cunard disapproved deeply of Mrs Corrigan's obscure origins, her jolly vulgarity and her popularity among the well-heeled philistines, though Laura bought her way into her social circle by making generous contributions to Sir Thomas Beecham's operatic projects. It was Mrs Corrigan who pioneered the novelty party, an idea she had garnered from her burly American friend Elsa Maxwell in Paris. Elsa's parties involved the complex staging of country house murders and treasure hunts for such diverse objects as a swan, a pompom from a sailor's hat and an autographed portrait of royalty. Elsa and Laura shared a passion for fancy dress, and before long photos of aristocratic party-goers dressed as Mozart, Cleopatra or Nelson were gracing the gossip columns of *Tatler* and the *Daily Sketch*. The *Daily Mirror* reported that modern hostesses were competing:

> to provide boxing matches or private cinema entertain-ments or music-hall shows if they wish to keep their guests from yawning. The Hon. Mrs Greville, for instance, had quite a variety of entertainment at her dinner party. There was a conjuror and a ventriloquist, who carried on a conversation with his painted fist, and an Hawaiian orchestra which provided languorous tunes.

Mrs Greville threw a railway-themed cocktail party at her London house in Charles Street. The ivory and gold ballroom was transformed into a station, waiting room, restaurant and bar with the addition of LNER posters, ticket collectors in uniform, a station master and a troupe of variety artistes. The furniture had been borrowed from a first-class waiting room, and refreshments were served in familiar LNER glasses. Judging by the glazed expressions on the faces of the partici-pants in surviving photographs, the novelty railway party failed to generate enough steam to capture their imaginations. Similarly, Emerald Cunard organised an experimental night out for her friends at the White City Stadium, including greyhound-racing; she even had a modest win on the hound that she had backed.

By the late 1920s the social scene had expanded; no longer was the aristocratic marriage market a 'closed shop', where families knew one another's offspring, lineage and likely inheritance. The regulated social world of the pre-war era collided with the easier manners of the younger generation in the 'Great Mayfair War' of 1928. Lady Violet Ellesmere, an aristocratic figure with traditional views, gave a ball at Bridgewater House at which there were three hundred guests, most of whom she did not recognise. She asked four of the guests to leave, which they did. Lady Ellesmere wanted to make an example of the 'gate-crashers' and so supplied their names to the press, in order to stop the nuisance that was becoming prevalent in society. In the subsequent newspaper debate, opinions were sought from the Ellesmeres, the evicted offenders (including Cecil Beaton's sister Nancy and Stephen Tennant), their families, other uninvited guests who were not turned out and rival hostesses. Public opinion was largely sympathetic to the gate-crashers, as it had become quite normal, when invited to a cocktail party, to bring a few friends along as well. Lady Cunard's view was solicited, but she claimed she never had difficulty with gate-crashers. 'Why should I? I only ask the people I like.'

It was a flippant story, but it revealed some startling truths. Before the war, the boundaries of society were well defined, and no young man would have been invited to a ball unless he had the appropriate credentials of birth, breeding and, therefore, behaviour. But the war had changed everything; presentable young men were scarce, and those who would once have been 'outsiders' were now accepted to make up the numbers.

In addition, humble readers now avidly devoured the newspapers, with their tales of upper-class parties and celebrities' bad behaviour. Modern life provided ample opportunity for stories about technological developments, speed, travel, crimes, disasters and scandals, but there was also interest from the readership in society figures, whether the offspring of noble families or those whose antecedents were rather more murky. In the manner of tabloid papers today, there was a huge appetite for gossip and comment.

Fleet Street hacks would elicit opinions on contemporary issues from actresses and film stars, duchesses and archbishops. They needed nerves of steel and a good contacts list to phone a countess at midnight to garner her opinion on bobbed hair, to enquire after a dowager's ability to dance the Black Bottom or to ask a captain of industry if it was unpatriotic to sculpt the Prince of Wales in butter. It took charm and diplomacy to get a name from 'The List' shoe-horned into a gossip column.

However, the ambitious society hostess recognised the benefit of seeing her name in print, and would take every opportunity to cultivate the columnists. She would offer a sympathetic ear and a ready quote to a young stringer with a looming deadline and 800 words to fill on whether or not one should apply perfume to a Pekingese. As a *quid pro quo* she was also adept at getting coverage favourable to herself. Often she employed a secretary who would telephone a favoured journalist in advance of social events with all the information necessary to fill next morning's column inches with nuggets about their mistress's glamorous life, her jewellery, her magnificent home, her friends, her royal guests and her cuisine. In return, favourable aspects of an individual's nature would be immortalised in print, such as 'Mrs Greville is rich and hospitable. An invitation to one of her parties is an honour and, if refused, is liable, like a royal command, not to be repeated.'

The hostesses also provided an informal introduction agency for young journalists keen to get a foot on the ladder; Mrs Keppel, for example, arranged an introduction between

Oliver de Reuter and Roderick Jones, and the latter eventually became the head of the family's international news agency. It was a symbiotic relationship in an era when the reading public were fascinated by the doings of the celebrities, from the younger royals and Amy Johnson the aviator to Mrs Kate Meyrick, queen of the night clubs.

The most influential gossip columnists, especially those who looked good in a black tie and tails and had the right accents, not only wrote about the hostesses in their columns but were often guests at their parties. Notable examples included Patrick Balfour (later Lord Kinross), who wrote for the *Daily Sketch*, the Marquess of Donegall and Beverley Nichols, both of whom wrote for the *Sunday Dispatch*, and Harold Nicolson and Robert Bruce Lockhart, who collaborated on the Londoner's Diary column at the *Evening Standard*. Viscount Castlerosse was a gossip columnist for Lord Beaverbrook's *Daily Express* for thirteen years and, like his peers, was carefully cultivated by Lady Astor, Mrs Greville, Sibyl Colefax and Emerald Cunard. He had a caustic wit and was enormously fat; as he puffed up the stairs at St James's Square to be met by Nancy Astor, his hostess, she leaned forward and patted his vast paunch, saying, 'If that was on a woman we should know what to think.' He countered, 'Well, it was last night, so what do you think?'

Some hostesses continued to entertain in the traditional manner; at the 1927 political reception at Londonderry House, Lady Londonderry wore a crinolined Queen Anne style dress of primrose-yellow, brocaded satin. 'Men go down like ninepins before a woman in an ancestral frock', commented the *Daily Express* approvingly. The following year, on 6 February 1928, Edith wore a full-length Velázquez-style gown of black velvet, a diamond necklace and *rivière*, and long diamond drop ear-rings. She stood with Stanley Baldwin, the Conservative Prime Minister, and her husband at the top of the famous staircase to receive her guests. The air was thick with the scent of mimosa, which decorated the mantelpieces and fireplaces of the long picture gallery and reception rooms. There were more than a thousand people present. It was a grand occasion in every sense; the most powerful and influential people in Britain were gathered for one of their regular tribal meetings, as the guests of the archetypal Tory lady.

Lady Londonderry not only hosted political events; she also cultivated literary and artistic types too, especially Irish writers such as George Bernard Shaw, Sean O'Casey and Oliver St John Gogarty. The ballroom was not her natural habitat, as she preferred outdoor life. She was a keen shot; on one occasion she was a guest at Sandringham, when peppery King George V complained that women should not hunt with guns. He claimed it was 'disgusting, horrible, unworthy!' Then he showed Edith a vast number of mounted hunting trophies; 'My daughter-in-law's!' he chuckled, meaning the Duchess of York, who could do no wrong in his eyes. On one occasion Edith's quick reflexes and physical strength probably saved a man's life. In 1928 the Londonderrys were staying with King Alfonso and Queen Ena of Spain at Santander, on the Bay of Biscay. They had eight-metre sailing yachts, which they would race against other Spaniards who were members of the local yacht club, at high speeds and often in quite choppy conditions. Lady Londonderry was out on the Queen's boat with a heavy swell running, moving at speed. One of the deck hands, a Basque sailor, lost his footing and fell into the sea at the bow. With remarkable presence of mind Lady Londonderry grabbed his arm as the yacht shot past and managed to haul him back on board.

Nancy Astor was similarly energetic and physically active, and enjoyed vigorous sports and exercise. She would swim in the Thames at Cliveden every day when she was in residence there, and while in London would retire to the top floor of 4 St James's Square to practise her strokes on the squash court that Waldorf had installed for her under the roof. She found such activities relaxing after her social commitments, which were considerable. When entertaining in London, the Astors preferred formal dinners, followed by a reception for up to a thousand people; their 'Town style' parties were extremely well run by Mr Lee, the butler. The silver would be delivered from the safe at Cliveden; the *placement* was decided by Lady Astor with Miss Kindersley, her controller. Precedence of rank was vital; royalty, then dukes and duchesses, followed by the 'other ranks' of aristocracy. The *placement* issue was often resolved by consulting Burke's Peerage, but they also had invaluable advice from Mr Lee, who knew which individuals loathed each other. Rivals were kept apart, while like-minded types were seated together. Married couples were sundered for the evening, but younger single people would be provided with others of their own age. Lady Astor always tried to claim the most interesting guests to sit close to her. The complex menus were decided and rehearsed in advance, and extra chefs and kitchen staff engaged if necessary.

The Astors' menservants wore everyday livery of brown coats with yellow and white striped waistcoats, with red and yellow piping down the trousers. Dress livery was brown jackets, striped waistcoats, breeches, white stockings and black pumps with old buckles, and white gloves for all except

Mr Lee, who was in charge of dispensing wines and liqueurs and needed ungloved hands. He wore a navy blue tailcoat, black breeches, black stockings and the same black pumps. Split-second timing was crucial to the running of a successful dinner party, and Mr Lee had very high standards. Dinner would often be followed by a vast reception in the ballroom. Mr Lee was superlative as the organiser of these events.

The police were always informed in advance in order to manage traffic in the surrounding square. Dinner guests were received in the hall as they arrived and divested of their cloaks and coats, which were stored in a staffed cloakroom. (Later, in the servants' hall, versatile Arthur Bushell would provide an excellent impression of statuesque Queen Mary being de-coated with great ceremony.) Aperitifs were served in the small dining room, and then the guests would move to the next floor for dinner. The guests arriving for the reception would be announced as they joined the throng by a master of ceremonies engaged for the evening. During the reception footmen served drinks and canapés. Wine was supplied by Hawker's of Plymouth (Mr Hawker was the Conservative agent for the Astors' constituency), and Mr Lee was allowed by Waldorf to buy in wines, sherries and ports for their guests. He ordered the very best quality, rather to the surprise of many of the Astors' guests, and took great pride in the care of the cellars. For large parties and receptions in London, 200 champagne bottles were delivered to a bathroom conveniently located near the drawing room, and fifty bottles at a time would be chilled in crushed ice in the bath.

Some guests, fearing that they might not be offered an alcoholic drink at the Astors', brought hipflasks for discreet consumption while visiting the bathroom. Others had their servants deliver their favourite tipple to Mr Lee before the party started. George V's equerry, on arrival with the King and Queen Mary at a dinner party in 1923, discreetly handed over to Mr Lee two decanters, one of port, the other sherry. Both monarchs were fond of a drop, but at the end of the evening Mr Lee slipped the untouched decanters back to the equerry, remarking 'Hardly necessary, I think you'll agree, sir.' Similarly the Prince of Wales's equerry, Major 'Fruity' Metcalfe, phoned Mr Lee in advance of a dinner party offering to send over brandy for HRH's consumption, but was suavely assured that would not be required. Parties at Cliveden were much less formal, though again some arrived with their own supplies of alcohol in case it was unavailable. Bob Boothby remembered that it was difficult to obtain any more than a single glass of wine with dinner. On one occasion Oswald and Diana Mosley brought a petrol tin to Boothby's bedroom; it was full of martini, and they all fortified themselves against an evening of Lady Astor's mimicry and impersonations with a stiff pre-dinner cocktail.

Nancy Astor's guests at Cliveden naturally included politicians, but also encompassed in the 1920s ambassadors such as the Japanese and Russian, though not the Germans, memories of the last war being all too recent. The Astors liked the company of artists, such as Philip de László, the portraitist, who had painted Lady Londonderry, and the brothers Rex and Laurence Whistler. Alfred Munnings, the equestrian artist, was a particular favourite of Waldorf's, and he was often commissioned to paint portraits of his racehorses. Nancy was particularly drawn to literary types, and the playwright George Bernard Shaw was to become a favourite sparring partner and regular guest at Cliveden, spending Christmas 1928 at the house. They first met in 1927, and argued with vigour and genuine enjoyment on many points of view. Shaw was of the opinion that if only Lady Astor was able to think consecutively for sixty seconds she could be the greatest woman in the world. It was through 'GBS' that Nancy met the charismatic T. E. Lawrence, better known as 'Lawrence of Arabia'. He had adopted the surname of his literary mentor (and, coincidentally, of Nancy's first husband) to serve incognito in the Royal Air Force as Aircraftman T. E. Shaw. He would tease her and she would banter back. He was stationed near Plymouth, so was a regular guest when the Astors were resident in the constituency.

Nancy was never a martyr to boredom. Every year while the children were young the whole family went to stay on the remote island of Jura, in the Inner Hebrides. The children loved it for its fishing, swimming and boating, but both Rose and Nancy would become very bored. On one occasion Nancy was practising her golf putting in front of the lodge, and in a blast of temper she suddenly turned and struck four golf balls at the house in quick succession, breaking two windows in the process.

The Astor children were brought up as Christian Scientists, and Nancy proved to be a rather domineering mother. She could entertain them, usually by making them laugh, but she could also be impatient and very critical, which bewildered them as youngsters. In 1925 Bill, while a pupil at Eton, was appointed the cox to the rowing eight, a prestigious role in that sports-mad school. At the Henley Regatta that summer, with Bill as cox, Eton lost the rowing race; Lady Astor, instead of commiserating with her crestfallen son, accused him of having neglected his Christian Science practice and thus having lost the competition for his school.

Nancy's devotion to Christian Science nearly had very serious consequences for her daughter Wissie, who in 1929 had a serious hunting accident in Leicestershire that damaged her spine. Under intense pressure Nancy and Waldorf reluctantly agreed to consult a medical practitioner, but insisted on summoning Sir Crispin English, an abdominal surgeon who had treated Nancy before her conversion to Christian Science. When he arrived, he was furious as it was evident Wissie urgently needed an orthopaedic specialist, and precious time had been lost in treating her injuries. Wissie, then aged twenty, never fully recovered her health, and her relationship with her mother suffered as a result. As soon as possible, she moved into a house of her own and for a while avoided contact with Nancy.

6

The Great Depression: 1929–1933

The worldwide financial crisis of the early 1930s had profound implications for all classes of British society. The Great War had brought in new methods of factory production, but by the end of the 1920s over-production had led to a falling-off in consumer demand. The American stock market overheated in October 1929, and the Wall Street Crash wiped out vast paper fortunes overnight. Land rents in Britain stagnated, and unemployment loomed for many.

Because of the crisis, many countries had placed large sums of money on deposit in London, regarded as a safe place for their reserves. But the worldwide slump and massive unemployment caused some nations to withdraw their deposits, and in August 1931 a serious run began on the Bank of England. The institution did not have enough gold reserves, so it borrowed £50 million in dollars and francs from the USA and France, but that was quickly exhausted. The Labour government resigned rather than cut the dole payments, and the National Government was formed; it borrowed a further £80 million, but that also went to foreign creditors. On 20 September 1931 Britain abandoned the gold standard, and the Bank of England no longer guaranteed to give gold in return for its paper notes. The value of the pound dropped to 13 or 14 shillings, but this had the benefit of making British exports much cheaper overseas, which eased unemployment at home.

The moneyed classes were not immune to the global financial crisis. Many faced a drastic reduction in their incomes from investments, shareholdings and property. Nancy Mitford recommended the Wall Street Crash as the ideal conversational topic for those attending a weekend shooting party at a country house, as it was far less contentious than discussing the relative merits of modern and traditional artists, and less risky than asking about the origins of one's fellow guests. It had the virtue of eliciting opinions and gossip, and was therefore a means of expressing solidarity.

At one country house the inhabitants could speak of little else. Sacheverell Sitwell and his wife, Georgia, abandoned their holiday in Amsterdam, having seen the English papers, returned to England and drove down to Polesden Lacey on 27 September 1931 with Emerald Cunard. (Only a global financial crisis could persuade Emerald to spend a Sunday in the shires, after her sixteen years with Sir Bache in rural Leicestershire.) They joined Mrs Greville's house party, which included Austen Chamberlain, Sir Robert Horne, Professor Lindemann and Beverley Nichols, to discuss the situation. Wealthy but eccentric Gerald Berners was reduced to tears, suggesting that Sachie and Georgia Sitwell should share Faringdon with him to help them financially, and in October they moved into his Berkshire manor house.

Even Mrs Greville, one of the richest women in Britain, was shaken; she confided in Beverley Nichols, as they sat in opulent splendour in Polesden Lacey's drawing room, surrounded by crimson silk wall coverings and eighteenth-century gilt *boiseries*, museum-quality Chinese ceramics, jade carvings and Fabergé bibelots, that if she was reduced to comparative poverty, perhaps a mere £10,000 a year (the equivalent today of approximately £500,000), she had a strategy for her twilight years:

> I think I should leave the country, and take a tiny apartment in Paris […] I hope my maid would come with me. Indeed, I am sure that she would. And though, naturally, I should not be able to entertain, I could have a few people to tea, once a week. And perhaps […] though one cannot be sure […] perhaps some of the people whom I have entertained in the past would invite me back.

Her visions of romantic penury were fortunately interrupted by the arrival of yet another ambassador. Mrs Greville's fortunes were affected by the worldwide slump, though the devaluation of the pound made British exports, such as McEwan's Pale Ale, more affordable on international markets. As a major shareholder in the brewery set up by her millionaire father, who had schooled her in commerce, she was a formidable businesswoman. Kenneth Clark recalled how he glimpsed the brewery directors arriving at Polesden for a board meeting. Mrs Greville was ill in bed, but he watched as each of them was summoned in turn, and later emerged visibly shaken.

Nevertheless Mrs Greville economised in a way that only the truly rich would; she owned very valuable emeralds, which had once belonged to Empress Josephine, and magnificent ropes of pearls, but had to pay considerable insurance premiums whenever they were worn. So she had replicas made and often wore those instead, especially when she was travelling. Only an expert could have told them apart, and her insurance premiums were much reduced as a result. However some of her contemporaries faced far tougher financial decisions and less palatable alternatives.

Sibyl Colefax needed to supplement the family's income in order to continue entertaining. Arthur's increasing deafness now limited the fees he could command from his work at the Bar, and they had a shortfall of around £2,000 per year, the equivalent of approximately £70,000 today. Sibyl was a reluctant businesswoman, but she had a great flair for interior design, largely self-taught, and excellent taste. She also knew people who were prepared to pay for bespoke interiors, and she had good contacts with antiques and fine art dealers. In addition, she was acquainted with women who were successful interior designers, including the American Elsie de Wolfe, otherwise known as Lady Mendl.

The decorating company of Sibyl Colefax Ltd was established in 1933, with premises at 29 Bruton Street, in Mayfair. There was demand in 'smartistic' London for interior designers. Syrie Maugham, the former wife of the writer Somerset Maugham, had established a distinctive style, setting up her firm in 1922 in Baker Street. In reaction to the cluttered, dark Victorian interiors of her youth she created rooms in various shades of white, cream, oyster or pearl. She also used mirrors extensively, to reflect the soft light of 1920s London. Vast white flower arrangements added texture, and even her books were rebound in vellum. Against the white walls would stand 'pickled' furniture, elegant antique pieces that had been stripped and bleached. Her house at 213 King's Road in Chelsea was 'as pretty as a narcissus in snow, as pretty as the silver feathers on a pane of winter's glass'. Syrie Maugham and Sibyl Colefax were near neighbours and knew one another socially. The two women's distinctive styles were very different, and they did not regard each other as business rivals.

Sibyl's decorating style was rather more conventional and historical in inspiration; she favoured a soft colour palette of light greens and greys with judicious touches of gold and rose. She liked antique lacquer and Oriental ceramics, both of which typified the English 'country house' style, especially when combined with floral chintzes, which she used to brighten drawing rooms. She provided pleasant, comfortable and functional interiors decorated with timeless good taste. Some preferred the angularity of Modernism, but Sibyl's accessible style worked well in grander country or town houses, where existing furniture could be reupholstered and better lit, supplemented with carefully chosen antiques and art works, to make pleasing, comfortable interiors.

Her first business partner was Peggy Ward, who later became the Countess of Munster. Sibyl used her social connections to advance her career, and her own house in Argyll Street acted as a showroom for her talents. Sibyl's determination and enterprise provided the motivating force behind the company. Her workload was immense, with twelve-hour days starting at 7 a.m., so that she could continue to entertain in the evenings. To save time she often changed her clothes in the back of her chauffeur-driven Rolls while travelling between appointments. Her weekends in country houses were arranged so that she could check on progress on the firm's various projects *en route*. Prestigious commissions rolled in, but at first Sibyl tended to under-estimate the hidden costs, so her profits in the early years were not huge. Her response was to work even harder, and her ambition was to be commissioned by the Prince of Wales to decorate his home, Fort Belvedere, an early-nineteenth-century country house in the Gothic Revival style, situated in Windsor Great Park, which he occupied from 1929 to 1936.

Meanwhile, she maintained a frenetic pace in her social-ising. She had immense stamina, but also a desire to be everywhere and meet everyone of interest. A typical day from her diary was parodied by the novelist Mary Borden in her story 'To Meet Jesus Christ':

> To go from a Pirandello play to a ball in Park Lane, a musical At Home at an Embassy in Portland Place, a reception at the India Office, and a supper in Soho, and to mark down a new quarry in each place, and roll home exhausted at four in the morning with half-a-dozen new intimate friends, who include the great Italian dramatist, a Crowned Head, the French writer of the day, and some woman who had snubbed her for years, was something of an achievement, but this was her average nightly bag.

However, not everyone wished to be drawn into her social circle; Vita Sackville-West insisted her two sons share a bedroom at Sissinghurst, so that one of them would always be occupying that room even if the other was away, and refused to install a separate guest bedroom, so that she need never have Sibyl to stay for a weekend. Sibyl's relentless desire to know everyone also grated on some; a tale spread around London of a contest between a young man and a Chelsea hostess in pursuit of an electric lion. The young man won the race because the woman kept turning round to explain to the spectators that she had known the lion as a cub.

She was adept at collecting what she called 'my young people'. Kenneth Clark's meteoric curatorial career started with the success of the Italian Old Master exhibition, which opened at the Royal Academy in January 1930 and had been organised with Sibyl's assistance. It was such a popular success that fashionable Londoners would go to any lengths to obtain tickets, Clark recalled. He and his wife, Jane, were taken up by Sibyl, and her invitations with their angular, almost illegible handwriting arrived in droves. She was impressively organised, spending three hours every Saturday and Sunday morning starting at 5 a.m., writing hundreds of invitations and posting them in huge bundles. She also seized every possible opportunity to garner new people for her collection; the actor Alfred Lunt accompanied her to the theatre and was so annoyed by her restless scrutiny of the audience that he threatened to leave.

Lunch or dinner at Sibyl's was not always an unmitigated pleasure. Unlike the spouses of most of the hostesses, Sir Arthur Colefax was a regular feature at the dining table. Flanked by the more patient guests, he would hold forth on the issues of the day. Sibyl's glittering social circle were very hard on poor Arthur, but there was a striking unanimity in their descriptions. Virginia Woolf claimed she had unwillingly become the second leading authority in Britain on the Dye-Stuffs Bill, Sir Arthur being the greatest. Maurice Bowra, a keen cricket enthusiast, compiled an imaginary First Eleven of Bores, making Arthur captain. Beverley Nichols wrote:

> if it had not been for Sibyl her guests would have scattered at the very sight of him. He knew a great deal about the laws of England and also about the laws of France, and at one time he had some sort of advisory post connected with the construction of the Channel Tunnel. Once, walking home with Max Beerbohm after lunch, I asked what Sir Arthur had been talking to him about for so long. Max heaved a deep sigh. 'Surely you need not ask? He was boring the Channel Tunnel.'

Sibyl's literary regulars included T. S. Eliot, the Kiplings, Rebecca West, Harold Nicolson, H. G. Wells and André Maurois. She also had a penchant for theatrical types, especially John Gielgud, Tilly Losch and Alexander Korda. Musicians such as Noel Coward and Artur Rubinstein came as guests, but were often persuaded to 'sing for their suppers'. One of her greatest coups was the actor Charlie Chaplin; Sibyl had met him in Hollywood, and when he visited Britain, she enticed him to Argyll House. Harold Nicolson wrote:

> Lunch with Sibyl Colefax. A good party. Lady Castlerosse, Diana Cooper, Charlie Chaplin, H. G. Wells, Tom [Oswald] Mosley. We discuss fame. We all agree that we should like to be famous but that we should not like to be recognised. Charlie Chaplin told us how he never realised at first that he was a famous man. He worked on quietly at Los Angeles, staying at the Athletics Club. Then suddenly he went on a holiday to New York. He then saw 'Charlie Chaplins' everywhere – in chocolate, in soap, on hoardings, 'and elderly bankers imitated me to amuse their children.' Yet he himself did not know a soul in New York. He walked through the streets where he was famous and yet unknown. He at once went to the photographer and had himself photographed as he really is.

The financial crisis of the early 1930s alarmed Emerald Cunard. She discreetly disposed of some of her diamond and emerald jewellery, but had good-quality paste replicas made first, so that no one would notice. Her financial worries were eventually alleviated by a substantial inheritance from her old admirer George Moore, who died on 21 January 1933. The bulk of his estate, worth £80,000 (approximately £2.9 million today), went to Lady Cunard, whom he had loved for thirty-nine years. He had never married but had spent his life adoring her from afar. She was an infrequent visitor to his house in his last years, usually turning up unannounced, clutching an orchid in a pot as a gift. He relished her company: 'Dearest and best of women. Life would be a dreary thing without you. Come to see me soon', he wrote. In one of his last letters to her, on 14 October 1932, he referred to his own book *Heloise and Abelard*, and told her that in the text he was Gaucelm D'Arembert (G for George) and she was Lady Malberge (M for Maud). Chapter XXII contains the following passage, narrated by Gaucelm:

> 'It has fallen out that Malberge has wept naked in my arms, telling me that I must help her to obtain some man who has caught her fancy, reminding me of our long love, her tears flowing on her cheeks. Thou wilt help me, she has said, for I must have both of you […] sometimes I mingle with the crowd and catch sight of her, and sometimes a whim brings her here to me, and I look upon my life as it has come to me through Malberge as a perfect gift. My death, which cannot be far away now, only affects me in this much, that I shall not see Malberge any more; and not seeing her, I am indifferent to all things after death as I am during life, indifferent to all things but Malberge.' And on these words Gaucelm D'Arembert turned away, thinking that he had said enough.

Moore also left Emerald his letters to her, many of which she destroyed, but those she retained were later inherited by

Sacheverell Sitwell. Emerald's missives to Moore have not survived, so it is difficult to know to what extent she ever reciprocated his grand passion. However, Nancy Cunard was very fond of 'GM', even asking him once if he might be her biological father. Emerald's cavalier treatment of 'the Hermit of Ebury Street', as he was disparagingly called by Sir Thomas Beecham, was another factor in Emerald and Nancy's deteriorating relationship.

Kenneth Clark first met Emerald in 1930, when she arrived late for a concert. The audience had been kept waiting by the conductor, Beecham, and as Emerald chattered away blithely to the embarrassed Clark, who was showing her to her seat, Sir Thomas turned round and snapped, 'You're late. Sit down.' Her perennial unpunctuality was famous; audiences at academic lectures would often see the shadow of a headpiece of osprey feathers bobbing along the lower edge of the illuminated screen and recognise the unmistakably beaky silhouette of Lady Cunard.

By now Emerald had refined her lunch and dinner parties to a fine art. Peter Quennell, a great gossip and prolific biographer, remarked that she liked to mix her guests 'like cocktails', surrounding herself with an assortment of the *prominenti* from diverse fields. She delighted in intelligent eccentrics such as Lord Berners, writers such as Somerset Maugham or Michael Arlen and suave statesmen such as Duff Cooper and Henry 'Chips' Channon. Visiting heiresses such as Barbara Hutton were welcome, as was prickly Virginia Woolf. Emerald was adept at discovering those who had the potential to amuse, inform or delight her other guests. She especially enjoyed teasing the more serious VIPs who turned up at her table. As Kenneth Clark recorded, one evening her victim was a ponderous American millionaire called Myron Taylor.

'Now, Mr Taylor, what do you think about incest?' 'Well, er, ah, there seems to be no doubt at all that biologically the results are deleterious. In some of our small prairie towns statistics show …' 'But, Mr Taylor, what about Siegmund and Sieglinde?' and Emerald began to sing in her small sweet voice, with impeccable diction, the end of Act I of *The Valkyrie*. Mr Taylor, only slightly shaken, continued inexorably, '… and it is proved conclusively that in some Near Eastern countries …' 'Kenneth, what do you think about incest?' 'I'm in favour of it, Emerald.' 'Oh, Kenneth, what a wicked thing to say! Think of the Greeks! … But all the same it was just a silly old taboo, like Pythagoras saying that it was wicked to eat beans.' Emerald delighted, 'Mr Taylor, do you think it wicked to eat beans?' Emerald's rooms were always very warm, and by this time the wretched Myron Taylor was sweating profusely. All he could do was to cover his large senatorial face with a table napkin.

Conversation at her table was general, stimulating and occasionally scurrilous though rarely vulgar, and the reputations of others were mercilessly shredded. Emerald remarked that one should be kind to the poor; only Mrs Corrigan was kind to the rich, with her tombolas and Cartier knick-knacks. Emerald called her rivals Mrs Greville and Lady Colefax 'The Dioscouri of Gloom', and alleged that Mrs Ronnie instructed her chef to inflate the quails to be served at dinner with a bicycle pump. When Somerset Maugham, widely known to be homosexual, was preparing to leave one of her parties early, he made the excuse 'I have to keep my youth'. 'Why didn't you bring him with you?' she retorted.

On one occasion her needling was publicly rebuked. The

elderly playwright George Bernard Shaw and his wife, Charlotte, were the guests of Lady Lavery, and Lady Cunard brought up the sensitive subject of a new publication, a collection of love letters written many years previously between Shaw and Mrs Patrick Campbell, before he had met and married Charlotte. Shaw had expressly forbidden 'Mrs P' from publishing them, but she had ignored his wishes. Now he was highly embarrassed, and Lady Cunard pressed home her advantage. 'You must read them', she insisted to Mrs Shaw. 'As love letters they are unsurpassed. Promise me you'll read them.' Charlotte Shaw replied, 'I shall certainly read them, and when I have read them I will tell you what I think of *them,* and what I think of *you.*' Even Emerald was silenced.

She was once discomfited at her own dining table. The conversation had turned to the resemblance between people and certain animals. Emerald made the tactical error of asking a question to which she could not predict the answer: 'What am I like?' she trilled. The guests sat in silence, each thinking inevitably of some species of bird. Archie Clark Kerr, a professional diplomat who appeared to have nodded off, suddenly pronounced 'A fruit-eating bat', and immediately closed his eyes again. Of all flying creatures, the unprepossessing nocturnal mammals with leathery wings, pointed faces and sharp teeth were probably the least flattering he could have suggested. Emerald changed the subject adroitly.

Emerald was obsessed by her appearance, and she reacted badly to having her photographic portrait reproduced in Cecil Beaton's *Book of Beauty* in November 1930. Somewhat theatrically, she thrust her copy of the book into the fire during lunch, to the amazement of her guests, and held it down with a poker, exclaiming, 'He calls me a hostess, that shows he's a low fellow!' However, she may have been secretly flattered to be featured in the book, and she had consented to having her photograph taken – unlike Virginia Woolf, who was furious to discover that Beaton had included two sketches of her he had made from photographs taken by others, without permission. Sibyl Colefax wrote nervously to Beaton, 'I do wish you hadn't put in Virginia – she will never forgive it – & she's so worth having for a friend.' Mischievous Lord Berners acquired a copy of the book and amused himself by making subtle changes to the portraits of female celebrities, blacking out the occasional tooth in an otherwise flawless smile or hatching in pimples or a discreet moustache above luscious lips. However, he never defaced the portrait of Emerald; he was too fond of her.

Even the Astors were shaken by the Great Depression, although they weathered the storm better than many, as their principal portfolio by 1929 was $100 million worth of real estate on the island of Manhattan in New York City, where property prices and rents stayed buoyant. However they had a great many charitable commitments they wanted to honour, such as supporting the Margaret McMillan nursery schools. With reluctance they economised by 'letting go' a number of household and estate staff, and mothballing some of their cars. They also decided to close up large parts of Cliveden until the financial situation improved substantially.

Despite its promising start, Nancy Astor's political career hit some obstacles in the late 1920s and early '30s. She narrowly held her seat against a strong Labour candidate in the election of 1928 with a majority of only 500. In February

1931 Nancy spoke in the House in support of a private members' bill on the total prohibition of alcohol. This was always a controversial stance, but Nancy caused national uproar by claiming that the reason why England's cricket team had narrowly lost the Ashes to the Australians the previous summer was that the Antipodeans were teetotal. It was hard to think of a greater insult to both English and Australian cricket enthusiasts, and Nancy was castigated by the press.

Despite their ideological differences, Nancy Astor and George Bernard Shaw were great friends. He was renowned the world over as an Irish socialist and radical playwright. His personality appealed to Nancy, being accomplished, witty, entertaining and sincere. Like Nancy, his passions were very private and ran deep. Through GBS Nancy had met Lawrence of Arabia, now known as Airman Shaw, who became a frequent visitor to Cliveden and St James's Square, roaring up on his motorbike whenever he could get leave. On one occasion he was late returning to his barracks, and in mitigation he explained he had been held up at dinner with Lord and Lady Astor and George Bernard Shaw; this was taken by his commanding officer as just a witty fantasy, and he evaded punishment.

Occasionally Lawrence would take Lady Astor for a high-speed spin on his motorbike, racing up the drive to Cliveden and sending up a spray of gravel as they roared past the Fountain of Love with Nancy riding pillion behind him. Waldorf could hardly bring himself to watch; he had managed to persuade Nancy to give up hunting when they married, but she retained a love of speed all her life. She was an impatient and impulsive driver, on one occasion driving far too fast down the Mall on an icy morning and unexpectedly encountering the Guards band marching up the middle of the road towards her. She braked, but the wheels locked and the car skidded on the frosty surface. The Guards scattered in all directions; Nancy regained control of the wheel and drove on at speed, laughing manically. She frequently ignored red lights and was occasionally stopped by police, but it was a more deferential age, and she was never charged with any driving offence.

Even such a wealthy family as the Londonderrys were feeling the financial breeze. In September 1931 Edith was staying as a guest of her friend Laura Mae Corrigan in her rented Venetian palazzo, and expecting Ramsay MacDonald to come and join them. He declined the invitation because of the seriousness of the international situation; politicians and economists were acutely aware that the German mark had recently collapsed, a disaster for that country's economy, and the pound was now under pressure. When Britain abandoned the Gold Standard on 21 September 1931, Charley wrote to Edith urging her to hurry home without lingering in Paris, as she and Laura Corrigan had planned, because the value of the pound was plummeting. He sold a large number of horses to reduce their outgoings, and the family economised by consolidating their servants around their three main homes: Londonderry House, Mount Stewart and Wynyard. They had already sold 9,000 acres of land in Merioneth in 1930, but now they also put the family's Welsh mansion, Plas Machynlleth, on the market, advertising it as 'highly suitable for a hotel or school'.

In the 1930s the Londonderrys' domestic staff typically

numbered around thirty people, many of whom travelled with them in the grand manner of a previous age. In addition there were the gardeners, still occupied in transforming Mount Stewart. Work continued on the fantastic gardens and grounds to Edith's scheme. The twin towers and flanking wall of the family burial ground had been constructed in the late 1920s. Lady Londonderry had also been provided with a flock of flamingos by King Fuad of Egypt – they did not like the climate of Northern Ireland and had to spend most of their winters moping in a heated shed.

Ramsay MacDonald regularly visited his dear friend Lady Londonderry. In political circles this unlikely friendship was thought to have moderated his Socialist views. They often wrote to each other in affectionate terms of endearment, and it was rumoured that when they both stayed as guests of the royal family at Windsor Castle he would visit her bedroom between 11.30 and 2 in the morning 'to talk'. Speculation about their relationship was rife, but it was almost certainly no more than friendship; he had been widowed in 1911, and was lonely. She was attractive, funny and good company, and her handsome husband was notoriously unfaithful, though she chose to make light of 'his girls', as she called them. Understandably, she found Ramsay MacDonald's Hibernian gallantries flattering. In addition, he was the leader of the National Government, and in 1931 he made Charley Londonderry a minister in his Cabinet, a role he was to hold until 1935.

Mrs Greville continued to entertain in lavish style at 16 Charles Street, where the eighteenth-century terraced house facing the main road had been extended at the back to incorporate mews buildings in the street behind, creating an open-air terrace, an enormous ballroom and quiet self-contained apartments for the hostess. It is a tribute to her dedication to entertaining that *Vogue* magazine on 26 July 1933 gave her the following accolade, just six months away from her seventieth birthday:

> At Season's Ending it is tempting to look back and decide that this year's best post-Ascot evening party (Class A Certified) was – Mrs Ronnie Greville's [...] A wonderfully wide crowd – royal, political, intellectual, and after the tired elder statesmen had gone home, animated groups of the younger people remained – we strayed through the rooms, admiring the beautiful Sir Joshuas [Reynolds], and thinking how pleasant an uncrowded party can be, ended up at the elaborate buffet in the courtyard.

Her capacity for intrigue was growing. She was very loyal to her old friend Rufus Isaacs, Lord Reading, the Viceroy of India, with whom she had stayed at the Viceregal Lodge in Delhi. He had clashed with one of his staff, George Lloyd, who had ambitions to succeed him as Viceroy. Mrs Greville invited George Lloyd to stay at Polesden Lacey, and he part-nered Mrs Greville's great friend, the impecunious Queen Ena of Spain, at bridge. Due to his impulsive card-playing, they were soundly defeated. Mrs Greville had influential contacts in the Foreign Office and the India Office, and revenge was sweet. She later purred, 'There was a time when George Lloyd thought he might get India. But I soon put a stop to that.'

Mrs Greville was very fond of Queen Ena, the grand-daughter of Queen Victoria, and rather protective of her. She took a dim view of Ena's estranged husband, King Alfonso, who was exiled from his native country in 1931. She felt he was not a gentleman; 'although he was a Hapsburg, one always felt he had only just *arrived*' was her considered verdict.

Mrs Greville had friends in America, and although she eventually lost her enthusiasm for New York, preferring Chicago, the West Coast and Hollywood, she always enjoyed an opportunity to catch up with the Vanderbilts. She had a long-standing rivalry with Grace Vanderbilt, whose seventy-room mansion on Fifth Avenue was the social centre of New York and was run as the stateliest of stately homes. Grace had a reputation as the supreme American hostess; in a single year she entertained 37,000 guests, either in New York or at her enormous 'holiday cottage' at Newport. Like Mrs Ronnie, her success as a Queen Bee was due to her combination of money, snobbery, energy and attention to detail. She was also adept at side-stepping criticism; 'Mother was always careful to silence potentially envious tongues with small acts of thoughtfulness and gentility,' recalled her son Cornelius Vanderbilt the Fifth.

Grace was known in New York as 'The Kingfisher' because she liked to think of herself as a great friend of all monarchs, especially the British royal family. When asked if there was anything a visitor could do for her on his return to London, she said, 'Only give my love to the dear boys', meaning the Prince of Wales and his brothers, the Dukes of York, Gloucester and Kent. Mrs Greville resented Grace's proprietorial attitude to the House of Windsor; in later years, when Mrs Vanderbilt announced that she wanted to live in Britain, she replied icily, 'No, Grace, we have enough Queens here already'.

Perhaps Mrs Greville was thinking of her great rival Laura Mae Corrigan, who in the manner of a lepidopterist or philatelist ardently collected royalty. Even when introduced to John Gielgud, who was playing the lead role in *Hamlet*, Mrs Corrigan could not resist telling the bemused young actor that she knew the Danish royal family 'intimately'. She vied with Mrs Greville to befriend both the exiled Queen of Spain and the King of Greece, and made every effort to associate herself with court circles. The intricacies of *placement* remained mysterious; at one of her dinner parties she had mistakenly placed a plain Mr Lancaster at her right hand, having mistaken him for the Duke of Lancaster, a genuine title that was used as a thin disguise by the Prince of Wales. Discovering the error, she ousted the unfortunate commoner from the position of most honoured guest and yelled down the table, 'Who's the next-ranking Dook?'

Many envious people resented Laura Corrigan's social success and took every opportunity to snipe at her, even while they lapped up tales about her excesses in the press; the journalist Valentine Castlerosse, who had enjoyed her lavish hospitality many times, pontificated in print that she should use her fortune to support some cultural cause, such as encouraging the young in the fields of art or architecture, but she took no notice. She was a veteran who had survived being frozen out in Cleveland and ignored in New York; minor carping in London was nothing by comparison. In addition, by this point she was becoming genuinely popular with people who recognised the fact that she was generous, kind and loyal.

In the 1930s E. F. Benson, the author of *Mapp and Lucia*, portrayed the change of ownership in London mansions and expressed the general relief that American millionairesses were glad to take on the mantle of holding vast parties. He could have been writing about Laura Corrigan:

A few only of the great London houses were still in possession of their owners [...] most of the big entertaining was done by Americans and other aliens who, in the old-fashioned way of the New World, still delighted in Duchesses and took the vast empty houses in the country from owners who had not been able to dispose of them to such advantage [...] In London these hospitable folk gave innumerable dinners, and had cotillions and cabarets, and were an immense godsend to those who thought that every hour not spent in a crowd was sixty minutes wasted.

Laura was involved in an unfortunate spat on 17 July 1930. Lady Mountbatten had organised a Midnight Revue at the London Pavilion, in support of the British Legion, with the Prince of Wales as the guest of honour. Boxes cost 250 guineas each, and American millionaire William Randolph Hearst paid £300 for tickets for himself and his mistress, Marion Davies. Competitive Lady Cunard bought forty tickets, but was outdone by Laura Corrigan who snapped up seventy-five seats in the front row, and invited her seventy-four guests to dine at her house before the show. Edwina Mountbatten's sister Mary Cunningham-Reid asked Laura if she could join the dinner party and bring a number of her own friends too. Laura politely declined, as she couldn't accommodate any other guests, so when Mary arrived at her door with her friends, Laura had them turned away. Like every other hostess, her formal dinners had a finite number of seats. However, the two sisters were furious, and Lady Mountbatten sabotaged Laura's next party by announcing a rival event on the same evening. Edwina persuaded Prince George of Kent to 'chuck' Laura in favour of her party. Society fixer Charlie Stirling appealed to Lady Londonderry's innate sense of fairness, and she stoutly went to Laura's party, taking with her the King of Spain. Laura was supported by many who felt she had been right to turn away the gate-crashers. However, the Prince of Wales sided with the Mountbattens, and when Laura subsequently sat next to him at a dinner given by Lady Cunard, he did not address a single word to her, a public humiliation that might have crushed a less resilient spirit. He stipulated afterwards that Mrs Corrigan's name should not feature on the guest list for any party he was to attend in future, a distinction that she shared with Mrs Greville.

Laura Corrigan had a gift for almost childlike candour, and could douse any small spark of male interest instantly. A man made a pass at her in the back of a taxi, and when she related the experience she said she didn't know whether to hold on to her skirt or her wig. Skittish Lord Weymouth offered to go to bed with her if she bought him a Rolls-Royce; she replied she would buy him two Rolls-Royces if they could both be spared that experience, which dampened his ardour. Every spare minute she spent with the moody Duke of Devonshire at his country house, Compton Place, she wielded an axe, chopping wood, surely a deterrent for any potential suitor.

Lumberjacking aside, Laura liked to spend part of each summer staying at an Italian palazzo surrounded by her friends. In August 1931 she rented the Palazzo Mocenigo in Venice. Situated on the Grand Canal, it had been the home of Lord Byron and the place where he wrote *Don Juan*. Laura caused a sartorial sensation by wearing 'short trousers' on the Lido, but the following year she and her guests were the talk of Venice for different reasons. Laura had hired the Palazzo Brandolini, and staying with her were Evelyn Waugh, the Duff Coopers and 'Chips' Channon. Also in town were

Cecil Beaton, Emerald Cunard and Sir Thomas Beecham, Lord and Lady Castlerosse, Bob Boothby, Oliver Messel and Winston Churchill's son Randolph. To add to the tension, Oswald Mosley and his wife, Cimmie, and Diana Guinness and her husband, Brian, were also staying in Venice; a raging affair had developed between Diana and Mosley, who would disappear together for hours at a time, reappearing at mealtimes to be met with pursed lips, raised eyebrows and leaden silences.

On 29 August 1932 it was Lady Diana Cooper's fortieth birthday. Ever generous, Laura Corrigan gave her a diamond clip for her birthday, but Diana leaned over the balcony and it disappeared with an expensive plop into the Grand Canal. That evening 'Chips' Channon held a birthday party for Diana in a restaurant on the island of Murano. All of 'smartistic Mayfair' seemed to be there, as well as glassblowers, gondoliers and musicians. Randolph Churchill urged his friend Richard Sykes to patch up an argument he had had with a former girlfriend, Doris Duke, an American tobacco millionairess. But she bristled at his approach, sharp words were exchanged and Richard whipped the cigarette from between Doris's lips and stubbed it out on her hand, a particularly insulting gesture, given the source of Doris's millions. Randolph threw a punch at Richard for his unchivalrous behaviour, but blameless Sir Alfred Beit was in the way, and a mêlée ensued, involving the choir of fifteen gondoliers and an audience of fifty interested bystanders. Cecil Beaton lobbed Prosecco bottles onto the heads of the protagonists and was promptly thrown to the ground by Oliver Messel. Duff Cooper waded in, and a rolling scrum of some eight men fought their way across the floor, dragging linen and crockery from the tables and overturning the furniture.

Stepping over the prone figure of a baronet in the doorway, Emerald Cunard made her customary late entrance. 'What a lovely party!' she trilled.

Laura might have been spurned by American high society, but she did not forget her own humble origins, and in 1933 she sent generous cheques to charitable bodies in and around Waupaca, Wisconsin, including the Red Cross, local churches and hospitals, education boards, the library and a fund for unemployment relief. Cleveland, the city that wouldn't accept her marriage to James, was provided with a double-edged gift. Laura organised a safari to Africa, hiring three planes in which she travelled with a journalist, a photographer and film cameraman, two secretaries, two maids, a doctor and a nurse, two cooks, three waiters, a hairdresser, a manicurist and a dressmaker. On arrival, she hired the services of big game hunters; rather than slaughtering wildlife for entertainment, the aim of Mrs Corrigan's expedition was to capture fourteen rare animals alive, and these were despatched to the Cleveland Zoo, along with instructions for their care and a cheque for £5,000 to pay for their welfare and food.

Back in London the parties continued, both the traditional and the novel. On 1 July 1929 there had been a rather subdued reception at Londonderry House, as the Conservative Party had been defeated in the election. Many of the guests were glad to make their excuses early and go on to a very different event, a circus-themed party at 17 Bruton Street, the former home of the Duchess of York. The young couturier Norman Hartnell had booked performing bears and Siberian wolf cubs, and Lady Eleanor Smith led a white pony up the staircase while Nancy Mitford and a host of other Bright Young People enjoyed the syncopated charms of a jazz band and a circus orchestra. The following night, many of the same sensation-seekers were the guests of Mrs Rosemary Sandars, whose party theme was babies. Guests converged on her house in Rutland Gate dressed as giant infants, complete with teddies and comforters, and swigged cocktails from feeder bottles supplied by the bar, which was set within the confines of a baby's play-pen. 'This is the type of behaviour which leads to Communism,' harrumphed one commentator. However it was bumptious, well-upholstered American Elsa Maxwell, a friend of Laura Corrigan, who created the most successful themed party; on 13 May 1930 she threw a 'murder' party at Lady Ribblesdale's house in St James'. Professional actors were engaged to play the part of detectives, and they quizzed the guests about the 'victim's' demise. The discovery of an artful trail of clues led to a thrilling denouement, the arrest of the bemused Duke of Marlborough as the perpetrator of the foul deed. The 'murder mystery' party had arrived; it thrived on the particularly British sensibility for a juicy scandal and a thrillingly sticky end in the cosy, clubbable setting of an upper-class house.

The nature of British nightlife was changing as a response to the Depression; many formerly wealthy people now could not afford to run a large home, staffed with servants, and they moved into smaller houses around Westminster and Knightsbridge. One after another the big mansions gave way to flats; Devonshire House went first, Grosvenor House soon followed. In Portman Square blocks of comfortable, modern service flats supplanted unwieldy houses, until even the rich began to favour life in apartments or converted mews. There was little space to entertain at home, beyond a few guests for cocktails or an intimate supper, so people increasingly took their friends out for dinner, going on afterwards to a night club. Even those who still lived in big houses adopted the habit of entertaining in restaurants and dance clubs, and the pre-war private parties that had been held in mansions large enough to have a ballroom became less frequent. Mothers keen to launch their daughters on society and hopefully to find them a suitable husband were no longer willing or able to spend £1,000 on a single ball, as they had done in the past; in these more straitened times smaller entertainments, such as a few weekends in the country, theatre parties or supper parties in dance restaurants were wiser investments. The relative dearth of large parties, however, had the effect of making them seem even more desirable, and those hostesses still able to provide them, such as Mrs Greville, Laura Corrigan and Lady Astor, were more popular than ever.

Invitations to stay at well-connected country houses were also very welcome in the early 1930s. Cliveden had a reputation for comfort and stimulating company, and could accommodate forty guests, who arrived on Friday evenings. Weekend parties attracted friends, family members, visiting Americans, personalities and celebrities, rather than the overtly political and 'High Society' cast who frequented the Astors' London house. Nancy liked literary people and actors, but musicians largely left her cold. She had no interest in classical music and preferred popular songs of the American South, which gave her the opportunity to play the mouth organ as accompaniment.

Ascot week was intensely social at Cliveden, as the house was close to the racecourse. Although Nancy enjoyed riding herself, she was too impatient to enjoy a day at the races, even though Waldorf owned a high-class stud and bred racehorses, so she would often wave off her guests as they left every day for the course, sporting buttonholes in the Astor colours, and occupy herself more profitably at home till they returned around 6 p.m. The dressing gong was rung at 7.45, and everyone would change into evening clothes with the help of their valets or maids. Ascot week would end with the Royal Ball at Windsor Castle, an opportunity for Nancy to wear the famous Astor tiara.

Not everyone was assured of a warm reception from the doyenne of Cliveden. The journalist Beverley Nichols was invited to lunch after mentioning Lady Astor in one of his regular columns for the *Sunday Chronicle*.

> Cliveden struck me as a house of the dead. The immediate effect was of a luxury hotel. It reeked of money but it had no feeling of welcome. And though every room brimmed with flowers they were arranged with less taste than the bouquets in the foyer of the Savoy. Nor was there any warmth in the greetings of our hostess. There were about twenty of us and as she strode into the room she waved her hand towards the drinks tray. It was loaded with every conceivable variety of alcoholic refreshment, from vodka to Pimm's Number One. 'If you want to poison yourself,' she announced in strident tones, 'you know where it is.'

Some were also critical of the Astors' luxurious lifestyle at a time of economic depression and hardship, but Rose Harrison, Nancy's maid, defended them:

> Entertaining for the Astors wasn't just something that they did, it was indeed an industry. Now there will be people who will criticise them and talk about poor people and the unemployed. But this was the accepted way of life at that time, people spent where it gave them the most pleasure. They also provided employment and kept money

circulating. Workmen and tradesmen alike were grateful to them.

There were tensions within the Astor family too. Nancy's eldest son, Bobbie Shaw, was a drifter and although brought up with the younger Astors, he felt excluded. He was sent to school at Shrewsbury, while his half-brothers went to Eton. In September 1921 he joined the Household Cavalry; he was an excellent rider and race jockey, but he had three bad falls and sustained head injuries that left him both volatile in temperament and with a bad reaction to alcohol; like his father, he was fond of the bottle. He inherited his mother's tendency to make caustic remarks – on one occasion he declaimed to an embarrassed dining table, 'Why did Mama marry Uncle Waldorf? Because she wanted a million-aire who said nothing.' Nancy snapped back sarcastically, 'There he is; there's my son. Wouldn't anybody be proud to have him?'

Bobbie was very good-looking and entertaining company, so he was attractive to women. Alexandra Curzon, known as Baba, daughter of the former Viceroy of India, was very keen on him but he explained that he was 'not the marrying kind'. In truth, he was bisexual and found fleeting physical encounters with like-minded men preferable to relationships with women. Perhaps he was also anxious to avoid the type of marriage exemplified by his domineering mother and acquiescent stepfather.

It was not illegal to be homosexual between the wars, but sexual activity between two men was both illegal and vilified by many. George V had muttered darkly about 'men like that' shooting themselves. Punitive laws did not prevent people from seeking out illicit sex, as the more salacious newspapers of the time were keen to report, but blackmailers could ruin their professional and personal lives. (Even the Duke of Kent made the fundamental error in 1932 of sending compromising letters to a male lover in Paris, and Buckingham Palace officials had the delicate task of buying them back, at great expense.) So when Bobbie was caught with a soldier 'in conduct unbecoming to an officer and a gentleman' in the summer of 1929, he was forced to choose between resigning his commission and facing a court martial. The regiment disguised the real nature of the offence, claiming that Bobbie had been drunk on duty, a plausible story, given his history. However, this 'fig leaf' of alcoholism was embarrassing to his mother, the fervent teetotaller.

Two years later, in 1931, Bobbie was accused of propositioning a guardsman. The police warned him they were planning to charge him, giving him ample opportunity to follow the time-honoured route across the Channel to seek sanctuary in France. If he had escaped, the charges would have been quietly dropped and he could have returned to Britain a few years later with an unblemished record, a better appreciation of the wisdom of discretion and, presumably, competent colloquial French. However, like Oscar Wilde, Bobbie decided to stay and face the ordeal of a public trial. He was sent to prison on 17 July 1931 for four months, as incarceration in a male-only environment was deemed the appropriate deterrent for active homosexuals. A single terse line in the *London Gazette* announced that His Majesty had 'no further occasion for his services'. The Astor family controlled the *Observer* and *The Times*, and Lord Beaverbrook agreed to Nancy's request to omit any reference to Bobbie's conviction in his many papers.

In some respects it was fortunate that Bobbie's prosecution

was just before the Astors' trip to the Soviet Union. While he was awaiting trial, Nancy gritted her teeth, visited her constituency, opened a fête and hosted a visit from the Prince of Wales. The Prince wrote her a kind letter saying 'how absolutely marvellously I think you behaved and bore up [...] It does seem a cruel shame that a minute's madness should be victimised when we know many who should have "done time" in prison years ago.' Despite her distress at Bobbie's problems, on her return from Russia she stood by him, visiting him in prison, and took him to Rest Harrow for a holiday after his release.

Meanwhile, Nancy's professional interests were changing. She had championed the interests of her Plymouth constituency, defended the rights of women and children and campaigned against the evils of alcohol. But in the early 1930s she took up international concerns. Through her friend George Bernard Shaw she had the rare opportunity to visit the Soviet Union, and although she had little sympathy with the Communist regime, she was determined to go.

Shaw and his wife, Charlotte, had been invited to visit the Soviet Union by the Russian Ambassador in London, Grigori Sokolnikoff. Charlotte was unwell and couldn't face the lengthy journey to Moscow by rail, so Shaw asked if he could bring a party of his friends instead. The group consisted of Lord and Lady Astor, their son David, Philip Kerr (now Lord Lothian), Charles Tennant, a writer and Russian expert called Maurice Hindus, and Nancy's American friend Gertrude Ely, a railroad heiress. With the exception of Shaw and Hindus, the entire party were Christian Scientists. Perhaps surprisingly, consent was forthcoming; but it was typical of Shaw to invite wealthy and titled friends to accompany him to Moscow, and he introduced them with relish as 'very rich capitalists' when he gave a speech to the Soviet high command at an official banquet.

They departed for Moscow on 18 July 1931, the day after Bobbie was convicted and jailed. GBS was convinced that, on balance, the Soviet Union was a successful social experiment, despite the Stalinist purges that were terrorising the populace, but Nancy remained sceptical. It was rumoured she had packed enough tinned food to feed the party for two weeks, in anticipation of the austere conditions ahead. The highlight of their visit was a two-hour meeting with Stalin himself. Nancy Astor tackled the 'Man of Steel', asking him: 'When will you stop killing people?' He answered, 'We are living in a state of war. When peace comes we shall stop it.' In return, Stalin asked why the English-speaking peoples governed so much of the world. Nancy told him it was because of the translation of the Bible into English, which had both enriched the demotic language and promoted independence of thought. Canny Stalin also asked about the future career of Winston Churchill, once again in the political wilderness; he had evidently spotted the potential in Nancy's rival.

Nancy returned to Britain to discover she was suspected of pro-Soviet tendencies, because Shaw had made speeches in support of the Communist regime. The writer declared that he had seen no signs of food shortages (despite a desperate famine in the Ukraine, caused by Stalin's measures) and applauded the Soviet system for having freed the workers from economic slavery, privation and unemployment. It was ironic that before long Lady Astor was also suspected of being a supporter of Nazi Germany, diametrically opposed to the Soviet Union.

The early 1930s also brought personal and family problems for Emerald Cunard. Her daughter Nancy, now living in France, was becoming increasingly estranged. Emerald disapproved of much of Nancy's behaviour, including arranging a private screening in London of a banned French Surrealist film, *L'Age d'Or*, on the grounds that it was blasphemous and obscene. In 1928 Nancy took a trip to Venice with her cousin Victor Cunard. There she met a handsome black American jazz pianist, Henry Crowder, and was instantly attracted to him. Before long they were living together in liberal Paris. Henry helped her operate the printing press she had set up, and played piano in bars. There is no doubt that the attraction was genuine, though it is difficult to know whether Nancy was actually in love with Henry as an individual or whether taking a black lover was a political statement for her; she was often recklessly and overtly unfaithful to him, even seducing one of his fellow band members. Tellingly, Nancy often exhorted Henry to be more 'African'. The mild-mannered musician would protest, 'But I ain't *African*. I'm *American*.'

Typically Nancy Cunard challenged a number of contemporary taboos, including bringing Henry to London as her lover, to test the reactions of English society. In the late 1920s most British people's knowledge of African Americans was superficial; they were seen primarily as entertainers in various fields, and as the creators and performers of exciting new music. Evelyn Waugh noted the increasing fascination with black performers, and even Lady Astor, who had grown up in Virginia, engaged a group to sing 'Negro folk songs and spirituals with banjo accompaniment' to follow the dancing at one of her balls at Cliveden. But dancing with one's peers to the music of a band of 'exotic' black Americans at a

London night club was very different from forging an intimate relationship that transgressed the 'colour bar'.

The couple visited London in the summer of 1929; Henry was staying in a hotel in Bloomsbury, while Nancy saw her mother most days. In the evenings the couple would attend parties together. Lady Cunard gave no sign she knew of the relationship, but secretly she engaged private detectives to follow Nancy and Henry. They returned to London in the summer of 1930 and were seen together at a cocktail party. Nancy's last appearance at her mother's house was on the evening of 21 July 1930, for dinner. The mood was sombre as a plane crash that day had killed the Marquess of Dufferin and Ava and five friends. Many of the guests also knew of Nancy's relationship with Henry, and felt awkward keeping that information from Emerald.

But Emerald was forced to react in December 1930, when Margot Asquith burst into one of her grand lunch parties and boomed, 'Hello Maud, what is it now? – drink, drugs or niggers?' The other guests were aghast, and Emerald was mortified; she first denied that her daughter 'even knew a negro', then threatened to have the police arrest and deport Henry. Sir Thomas Beecham despatched a telegram to Nancy in Paris, telling her not to come to London till she received an urgent letter he had sent her explaining the situation. Nancy ignored his warning and set out for London with Henry; they stayed at the Eiffel Tower restaurant, but were harassed by phone calls and police visits. On their return to Paris, Nancy received a letter from her bank stating that her mother's allowance to her would be reduced by a quarter, due to Emerald's straitened financial circumstances. Her substantial American investments had been badly affected by the Wall Street Crash of 1929, and her large fortune had been

whittled away by her twin passions for Beecham and entertaining. However, Nancy saw this as an attempt to punish
her for her transgressive love affair with Henry, and mother
and daughter were never to meet again.

As revenge, Nancy publicised her relationship with Henry
to her mother's friends. She printed a pamphlet, entitled *Black
Man and White Ladyship*. Nancy described her 'negro friend
– a very close friend' who had often accompanied her to
London. She referred to her mother as 'Her Ladyship'
throughout, and called her 'the most conscientious of
ostriches', a snob, a hypocrite and a racist. 'Her Ladyship
may be as hard and buoyant as a dreadnought but one little
touch of ridicule goes straight to her heart. And she is so
alone – between these little lunches of sixteen, a few callers
at tea and two or three invitations per night.' The pamphlet
also detailed the cruelties and indignities to which black
people had been subjected by Western societies. It was
December 1931, and Nancy posted copies to about a hundred
of her mother's friends and acquaintances, including the
Prince of Wales, as a shocker of a Christmas card.

Even Nancy's loyal friends felt that such a vicious personal
assault on her mother detracted from her worthy advocacy
of better treatment for black people. Henry told her it was
'idiotic'; disagreeing in private with a parent was a different
matter from defaming them publicly. Nancy's recent behaviour had been incomprehensible to Emerald, and though she
said little on the subject, she thought that Nancy was mentally
unbalanced.

British society took a mixed view of Nancy's campaign
in support of the Scottsboro Boys. Nine black youths had
been arrested in Alabama and charged with raping two white
girls; the eldest eight had been sentenced to death, and their

fate became an international *cause célèbre*. Nancy organised a fundraising dance at a London hotel, and the Marquess of Donegall ran an inaccurate story in his regular gossip column in the *Sunday Dispatch* on 9 July 1933, suggesting that the police had intervened in the multi-racial bathing party that followed the dance, and suggesting that Nancy return to her 'spiritual home in Harlem'. The paper was forced into an apology the following week because the police had not been called. Nancy also successfully sued a number of British newspapers for libelling her in their coverage of her 1931 trip to London with Henry.

She used the money to commission and produce a massive illustrated book entitled *Negro*, tackling the injustices suffered by black people and celebrating black achievements. It was published in 1934, and was two inches thick and 800 pages long. Once again Nancy railed against her mother, 'an American-born frantically prejudiced society woman', who was willing to be photographed with 'an Indian rajah', because he was rich and therefore powerful. *Negro* was passionate; it raised important issues about harrowing inequalities, past and contemporary. If it was occasionally incoherent, there was no doubting Nancy's sincerity, and it garnered favourable reviews in the *New Statesman* and the *Daily Worker*. However, it was expensive, costing 2 guineas, and did not sell; when London was bombed by the Luftwaffe in 1940, hundreds of remaining copies were destroyed in a warehouse fire.

7

Parties and Politics: 1933–1936

Even the grandest household had its problems. The heir
to the throne, known to his family as David, was a concern
to his parents and the courtiers who sought to check his
behaviour. While the public followed the career of the Prince
of Wales with benign interest, those who knew him better
tended to be less enthusiastic. The golden-haired Prince
enjoyed all the benefits of a playboy existence, from night
clubs and cocktail parties to bagpipe-playing and glamorous
travel. Like a more worldly Bertie Wooster in P. G. Wodehouse's
novels, he even took up the ukulele.

He was bored rigid by the role that he was to inherit. King
George V was dutiful, critical and uxorious; the Prince was
averse to discipline. He was modern; he not only followed
fashion but led it with sartorial innovations that enraged his
father. For formal occasions he preferred soft collars and
dinner jackets; informally he wore loud checks, plus-fours
and assertive Argyll socks. On Saturday evenings he would
parade around his home, Fort Belvedere, in a blue and white
tartan kilt playing the bagpipes. He could be petulant and
unreliable, complaining in letters to his mistresses about the
business of 'kinging', as he called it. The Prince's Assistant
Private Secretary, Alan Lascelles, criticised him to the Prime
Minister in 1927. He said that the heir to the throne was
unfit for the role because of his selfish preoccupations, his
drinking and his womanising, and opined that the best

possible outcome for the country might be if the Prince were to break his neck in a riding accident. 'God forgive me, I have often thought the same,' replied Baldwin.

Although the Prince claimed to have at heart the interests of the working classes, he preferred to spend his time with the wealthy, especially amusing Americans such as Henry 'Chips' Channon and Emerald Cunard. 'Chips' was from Chicago; he moved to London, became an MP and married a brewing heiress, Honor Guinness. He kept a diary that recorded his ambitious socialising; he cultivated both the Prince of Wales and his glamorous younger brother, the Duke of Kent, and would have his butler add Benzedrine to cocktails served at his beautiful house. 'Chips' personified the new transatlantic social elite who entertained the Prince. As Stanley Walker wrote:

> International society is not always difficult to crash. To be the guest of the Prince of Wales at his country house, Fort Belvedere, is regarded as a high honor. Many of the members of what is known in New York as the 'international set' are accepted in London, and shuttle back and forth between England and America.

The Prince liked America, and he liked married American women. He had been involved for a number of years with Freda Dudley Ward, who was half-American; they had met during an air raid in the Great War, and by a strange quirk of fate they had been introduced by Mrs Maud Kerr-Smiley, the sister of Ernest Simpson. Then in 1929 he met Thelma, another semi-detached American, who was unhappily married to Marmaduke, the first Viscount Furness, known as the 'Fiery Furness' for his red hair and temper. This time it was Edith, Lady Londonderry who effected the introductions; the

Prince promptly dropped Freda in favour of his new passion for Thelma.

It was Thelma's older sister who brought Mr and Mrs Ernest Simpson into the Prince's social circle in 1932, though he had met them the previous year, first at an informal cocktail party and later at a weekend house party in Leicestershire. They became regular members of his entourage, staying for weekends at his home, Fort Belvedere, or entertaining him in London.

Ernest Simpson had an English father and an American mother; he was not particularly well off, but in the early 1920s he was much in demand on the London scene, and a regular dance partner of Barbara Cartland, who described him as 'a handsome young bachelor, who was to figure dramatically in the history of England seventeen years later'. It is interesting to speculate how different the outcome might have been for the British royal family if Ernest Simpson had married the future romantic novelist with the penchant for pink chiffon rather than Wallis Warfield Spencer from Baltimore. In 1916 Wallis had married a handsome American naval lieutenant, Earl Winfield Spencer. The marriage had ended in divorce as he was an alcoholic with a volatile temper. Her second marriage, in 1928 to Ernest, was far happier, and they lived in a modest but modish flat in Bryanston Court, near Marble Arch.

Those waspish social observers Cecil Beaton and 'Chips' Channon were initially dismissive of Wallis Simpson. Beaton first met her in 1930, and was unimpressed to find himself distantly related by marriage to her husband, Ernest. He described her disparagingly as being 'brawny and raw-boned in her sapphire-blue velvet. Her voice had a high nasal twang.' By contrast, 'Chips' described her as a 'neat, quiet, well-bred mouse with startled eyes and a huge mole'. (The mole, on her chin, was usually touched out in photographs.) Needless to say, both men rapidly revised their opinions when it became apparent that she had moved into the orbit of the Prince of Wales. But it was Emerald Cunard who championed her from the first: 'Little Mrs Simpson knows her Balzac', she observed approvingly, if probably optimistically. By 1932 the Simpsons often entertained Emerald, 'Chips' and the Duff Coopers at their apartment. The Prince of Wales became a frequent visitor too, dropping in for cocktails or intimate little dinners.

Early in 1934 Thelma Furness sailed back to the States to support her sister Gloria Vanderbilt, who was facing a scandalous court case. While she was away, Thelma asked her friend Wallis to 'look after the little man for me', implying that the Prince might be lonely without her. It was a fatal mistake; by the time she returned to London in March, Thelma was no longer the Prince's 'special friend'. She dined with the Prince and his other guests, and as he reached for a lettuce leaf from the salad bowl, Wallis playfully slapped his hand. Thelma shot her a glance of admonition, but Wallis met her eye and coolly stared her down. Nothing was said, but it was apparent that Viscountess Furness had been usurped by her friend. The Prince wanted to have the Simpsons invited to social events he was attending, and smart hostesses quickly took the hint. Some regretted the passing of Thelma, but Lady Cunard and Lady Colefax found compensating virtues in Wallis.

The 1914–18 war was long over and done with, but it had cast a heavy shadow over my adolescence and although in the nineteen-thirties the international skies were apparently cloudless and Europe was just one big cosy happy family, I was perceptive enough to realise that none of it quite rang true.'　　　　　(Noel Coward, *Autobiography*)

In the 1930s extremist movements were on the rise in many countries around the world. Mussolini had introduced Fascism in Italy, while Stalin retained a grip on Soviet Russia. Nationalism and militarism combined to venerate the semi-mythological figure of the Emperor in Japan, and in Germany the National Socialists, previously considered a fringe party of extreme right-wingers, had become a credible political force. Conservatives of all stripes started to see Herr Hitler as a bulwark against Communism in central Europe. Public spectacles were staged with propagandist intent; cinema newsreels, soundtracks and photographs showed the floodlit Nazi pageants at Nuremberg, with drilled battalions, the uniforms, the banners, insignia and light shows, and the monumentalist new architecture that acted as a visual shorthand for Nationalism and Fascism. Meanwhile Hollywood provided escapism from the Great Depression and the scourge of unemployment.

The dictators were charismatic and ruthless individuals with public images cultivated and promoted to disguise their ruthlessness. Stalin claimed to have achieved social equality; Hitler had revived the German sense of national pride and created autobahns; Mussolini had reunited the fractured regions of Italy and championed social order and punctual trains. With the benefit of hindsight, anyone with a moral compass would have condemned the ideologies of Stalin, Hitler, Mussolini and Franco, because of their subsequent actions, but in the early

1930s those acts were either unknown or in the future. To *bien-pensants* such as Nancy Astor the emergence of a clutch of strong leaders willing and able to take control of their individual countries seemed like progress, and a further step away from the possibility of another hideous European war. Nancy Astor was determined to get involved on the international scene, hence her much-publicised trip to Soviet Russia. Undoubtedly her motives were good; she desired peace, loathed war and had high moral standards in many aspects of her personal life. But in the early 1930s it was not apparent which of the emerging leaders of Spain, Germany, Italy and Russia were on the side of the angels, if any. The surging nationalist movements of China and Japan were even more of a closed book.

Nancy Astor embodied many of the prejudices of her age and class; she maintained a dim view of Communists and Jews, even claiming that these two (unlikely) ideological bedfellows were working together to whip up anti-Nazi feeling in the American press. In addition, she despised Catholicism, especially as it was practised in 'Latin' countries such as France, where she felt there was far too much interest in food, drink and sex. Her perception of the German national character was much more favourable, and she was worried that the Germans were being provoked into aggressive behaviour because of their treatment by the Allies. When, in 1933, Germany withdrew from the League of Nations, Nancy urged Britain to disarm as proof of a desire for peace. Remarkable as it may seem now, this pro-appeasement stance was not uncommon among the British aristocracy, the political establishment and the diplomatic corps until the mid- or late 1930s.

A number of the Mayfair set were intrigued by Adolf Hitler before he came to power. In March 1932 Virginia Woolf met Alice Keppel, now resident in Florence but temporarily staying at the London Ritz. She noted that Edward VII's former lover was going to Berlin to hear Hitler speak. Bob Boothby also travelled to Germany in 1932 to lecture on the economic crisis, and was invited to meet Hitler at a hotel. Boothby recalled that when he entered the room where Hitler was sitting writing, his quarry leaped to his feet, lifted his right arm and snapped 'Hitler!' The Scot returned the salute and shouted 'Boothby!' It became apparent to Boothby that not only did Hitler lack a sense of humour, he was also unhinged.

Hitler was appointed Chancellor of Germany on 30 January 1933. Within three months basic rights such as freedom of speech and assembly had been suspended, Dachau concentration camp had been opened, there was a boycott of Jewish-owned businesses and Jews were excluded from government employment, including teaching. The National Socialists were determined to quash any political opposition. They accused the Christian Scientists of distributing Marxist propaganda, and as a result in September 1933 Waldorf Astor was asked by the leaders of the Church of Christian Science to take a delegation to Berlin for discussions with the Minister of the Interior. They were informed that Christian Scientists had nothing to fear so long as they kept out of German politics, and Waldorf had a twenty-minute meeting with Hitler. This relatively early personal contact with the Führer identified the Astors with German interests, and was to prove damaging in later years when accusations were levelled against the 'Cliveden set'.

On 1 October 1933 Geoffrey Harmsworth's account of

his disconcerting interview with the Führer appeared in the *Sunday Dispatch*: 'The friendly, rather tired brown eyes, the warm smile (the moustache is smaller than Charlie's), and the firm handshake – unless this was part of "the business" – were disarming to say the least, and far from suggested a Frankenstein whose hands were barely dry from the morning's murders and Jew torturings.' However, as soon as Harmsworth mentioned Communism, Hitler apparently turned into a volatile firebrand, fiercely denouncing his political rivals and claiming that the New Germany had saved the whole of Europe from descending into 'Communistic chaos'. Unnerved by his encounter, Harmsworth ended his article with an optimistic comment:

> It was difficult to believe that these were the sentiments of that quiet little man with whom I had just spent one of the most interesting half-hours of my life. There are a lot of people in Germany who fanatically believe that he is a New Messiah; the rest of the world says that he is a Man of Straw. Perhaps he will disappear as suddenly and dramatically as he jumped into power. In ten years' time Adolf Hitler may be just a legend.

Duff and Diana Cooper attended the Nuremberg rallies in the autumn of 1933 out of curiosity, and Diana was profoundly repelled by seeing Hitler at close quarters: 'His dank complexion had a fungoid quality and the famous hypnotic eyes that met mine seemed glazed and without life – dead colourless eyes'. They could understand little of his ranting oration and so tried to leave early, which was taken as an insult by the German authorities, and they narrowly avoided spending the night in a cell. She called her first experience of the Nazis 'a dreadful revelation'.

It had always been the job of competent, professional ambassadors to act as mediators between the 'Men of Destiny' running their own countries and the foreign governments they wished to influence. In the 1930s the role of ambassadors in promoting the interests of the emerging dictatorships became paramount in Britain, and these individuals were aware that 'soft power' lay in the hands of the most important society hostesses. A *Vogue* article in October 1929 described how:

> One of the features of the autumn is the arrival of the new secretaries in the various embassies and legations [...] The society of every capital is ruled by the older women and led by the younger, but they are not altogether prepared for one of the charms of London – the wit and youthful *esprit* of our more important hostesses, none of whom resemble the elderly dragons of London times [...] Lady Londonderry [...] will give at least one big reception, in accordance with a tradition that is almost royal; Mrs 'Ronnie' Greville, whose caustic wit does not prevent her being our most dazzling unofficial hostess; and Lady Cunard, whose *esprit* has won her a special regard among intelligent people, for she is perhaps the most completely natural, and certainly the gayest of our entertainers.

The hostesses' favourite ambassador was undoubtedly Count Dino Grandi. He was appointed to head the Italian Embassy in 1932 by Mussolini, whom he had supported since the early 1920s. Grandi was handsome and charming; he was an Anglophile and wanted to further peace between Britain and Italy. He entertained the London *prominenti* frequently at the Embassy in Grosvenor Square. Grandi adored his wife and his children, but before long he was having an affair with

Baba Metcalfe, wife of 'Fruity' and one of the daughters of Lord Curzon. She was simultaneously involved in an affair with her brother-in-law Oswald Mosley. He benefitted from the triangular relationship as Mussolini subsidised the running costs of Mosley's political party, the British Union of Fascists, known as the 'Blackshirts'. When Mussolini lost faith in Mosley, he turned his attentions to the Nazi party in Germany, where his other mistress, Diana Guinness, and her sister Unity Mitford were close to Hitler and the Nazi high command.

Grandi made many friends in England; sensitive to the subtle undercurrents of London life, he was the first ambassador to invite both the Prince of Wales and Mrs Simpson to a dinner at the Italian Embassy. As a result Grandi became a regular visitor to Fort Belvedere for jovial weekends of dancing and cocktails. The Count valiantly attempted to represent his country's best interests, and hoped fervently (but vainly) that Il Duce would not be fooled by Hitler.

For some of the hostesses a visit to meet the dictators was a personal quest. In March 1932 Laura Corrigan set off for Rome, returning in triumph in May, having had an audience with Mussolini. A large signed photo of Il Duce had pride of place in her boudoir, jostling for space with images of the Spanish royal family. Mussolini appealed to the hostesses, though Mrs Ronnie found him 'pompous' on her trip to Rome and preferred her audience with the Pope. When Count Grandi was staying at Cliveden for the weekend, he made a few slightly caustic comments about Il Duce, but was told by Lady Astor: 'Young man, please remember that in this house nothing is *ever* said against Signor Mussolini.'

However, it was Grandi's German contemporary Joachim von Ribbentrop who made the most concerted efforts to cultivate the Queen Bees. Hitler sent this former sparkling wine salesman to mount a charm offensive on Britain's ruling classes. Initially he seemed personable and affable and spoke excellent English, which made him welcome in many a plush drawing room. The Führer knew little about foreign affairs; von Ribbentrop knew even less, and was impervious to the nuances and subtleties of diplomatic protocol. But Hitler valued fanatical personal loyalty above the skills of his country's Foreign Ministry, which was staffed by professional career diplomats.

Von Ribbentrop was encouraged to act independently of the official German Ambassador to London, the respected Leopold von Hoesch. Von Ribbentrop's message was that Germany and Britain had shared values and culture, and their beliefs and interests were also the same. He scored an early success with Mrs Greville; it seems she had encountered him socially before he became involved in politics, as one of the entries in her visitors' book for 11 November 1932 lists a 'Baron Ribbendrop' (*sic*) dining at her London home.

His first visit to London as Hitler's emissary was in November 1933, and he met Stanley Baldwin and Ramsay MacDonald, assuring them that Hitler was committed to peace, but pressing the case for German rearmament on the grounds of the threat to Europe from Soviet Russia. In an early indication of his subsequent style he was also invited to lunch by Roderick Jones, head of Reuters, and bored him, his wife and fellow guests into exhaustion for three hours by declaiming on the virtues of the Third Reich, allowing no interruptions.

In November 1934 von Ribbentrop returned to London for a three-week stay. His visit coincided with the marriage of the Duke of Kent and Princess Marina of Greece. It was a moment of euphoria in London society (and some relief within the royal family, given the Duke's rakish past.) Von Ribbentrop was relentlessly charming; he was now peddling the Third Reich to the British ruling classes, as he had formerly peddled his in-laws' cases of wine.

Mrs Greville invited von Ribbentrop to dinner on 25 November, and her other guests included Lady Cunard, the Aga Khan and Lady Churchill. He was taken up by Lady Londonderry and met opinion-formers such as Lord Lothian and George Bernard Shaw (both great friends of Nancy Astor), the Archbishop of Canterbury, the press baron Lord Rothermere and prominent journalists. He also targeted statesmen like Sir Austen Chamberlain, and succeeded in irritating Sir John Simon and Anthony Eden at the Foreign Office. Hints were dropped to von Hoesch at the German Embassy that Hitler's PR representative was making a fool of himself. In Berlin, Baron von Neurath, the Foreign Minister, wrote to Hitler claiming his protégé's visit to London had been 'a complete disaster'. Hitler dismissed the complaints.

Von Ribbentrop was authorised to offer lavish hospitality, and various British opinion-formers, such as Lloyd George and Lord Rothermere, travelled to Germany to meet the Führer; Lord Lothian interviewed Hitler in 1935. All-expenses-paid trips to attend the Nuremberg rallies were available to journalists and politicians. He also cultivated the key host-esses such as Lady Astor, and her satellites like Oswald Mosley. Lady Cunard, although she teased him, was a useful route to the Prince of Wales. Wealthy socialite Laura Corrigan was another desirable acquaintance, because of the people she assembled at her parties. And he was particularly keen to cultivate Lord and Lady Londonderry, at whose glittering political receptions he could meet the prime political movers.

Lord Londonderry himself was a special prize, as Air Minister. All these people favoured a *rapprochement* with Nazi Germany.

Rather more left-wing than her contemporaries, Sibyl Colefax was critical of those ambassadors whose only experience of genuine British opinion was filtered through the selection process of the other society hostesses. One of her prescient observations about foreign diplomats in London dates from 1933: 'They only dine with other ambassadors, with the House of Lords of any kind or sort – with occasionally members of the Cabinet [...] there's no doubt that Sara [h]Wilson, Alice Keppel *e tutti quanti*, have assured him [Alanson B. Houghton, the US Ambassador to Britain, 1925–1929] that England is down and out, because they spend all their time telling this to each other.'

Lady Cunard referred to von Ribbentrop behind his back as a 'delicious, real life Nazi'. She also teased him to his face, with questions such as 'What does Herr Hitler truly think about God?' or 'Tell us, dearest Excellency, why *does* Herr Hitler dislike the Jews?' She was similarly inflammatory in praising Mussolini to some Foreign Office officials at a lunch at Sibyl's on 11 November 1935. Emerald often made such statements just to provoke a reaction, but, like Mrs Greville and many of her circle, she was initially impressed by the new regime in Germany, and approved of their policy of imposing social order and tackling unemployment. The US Ambassador between 1933 and 1937, Robert Worth Bingham, described Lady Cunard's set as the 'pro-German cabal'. Von Ribbentrop was very keen to court Emerald, because of her close relationship with the Prince of Wales; she first introduced him to the Prince at a lunch at her house in June 1935, and he ingratiated himself with Wallis Simpson too. The first time Wallis and von Ribbentrop met was at a large luncheon at Emerald's, and Winston Churchill was also in attendance. Von Ribbentrop droned on unstoppably, listing the achievements of the Führer as Winston sat silently listening. After Hitler's ambassador had finally left, Churchill said, 'Emerald, I hope we never have to hear that broken gramophone record again.'

Lady Astor was less deferential, teasing von Ribbentrop: 'Aren't you a damned bad ambassador?' she yelled at him down the table. He asked what she meant, and she told him he had no sense of humour. 'You should see me telling jokes to Hitler, and how we both roar with laughter', he replied, somewhat implausibly. She also tackled him about the shortcomings of National Socialism, and told him that Britain would never take Hitler seriously because of his Charlie Chaplin moustache.

Von Ribbentrop's greatest desire was to influence the Prince of Wales into acquiescence with Hitler's aims. The heir to the throne was certainly pro-German in principle (his mother, after all, was German, and he had many close family ties), and he was fêted, courted and respected by the British public. However, his role was to be the symbolic head of a constitutional monarchy; Hitler and von Ribbentrop did not comprehend the limited power the prince could wield over the conduct of foreign affairs or international diplomacy.

Competition between the hostesses was fierce; they were aware of each others' activities and even socialised together, but each had at least one rival who encroached on her 'territory'. Blue-blooded Lady Londonderry, who had done so much for women's involvement in the First World War and now operated behind the scenes as a considerable political hostess, was not a natural ally of Virginian Lady Astor, the first woman to take her seat as an MP, whose Parliamentary potential was marred by her outspokenness and unorthodox behaviour. Mrs Greville, enormously rich through trade but with murky origins, bristled at any comparison with the even wealthier and more obscure mid-Western steel millionairess Mrs Corrigan, and the two of them relished cutting each other dead when their paths crossed. Perhaps the most needling of the duos were San Francisco-born Emerald Cunard and Sibyl Colefax; both of them had ambitions to run a salon for the musical, theatrical and literary elite, but they also had strong proprietorial feelings about the Prince of Wales and Mrs Simpson. Nigel Nicolson, the younger son of Harold Nicolson and Vita Sackville-West, recalled the 'undeclared competition' between Emerald and Sibyl:

> I once heard Lady Cunard pause mid-flow to say, 'I'm talking too much, like Lady Colefax', a comparison which was quite unjustified, for Sibyl was the less talkative of the two and kinder to the young. On another occasion Lady Cunard called to me down the length of her dining-room table, 'Nigel, tell us about your girl-friends', and twelve pairs of experienced eyes turned towards me. Sibyl would never have done that.

Sibyl was an inveterate collector of people and was often ridiculed for her insatiable drive to 'bag' some quarry or other. She fell out with Osbert Sitwell when she nabbed him in the street in order to be introduced to his companion, and invited the friend to lunch, but not Osbert. Realising her error, she invited him too at the last minute, but he declined. However, as her guests arrived at Argyll House, Osbert climbed onto a neighbouring roof clutching a megaphone and announced the arrivals in the manner of a Master of Ceremonies. A mature actress won the epithet of 'Miss Mary Pickford', a young politician was 'the ex-Kaiser of Germany', and a committed pacifist was described as 'Signor Mussolini'.

The Yorks lived rather quietly by comparison with Bertie's brothers. They tended to avoid glamorous places such as the Embassy Club, and they were overlooked by the smart set that gravitated to the Prince of Wales. As Elizabeth was to say in later years, 'Bertie and I were never *chic* enough for Lady Cunard.' However, they were much in demand among more conventional and aristocratic circles. Good conversation, dinner-dances with trusted friends and weekends on friends' country estates were their preferred environment, especially when their two small daughters, Elizabeth and Margaret Rose, were growing up. Mrs Greville made them her guests of honour whenever she entertained British or foreign royalty such as visiting Maharajahs, the Queen of Spain or the King of Italy. A typical evening in their honour was held on 29 June 1933 at a reception at Charles Street; the guests included the Aga Khan, Lord and Lady Londonderry, Senator Marchese Marconi and his wife, the Marchesa, Lord and Lady Reading, Sir John and Lady Simon, Lady Emerald Cunard, Maggie's god-daughter Sonia Cubitt, Winston Churchill, Sir Robert Horne, Sir Philip Sassoon and the Prime Minister of Canada. Mrs Greville wore the famous emeralds that once belonged to the Empress Josephine. She was described as:

one of the greatest hostesses in present-day London [...] no hostess stands higher in the esteem of the Royal family [...] she has vivacity and a multitude of interests. And she is interested in everything, from politics to housing schemes – from museums to the theatre [...] Above all she is a great mistress of the art of conversation. That is why her dinner parties attract such distinguished men and women.

Always astute in noticing the 'coming man', Mrs Greville also cultivated those already in prominent positions, especially during her weekend house parties. After a magnificent dinner she would draw aside the most important people present for an intimate chat in her study, while the other guests were entertained by professional performers in the salon. She was pre-eminent among the hostesses in wielding genuine political power, but her Machiavellian impulses were not always successful. She attempted to sabotage Duff Cooper's attempt to win a seat as an MP by offering to back an independent rival candidate to contest the seat and split the Conservative vote. She was annoyed when her stooge, Beverley Nichols, refused to co-operate; she threatened to cut him out of her will and fulfilled her threat, eventually leaving him nothing despite their decades of close friendship.

Her great skill was in combining interesting people from very diverse backgrounds, and she embraced the full spectrum of politics and philosophy. Professor Frederick Lindemann was one of her protégés. Born in Germany, he was a brilliant academic scientist, but she was able to tempt him away from Oxford University for country house weekends at Polesden Lacey by offering him dancing and tennis; he was the only professor to play competitively at Wimbledon. He stayed at

Polesden thirty times between 1926 and 1939, and also dined with her frequently in London. 'The Prof' was introduced to Winston Churchill by Mrs Greville in Charles Street on 11 February 1930, and the men became fast friends. Both were 'lone voices', advocating arming against a resurgent Germany, and in wartime they united to destroy the Nazis at any cost. Churchill referred to Lindemann as 'my scientific brain', and together they devised the policy of carpet-bombing Germany.

Mrs Ronnie Greville [...] must surely head the list of inveterate globe trotters of the feminine sex.'
(*Letters of Eve* column, *Tatler*, 10 January 1935)

By the early 1930s Mrs Greville was broadening her horizons to go international. In the previous decade she had 'embassy-hopped' to support her frequent overseas trips. She cultivated the London-based ambassadors of her target countries, inviting them and their homesick families to stay for cosy weekends at Polesden Lacey. As a result of her hospitality to the international diplomatic corps, she was given preferential treatment when she visited their home nations: a special train, an honour guard and interpreters, an introduction to the president or the royal family, or sumptuous banquets in her honour. Essentially, she was a status snob: she wanted to know the VIPs wherever she went, and she always made a beeline for whoever was running the show.

Now she was intrigued by Germany, with its enigmatic new leader, Herr Hitler. She was already a regular *habituée* of the German Embassy and a great friend of Ambassador von Hoesch. In August 1933 she toured Germany under her own steam, in her chauffeur-driven car, visiting Baden-Baden, Nuremberg, Stuttgart, Dresden and Berlin. She returned to Germany in August 1934 for a month; and she attended the Nuremberg rally in September as one of the 'Ehrengäste', or 'Honoured Guests' of the Third Reich, with a personal invitation from Rudolf Hess, Hitler's second-in-command. She even managed to engineer a meeting with Hitler himself through the Foreign Minister, Baron von Neurath. In 1941, when Britain was at war with Germany, she recalled that Hitler had spoken to her 'quietly and intelligibly'. When asked if she had found the Führer common, she replied, 'Not at all – one doesn't notice that with a truly great man […] now Mussolini, yes, the only great man I have ever known who was truly pompous.'

On 24 October 1934 *Tatler* reported: 'That brilliant powerful personality Mrs Ronald Greville is back. She was entertained by Hitler at the Nuremberg festivities last month, and is now enthusiastic over "the little brown shirts".' Those who lunched at Sibyl's on 14 September 1934 had been more critical, as Robert Bruce Lockhart recorded in his diary: 'Much talk about Mrs Ronnie Greville who has been at Nuremberg and who has come back full of enthusiasm for Hitler. Her influence is very strong with [Foreign Secretary Sir John] Simon. Her vanity is inordinate. In those countries where she is not given a special train, the local British ambassador or minister gets sacked.' Lockhart lunched at Lady Cunard's on 17 October 1934 and sat next to Mrs Greville herself, 'who talked pro-Hitler stuff with great vigour. She is a convinced pro-German and is very angry that no-one from the British Embassy went to the Partei-tag at Nuremberg. After all, the British Ambassador in Moscow attends the May 1st and November 7th celebrations in Moscow.'

Mrs Greville was back in Baden-Baden in August 1935 'for the cure', and entertained lavishly at the Hotel Stephanie, where she became friendly with the journalist Barbara Cartland; the two women would take chauffeur-driven rides in Mrs Ronnie's Rolls-Royce through the surrounding forests and gossip about their shared acquaintances. She was described in the *Daily Mail* as 'a great admirer of Herr Hitler and knows him personally' (8 September 1935). Through von Ribbentrop, Mrs Greville was invited to attend the Berlin Olympics and set out in August 1936; after some days in Berlin she travelled on to Baden-Baden and Dresden. The Berlin Olympics marked the high spot of Hitler's great PR push.

Although she was an enthusiastic and curious traveller, Mrs Ronnie Greville's declining health was starting to limit her activities. She held a weekend house party at Polesden Lacey in April 1935 for her guests of honour, the Duke and Duchess of York. Mrs Greville was unwell and was confined to bed, but she urged her guests to go ahead with dinner without her. With 'Madam' off the scene, her loyal but occasionally unruly staff took even more liberties than usual. Osbert Sitwell recalled the bacchanalian behaviour of the staff serving dinner to the house guests while his great friend 'Maggie' Greville was indisposed. The butlers and footmen were drunk and took pleasure in attempting to ply the Duchess of York with whisky throughout dinner.

Osbert was Mrs Greville's 'spare man' at many events. In July 1935 he joined a grand dinner party at her house in Charles Street with a stellar list of fellow guests, including Lord and Lady Londonderry and Emerald Cunard. There was a strong pro-Fascist atmosphere, with Prince and Princess Otto von Bismarck representing the German

Embassy. The Senator Marchese Marconi and his wife were ardent supporters of Benito Mussolini, who had been the best man at their wedding. The Rt Hon. Sir Eric Phipps and his wife were there; he was British Ambassador to Berlin when Mrs Greville engineered her meeting with Hitler. Other guests included Sir Evan Charteris, Viscount Hailsham and Sir Robert Horne. Sir Philip Sassoon, who was also present, may have felt uneasy; he was Jewish in origin, and his contacts in Europe were reporting growing anti-Semitism in the Third Reich. He had also visited Germany with Bob Boothby shortly after the Nazis had come to power, and had met Goering.

Unfortunately, anti-Semitism was rife in Britain between the wars, even in privileged and educated circles. Virginia Woolf, who had lunched with Philip Sassoon at Sibyl's in 1929, described him in a letter to her sister as 'an underbred Whitechapel Jew'. Oswald Mosley also made disparaging remarks about Lloyd George accepting hospitality 'from the voluptuous Orient', meaning Philip Sassoon; nevertheless when Mosley and Sassoon met over dinner at Emerald's house with the Prince of Wales and Mrs Simpson in January 1935, everyone observed the proprieties.

Sir Philip Sassoon was the Tory MP for Hythe, and during the summer months he would often entertain house parties at Port Lympne, his opulent house on the south coast. His regular guests included Lady Astor and three of her sons, Emerald Cunard, the Colefaxes and Mrs Ronnie Greville. Although a supporter of female suffrage in principle, he found Lady Astor's idiosyncratic behaviour in the House of Commons wearing. He also avoided the formal political receptions at Londonderry House. As Under-Secretary for Air between 1924 and 1929, and again

Mrs Margaret Greville, painted while on her honeymoon in Paris, 1891.

The Duke and Duchess of York on their honeymoon at Polesden Lacey, 1923.

Nancy Astor, two years into her marriage to Waldorf, 1908.

The Astors' home, Cliveden, on the banks of the Thames, painted in the late nineteenth century.

The hall of Argyll House, showing Sibyl Colefax's unique decorating style.

Sibyl Colefax photographed by Cecil Beaton at Ashcombe, his house in Wiltshire, in the 1930s.

Edith, Lady Londonderry, wearing the famous Londonderry tiara (above) and in her Women's Legion uniform (right).

Laura Mae Corrigan, sporting one of her many chic wigs.

Lady Maud and Sir Bache Cunard on a rare public appearance together, 1915, after their marriage broke down.

Their only child, intense but troubled Nancy Cunard, photographed by Man Ray.

Emerald Cunard, as Maud had renamed herself by then, photographed by Cecil Beaton, circa 1928.

The Duke and Duchess of Windsor, happily married after their relationship brought about the Abdication crisis, photographed by Cecil Beaton in 1938.

The ballroom entrance to the Dorchester Hotel protected by sandbags during the London blitz.

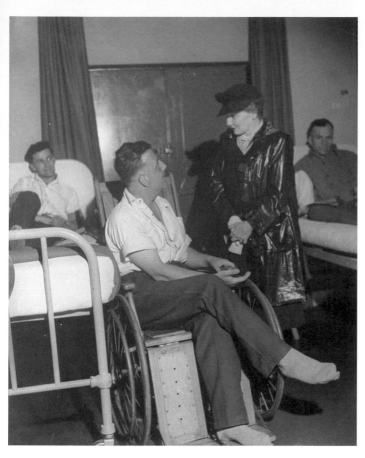

Lady Astor visiting wounded Canadian servicemen at the military hospital at Cliveden during the Second World War.

Lady Astor with George Bernard Shaw and Charlie Chaplin at the Dominion Theatre, 1931.

Harold Nicolson and Vita Sackville-West were both friends and sometime critics of all of the hostesses.

'A whim of steel': Emerald Cunard holds court in her later years.

from 1931 to 1937, he wanted to avoid any more social contact than was necessary with Lord Londonderry, Secretary of State for Air.

His influential political friends included Winston Churchill, Neville Chamberlain and Anthony Eden. Parliamentary contemporaries including Bob Boothby and 'Chips' Channon admired and respected him. Creative and literary types including Cecil Beaton, Noel Coward and T. E. Lawrence were visitors too, and Harold Nicolson and Vita Sackville-West regularly came over from Sissinghurst. A confirmed bachelor, Sassoon lived a discreetly gay life.

Throughout the rest of the year Sassoon held weekend country house parties at Trent Park, his vast estate 13 miles from London. There was a swimming pool, an orangery, a golf course, tennis courts and a lake, set in 1,000 acres of land. To travel between his two country houses Sassoon often flew in his private plane. In addition, he had a magnificent house on Park Lane in London. He was extremely wealthy, and had a particular interest in architecture and interior design. According to 'Chips' Channon, in 1937 Sassoon dropped hints to Emerald Cunard that he hoped to be appointed First Commissioner of Works, and his lobbying was successful; it was a role that included supervising the repairs to the Houses of Parliament and refurbishing and redecorating no 10 Downing Street.

Between 1931 and 1935 Ramsay MacDonald headed the National Government. Lord Londonderry benefited from Edith's friendship with the premier, being appointed the Secretary of State for Air, a role he relished because of his genuine enthusiasm for aviation and his war experience. In return, the Socialist Prime Minister MacDonald could rely on the arch-Tory aristocrat as a dependable ally within his truculent Cabinet. The close relationship between the Londonderrys and MacDonald was fractured when he resigned in May 1935, and Stanley Baldwin took over. Londonderry was sacked from the Air Ministry by the new Prime Minister, which made him bitter. In addition, Charley was Tory leader of the Lords, but he lost that prestigious post too, which he saw as an action of class hatred.

Throughout Charley's four years in the post, he advocated that Britain should have a strong air deterrent, by developing state-of-the-art offensive armaments, especially fighter planes and bombers. However, he anticipated that Soviet Russia would be the enemy, not Germany. Charley was convinced that it was Communism that represented a threat to civilisation, and therefore saw the nationalist European dictators as a desirable bulwark against revolution. His convictions were not unusual: the British upper classes were aware of the savage fate of their Russian counterparts following the Bolshevik revolution. The writer Gilbert Armitage summed up those views by stating that the Nazis 'have not yet assassinated an entire reigning family in a cellar and butchered some millions of "class enemies", as the nice, kind, almost democratic bolshies have done'. By contrast, the sense of social order and discipline, economic growth and technological progress instigated first by Mussolini in Italy and then Hitler in Germany seemed appealing.

Lord Londonderry was targeted by Hitler's special ambassador, Joachim von Ribbentrop, because he was exactly the type of aristocrat both Hitler and his representative erroneously believed still ran Britain. There were still many informal contacts between patrician families in Germany and Britain, as in both societies aristocrats tended to gravitate to each other. The Nazi high command was keen to recruit German dukes and princelings to trumpet the virtues of the Third Reich in British drawing rooms; they even employed Prince Otto von Bismarck, the grandson of the famous Iron Chancellor, as the First Secretary at the German Embassy in London. They over-estimated the influence British aristocrats could exert in a modern democracy, but that did not stop them trying.

Charley Londonderry was a former soldier who had served for three years in the Great War, and his memories of that conflict made him sincerely committed to ensuring that Britain and Germany never fought again. Charley was re-assured by the soothing platitudes of von Ribbentrop and Germany's apparent desire for peace. Cast aside in London, as he saw it, Lord Londonderry felt his experience and states-manship would be better appreciated in Berlin. He also recalled his ancestor, the statesman Viscount Castlereagh, who, at the Congress of Vienna, succeeded in brokering an agreement to bring back the world to 'peaceful habits' after the Napoleonic Wars.

Lord Londonderry plunged headlong into bringing about a better understanding between Germany and Britain, seeing himself now as a private statesman with a worthy mission and excellent connections. Charley and Edith, with their youngest daughter, Mairi, visited Germany in December 1935 and February 1936. He went stag-hunting with the Commander-in-Chief of the Luftwaffe, Hermann Goering (who bagged a bison), and they stayed for a week at his luxurious mountain retreat before going on to the Winter Olympics. Charley also had a two-hour audience with Hitler, who declared that he was most concerned about the world growth of Bolshevism. Charles found him 'forthcoming and agreeable', especially when assured by the Führer that 'Germany wants to live in close friendly alliance with England'. Londonderry described the Führer as 'a kindly man with a receding chin and an impressive face'.

Edith also wrote about Hitler as a 'man of arresting personality – a man with wonderful far-seeing eyes', and told Dr Paul Schmidt, Hitler's interpreter, that 'to live in the upper levels of National Socialism may be quite pleasant, but woe to the poor folk who do not belong to the upper orders'. She was careful in what she said, but Unity Mitford, a Hitler devotee, wrote to her sister Diana: 'Lady Londonderry [will] simply go back and say just as nasty things as before.'

After their first two visits Charley wrote to von Ribbentrop expressing the hope that Britain and Germany could unite to combat Communism. Von Ribbentrop became known as 'The Londonderry Herr' as a result of his apparent closeness to the Londonderrys, and Charley's enthusiasm for the Third Reich went down badly in British political circles – 'Londonderry just back from hobnobbing with Hitler,' recorded Harold Nicolson in a letter to his wife. 'I do deeply disapprove of ex-Cabinet Ministers trotting across to Germany at this moment.'

In May 1936 the von Ribbentrops and Laura Corrigan flew to Mount Stewart to spend Whitsun as the guests of the Londonderrys. The Londonderrys did not personally like von Ribbentrop, but they invited him to stay with them in order to influence the views he relayed back to Berlin. Lord Londonderry became a fully-fledged supporter of Anglo-German 'understanding'. When von Ribbentrop was formally appointed German Ambassador to London, in October 1936 he spent a weekend at Wynyard, Lord Londonderry's estate near Durham. During this visit von Ribbentrop attended divine service at Durham Cathedral, during which he leaped to his feet at the opening notes of 'Glorious Things of Thee are Spoken', the tune of which is also that of 'Deutschland, Deutschland, über alles', and gave a rigid 'Heil Hitler' salute.

Having conquered London, Laura Corrigan struck out for Paris. This time she knew to go straight to the professionals in order to get established. Another American expat, the legendary Elsa Maxwell, was the route to what Laura regarded as the *crème de la crème* (although she pronounced it to rhyme with 'dream'.)

Elsa, the party planner *extraordinaire*, had grown up in obscurity in California. She described herself as 'a fat, unattractive woman who was born in Keokuk, Iowa, and was reared in San Francisco without money, family position or even a grammar school diploma'. Having been told as a child that she wasn't invited to a friend's party because her family were too poor, Elsa spent her adult life persuading the wealthy to let her run their social lives for them, so that she need never miss another party. She was spectacularly successful at devising novelty themes, such as treasure hunts or scavenger hunts, and lived on 'gifts' from grateful clients and commissions from party venues.

Witty and inventive, Elsa spent fifty years in a lesbian relationship with Dorothy 'Dickie' Fellowes-Gordon, who was Scottish – they had met in 1912. She was so celebrated that Cole Porter wrote a song for Ethel Merman entitled 'I'm Dining with Elsa (and her ninety-nine most intimate friends)'. Her mantra to wealthy clients was 'Money doesn't make a good party. You do.' In return for substantial 'gifts', she launched Laura Corrigan in Paris, and Laura adopted many of her innovative ideas for her London parties.

Laura Corrigan had met and befriended Princess Marina of Greece some years earlier in Paris, when she and her exiled family were living in some austerity. She was delighted when Marina captured the heart of the Duke of Kent. Laura was one of the few people who could boast neither a title nor royal antecedents at the Kents' grand wedding, where virtually all of the guests were linked through the complex network of European royalty and strategic marriages. Laura took Marina shopping beforehand for her wedding present, a mink coat, which cost £6,000. It was a gift of great luxury, but also a practical present for a cash-strapped young woman suddenly marrying a prince.

At the ball to celebrate the Kents' marriage in November 1934, the royal fiancée wore a beautifully cut simple white evening dress that showed off her excellent figure. By contrast, Mrs Wallis Simpson, who was making her first appearance as a guest in front of the King and Queen, had chosen a dress in violet lamé, with a contrasting green sash, and a tiara borrowed from Cartier. The King and Queen were aware of the rumours that the twice-married American was romantically involved with the Prince of Wales. Her name had already been removed from the guest list, but reluctantly reinstated when the Prince insisted to his father that they were 'just friends'. Now the senior royals watched icily as this chic, rather metallic, whippet-thin interloper curtsied to them and to their small daughter-in-law the Duchess of York, who was decked out in traditional soft pink. At the wedding itself the Simpsons occupied good seats; the Prince's 'special friend' was starting to become a fixture in court circles.

Laura Corrigan did not take to Wallis Simpson, a fellow American divorcée, although Wallis was a guest at one of her dances in July 1935. The Prince of Wales and Mrs Simpson also avoided Laura's company after just one dinner party at Emerald Cunard's. It is also possible that Wallis was sensitive to any suggestion of similarities that might be drawn between her and Laura, both ambitious and rather hard-edged Americans from humble origins.

No such misgivings applied in the case of another American-born hostess. Emerald Cunard, aware of the growing attraction between the Prince and Mrs Simpson, had actively started to cultivate their relationship by 1935. In June, Wallis and Emerald stayed at Fort Belvedere for a week to attend Ascot. Emerald joined a house party at the Fort on 20 July 1935, and by midsummer Wallis was toying with the idea of going to Venice with Emerald, after her holiday in Cannes in a villa rented by the Prince. After returning to London in autumn 1935 there were regular dinner engagements, and Emerald was a constant feature in Wallis's life.

Wallis's growing importance to the Prince of Wales elicited varying responses from the Queen Bees. Emerald and Sibyl competed to cultivate her, though for different reasons; Lady Cunard enjoyed the excitement of fostering a royal romance, and entertained hopes of becoming the Mistress of the Robes, the trusted confidante of the queen. Sibyl seems to have had a more romantic view of the whole affair, though she was convinced Wallis had no intention of divorcing Ernest in order to marry the Prince. Lady Londonderry had some sympathy with her situation but disapproved on principle of the heir to the throne having a relationship with a married woman; even if Wallis were to divorce for a second time, there were serious constitutional issues for a monarch wanting to marry a woman with two former husbands still alive. Lady Astor was always sensitive to competition from other American women, seeing her own Virginian origins as vastly superior. She felt that Wallis's humble antecedents should bar her from any contact with royalty. Laura Corrigan and Mrs Greville had both been dropped by the Prince, and Margaret Greville, who had long held a low opinion of him, was furious about his behaviour on behalf of her protégés the Yorks, and her friends King George and Queen Mary.

In February 1935 Mrs Simpson returned to London following a skiing holiday in Kitzbühel with the Prince of Wales. She was now much in demand at the tables of those hostesses who wished to attract the Prince, especially Emerald and Sibyl. Her social life was extremely busy; even Lady Londonderry invited her to dinner. She described her new popularity in a letter to her Aunt Bessie as 'Wallis in Wonderland'.

She was not popular everywhere, though. Wallis was aware that Elizabeth, the Duchess of York, disapproved, and the relationship between them deteriorated when Elizabeth caught Wallis impersonating her to a giggling crowd of sycophants at Fort Belvedere. 'Chips' Channon invited Wallis to lunch in April 1935 following a hint from the Prince and found her to be a 'jolly, plain, intelligent, quiet, unpretentious and unprepossessing little woman', though he noted that 'she has already the air of a personage who walks into a room as though she expects to be curtsied to […] she has complete power over the Prince of Wales, who is trying to launch her socially'.

From early 1935 onwards, the Simpsons were under surveillance by Special Branch, the undercover division of the Metropolitan police, because of the couple's friendship with the Prince. The surveillance was authorised by the Home Secretary, Sir John Simon, a former beau of Mrs Greville. Visitors to Bryanston Court were recorded by Inspector Canning and his team of detectives. They noted Oswald Mosley, now leader of the British Union of Fascists, Alice 'Kiki' Preston, one-time girlfriend of the Duke of Kent, who was known as 'the girl with the silver syringe', and society hostess Emerald Cunard, who was sensationally 'reputed to be a drug addict'. It was noted disapprovingly that her daughter, 'the notorious Nancy […] was very partial to coloured men and created a sensation some years ago by taking residence in the Negro quarter of New York'. Detectives also recorded that Mrs Simpson and the Prince called each other 'darling' while visiting an antique shop in South Kensington; the shopkeeper remarking that the lady seemed to have the gentleman 'completely under her thumb'. The information collected by Special Branch was lurid and often incorrect; it was thought that Ernest Simpson was Jewish, and he was described as 'the bounder type', who was expecting to be given high honours. It was also alleged that Wallis Simpson, the veteran of many affairs, was having a relationship with a married car salesman called Guy Marcus Trundle at the same time as she was involved with the heir to the throne.

While Special Branch were keeping a beady eye on Wallis, the rest of the royal family were keen to avoid her. By the summer of 1935 battle lines had been drawn between the traditionalists (King George V and Queen Mary, the Duke and Duchess of York, Princess Marina, Mrs Greville, Lady Astor and Mrs Corrigan) and the pro-Wallis camp (the Prince of Wales, his brother the Duke of Kent, Emerald Cunard, Sibyl Colefax, 'Chips' Channon, the Duff Coopers, Cecil Beaton and Winston Churchill.) Demoralised, the old King avoided attending Ascot that year, leaving the Yorks to represent the formal royal presence, while the Prince of Wales strolled around the Royal Enclosure with Wallis on his arm. At the end of the summer, the Yorks and their two young daughters joined the King and Queen at Balmoral to shoot, fish, battle midges and dress up in tartan in the Ruritanian castle created by Queen Victoria. Meanwhile the thoroughly modern Prince, his best friend Mrs Simpson and his band of cosmopolitan socialites were soaking up the sun on the French Riviera. Once again, Ernest Simpson pleaded that the pressure of business made him unable to join them; those in the know remarked that he was 'laying down his wife for his king'.

Emerald Cunard was still supporting Sir Thomas Beecham's musical career, which was going from strength to strength. In May 1932 he conducted *Tannhäuser* at the Royal Opera House in Covent Garden, and the guests of honour were King George V and Queen Mary, who received him and congratulated him on the performance. Lady Cunard was in her usual box with her well-heeled friends to witness his triumph. However, all was not plain sailing between Emerald and Sir Thomas. Since 1926 he had been conducting a passionate affair with the gifted opera soprano Dora Labbette, who adopted the stage name of Lisa Perli (a tribute to her home town of Purley). Dora gave birth to their son in a Marylebone nursing home on 25 March 1933. The baby, Paul, was the third child of Sir Thomas, but his two older boys, born in 1904 and 1909, had grown up without him. This was a belated chance to be a father. The day after the baby's birth, a Sunday, was a rest-day for his orchestra. The great conductor took the train to London from Newcastle, where they had been performing, to see mother and baby, returning in time for rehearsals on Monday morning. Dora had managed to extricate herself from her marriage, and Beecham had proposed to her, even offering to get a quick 'Reno'-style divorce from Utica in an American court. But Dora was concerned that such an arrangement might not be valid in Britain. She urged him to persuade Utica to agree to a divorce through the British courts, but Utica refused to countenance it.

Although it is uncertain exactly when Lady Cunard learned the truth about Dora and baby Paul, in 1935 there was a furious row between Emerald and Sir Thomas. The diplomat and spy Sir Robert Bruce Lockhart recorded his somewhat terse version of events in his diary:

> Story goes back to last winter when Emerald discovered that Beecham had another girl around the corner. There was a row. Emerald threatened never to lift a finger for opera again unless Beecham gave up his fairy. Beecham agreed. Emerald discovered recently that he had not given her up. Hence these tears.

Lady Cunard recognised that Dora Labbette, twenty-five years younger than her, was a real threat to her relationship with

Sir Thomas, especially now they had a son. He would not relinquish Dora, and arranged a provision to give her an income when she was no longer able to work. Thomas also formally agreed to provide an education for Paul 'as befits the son of a baronet'. Dora and Paul now had a comfortable home in Hampstead Garden Suburb, and Beecham was a frequent visitor, encouraging young Paul to play the piano. At the end of 1935 Sir Thomas took up his prestigious role as conductor with the New York Philharmonic Symphony Orchestra. He was accompanied by Dora Labbette, and Emerald was left behind in London. Consequently Emerald sought distraction, and concentrated on fostering the relationship between the Prince of Wales and Mrs Simpson.

Emerald gave intimate little dinner parties, where the Prince and Mrs Simpson could meet in the company of others. The Prince liked the company of American women, their high standards of grooming, their charming informality, their sense of fun. With Emerald and Wallis he could dance, laugh, smoke, drink cocktails, voice his opinions; it was a contrast to the aura of palpable disapproval exuded by his Victorian parents.

By the mid-1930s Emerald was nearly sixty years old, though she always claimed to be five years younger, but she retained the conversational charms and personal chic that had first attracted Edward VII and now amused his grandson. She was tiny, wrinkled and heavily made up, very well dressed and often wore silver powder brushed through her hair. Harold Nicolson described her appearance as like 'a third-dynasty mummy painted by an amateur'. 'Chips' Channon commented on Emerald's intelligence and culture, her ambition to be at the heart of a kaleidoscopic circle of interesting people; as he wrote, 'The crown always frowned on so brilliant a salon; indeed Emerald's only failures were the two Queens [Queen Mary and, later, Queen Elizabeth] and Lady Astor and Lady Derby.'

The motivations of the two most politically committed Queen Bees, Lady Astor and Lady Londonderry, went beyond socialising for its own sake. Nancy Astor had long championed the causes of women and children. However, in 1936, when Lucy Baldwin, the wife of the Conservative Prime Minister, launched a campaign to improve the standards of midwifery, Lady Astor was critical, perhaps from jealousy. She mimicked Mrs Baldwin's voice, and made a *double entendre* of the campaigner's slightly naive appeal to her audience to 'make it your business to be responsible for one expectant mother'. In addition, Nancy Astor told Lucy Baldwin, 'When I see the sort of children we're all having, I'm for letting the mothers die!' Outrageous remarks of this kind damaged Nancy's reputation in an era when the mortality rates for mothers and babies were very high.

Edith Londonderry, by contrast, had been a founder member with Lucy Baldwin in 1928 of the National Birthday Trust Fund, providing anaesthesia for women in labour. In 1934, the NBTF set up the Joint Council of Midwifery, radically reforming the training and employment of midwives, who were so important in delivering babies in poor and urban areas. Neville Chamberlain, whose own mother had died in childbirth, supported this initiative. In July 1936 the Midwives Act was passed, thanks to Lucy Baldwin and Edith Londonderry. For the first time the national midwives service was funded by local government, and a new principle of medical treatment free to the needy was established. Families who could afford it were charged 30 shillings for the services of a midwife, but those who had no money would also be treated. The treatment and care of mothers and babies began to improve, and death rates came down. In these measures can be seen the origin of the National Health Service, the principle of care available at the point of need, and it is an example of the practical benefits for women of all classes achieved by the direct involvement of ladies of influence.

8

1936: The Year of Three Kings

1936 was a momentous year for British society, and the hostesses had ringside seats for the constitutional crisis, the fast-moving international developments and political and social upheavals that swept through the year. Some of them also endured personal tragedies.

As the year dawned, King George's health deteriorated. He was worried about the succession and his son's infatuation with Mrs Simpson. He predicted that the Prince would ruin himself within twelve months of inheriting the throne (in fact it took a mere 325 days). On 20 January he lapsed into a coma at Sandringham, surrounded by his family. His doctor, Lord Dawson, euphemistically stated: 'The King's life is moving peacefully towards its close.' The monarch's demise was actually hastened by an injection of morphine and cocaine, administered by Dawson to ensure that his death would be announced in the morning papers, notably *The Times*, rather than the less 'dignified' evening papers.

His heir, Edward VIII, felt woefully unprepared for the business of 'kinging'. He returned to London by plane to meet the Privy Council; this was a modern monarch embracing new technology. However, he was stepping into a very traditional role, and there were concerns about his aptitude. In addition, there was his relationship with the married American; surely now he was King, he would settle down with a suitable royal bride and give up Mrs Simpson? As his private secretary Alan Lascelles recalled:

> My impression is that the Prince of Wales was caught napping by his father's death [...] he had expected the old man to last several years more, and he had, in all probability, already made up his mind to renounce his claim to the throne, and to marry Mrs S. I know that, long before this, he had confided to several American friends of his that he could never face being king.

Edward VIII was livid when his father's will was read to the family; each of his brothers received about £750,000 in cash, worth about £28 million today, while he was left no money and was prevented from selling any of the inherited assets, such as the famous stamp collection or the racehorses. Edward telephoned Wallis to break the news that, while he had a crown, which he didn't want, he had no fortune, which both of them had eagerly anticipated. Lascelles was sure this was a factor in his decision to abdicate.

During the King's funeral the coffin was drawn through London on a gun carriage draped in the royal standard and bearing the Imperial State Crown. As the cortège entered New Palace Yard, the Maltese Cross on top of the crown fell to the ground, and was quickly retrieved by a sergeant major. King Edward VIII, walking behind the bier, muttered, 'Christ! What will happen next?' Those of a superstitious nature regarded the incident as an ill omen.

Urbane and intelligent career diplomat Leopold von Hoesch was the German Ambassador in London, and he disliked Hitler and National Socialism. The Foreign Ministry in Berlin provided him with a lavish entertainment budget, and he was personally popular both in London society and with his embassy staff. But Hitler did not trust him, and in 1934 he had sent von Ribbentrop to London to act as his personal emissary, to cultivate the influential and those around the Prince of Wales. Von Ribbentrop's heavy-handed charm made an initially favourable impression on some of the society hostesses, though others actively avoided him, especially Sibyl Colefax.

On 10 April 1936 Ambassador von Hoesch died suddenly in the bathroom of his official residence in London, apparently of a heart attack. Von Ribbentrop had just returned to Germany when the news broke; in London rumours quickly spread that he had been murdered, despite a statement from Prince Otto von Bismarck claiming the ambassador had suffered from cardiac problems. Von Hoesch's demise came just weeks after that of Roland Koster, German Ambassador to Paris, who also despised the Nazis. The rumours persisted; in the 1980s Baroness von Stohrer, who had been married to the German Minister in Cairo, alleged that friends in the Gestapo informed her that von Hoesch's toothpaste had been poisoned. Enid Bagnold, married to the head of Reuters news agency, was also told by someone claiming to be an eyewitness that von Hoesch had been murdered, and his body hastily embalmed to destroy the evidence.

The coffin containing his remains was taken to Victoria Station as part of a high-ranking cortège attended by Anthony Eden, Sir John Simon and Sir Robert Vansittart, Permanent Under-Secretary at the Foreign Office. A British destroyer took his remains to Germany, but his body was buried swiftly with almost no official ceremony. A decade later, while von Ribbentrop was on trial for his life at Nuremberg, he wrote in his self-serving memoirs of his regret at the death of 'this able ambassador'. However, in 1936, as he prepared to take over as ambassador in London, he noted smugly the demise of one of the Third Reich's greatest enemies.

Hitler's appointment of von Ribbentrop as Ambassador to London caused consternation among the Nazi high command. Some envied his preferment, but others complained that he had no ability for the role. Hitler defended his protégé, telling Goering that von Ribbentrop knew this British minister and that English aristocrat; Goering replied that the trouble was, they also knew von Ribbentrop. Even Unity Mitford, a fanatical admirer of the Führer, told him that von Ribbentrop would be a figure of fun in London. As early as October 1935 he had been described as a travelling salesman who 'scorns the English aristocrats for providing such a fine market, whether it be for his liquors or for the political crimes and lies of his country [...] Right now his commodities are wine and lies.'

With von Hoesch dead and First Secretary Otto von Bismarck 'babysitting' the London Embassy, von Ribbentrop was unimpeded in following Hitler's instructions to court British high society. In May 1936 he and his wife returned to London; on 29 May they were the guests of Laura Corrigan, who had taken Crewe House in Curzon Street, the Mayfair home of the first Marquess of Crewe, for the season. She also invited 'Chips' Channon, who revised his low opinion of von Ribbentrop when he realised the new German Ambassador could provide him with a luxury trip to the Berlin Olympics.

Meanwhile Germany was flexing its expansionist muscles by reoccupying the Rhineland in March 1936. Following a League of Nations conference in London, the Astors gave a dinner party for many of the delegates, key ambassadors and politicians. Attempting to break the ice, Nancy Astor organised a game of Musical Chairs after supper and told the English guests, *sotto voce*, to let von Ribbentrop and the Germans win. Allowing the more belligerent tribe to snap up the remaining assets while the music became faster and more frantic was a fitting analogy for the pro-appeasement lobby of the mid-1930s, whose maxim was 'peace at any price'.

Meanwhile von Ribbentrop conceived the unlikely idea of arranging for Hitler to meet the British Prime Minister, Stanley Baldwin, in secret. He recruited Waldorf and Nancy Astor and their friend Thomas Jones, former Deputy Secretary of the Cabinet, to achieve this goal. Von Ribbentrop, who loved subterfuge and dramatic gestures, felt that if only Baldwin could meet the Führer, he too would fall under his mesmeric spell. In June 1936 Jones and von Ribbentrop travelled to Rest Harrow, the Astors' seaside home in Kent, for a clandestine meeting with Sir Thomas Inskip, the Minister for the Co-Ordination of Defence, far from curious eyes or ears. Philip Kerr was there too, and talks continued into the night. The following morning Nancy Astor teased von Ribbentrop about the 'bad company' he had been keeping with rival hostesses Lady Londonderry and Lady Cunard. Von Ribbentrop assured her that they had always been generous to him, but the point was made; it was Lady Astor who really had political clout. Von Ribbentrop's plans for Baldwin and Hitler to meet were never realised, but as a result of their discussions Philip Kerr tried to persuade the Foreign Secretary, Anthony Eden, that Britain should support Germany as the dominant force at the heart of Europe, rather than siding with France and Russia.

But the Astors were not alone in apparently acquiescing in the rise of the Third Reich; there were many in society and court circles in the mid-1930s who appeared to approve the Fascist regimes that were gaining the upper hand in Italy, Germany and Japan. *Time and Tide* magazine publicly identified the Astors and the Londonderrys with the pro-German *rapprochement* initiative, in contrast to the 'realist politicians', including Winston Churchill, Duff Cooper and Austen Chamberlain, who could see through Hitler's promises to his real motives. Nancy countered in print, robustly claiming she was working for peace in Europe by treating Germany fairly. The singular ability to combine sincerity with naivety was one of Nancy Astor's most distinctive characteristics. Sibyl Colefax sternly resisted Nazi Germany's charm offensive; 'Chips' Channon noted her disapproval of his decision to accept an invitation from von Ribbentrop to attend the Berlin Olympics. Harold Nicolson also criticised 'Chips' and his wife for ignoring Germany's true motivations: 'The Channons have fallen under the champagne-like influence [...] they think Ribbentrop a fine man, and that we should let gallant little Germany glut her fill of the Reds in the East and keep decadent France quiet while she does so.'

Nicolson refused point-blank to go to Germany, as he was keen to tell a pro-Nazi German woman at Mrs Greville's dining table. His fellow guest was trying to persuade him to visit Germany, as the country had changed so much. He replied:

> 'Yes, I should find my old friends either in prison, or exiled or murdered.' At which she gasped like a fish. Maggie saw that something awful had happened and shouted down the table to find out what it was. In a slow strong voice I repeated my remark. As Ribbentrop's Number Two was on Maggie's right, it was all to the good. Old Willingdon, bless his heart [Lord Willingdon, Viceroy of India, 1931–36], backed me up.

Court mourning for George V formally came to an end in July 1936, six months after his death, but wider London society was keen to 'jump the gun'. On 11 June 1936 'Chips' and Honor Channon hosted an intimate dinner party for the new King at their extraordinary town house in Belgrave Square, to show off for the first time their newly created, opulent dining room. It was in the rococo style and modelled on the Mirror Room at the eighteenth-century Amalienburg hunting lodge near Munich. The project had taken over a year to complete, cost £6,000 and was 'a symphony of blue and silver', replete with crystals and mirrored glass, with an exquisite parquet floor brought in from Vienna. The privileged guests included, inevitably, Wallis Simpson (Ernest had tactfully claimed a prior engagement), Philip Sassoon, Duff Cooper and Lady Diana, and the Duke of Kent. Emerald Cunard, needless to say, arrived late.

With a theatrical flourish, the doors into the dining room were flung open. By the light of candles, the self-selected elite of London society enjoyed their own endless reflections in a magical room that glittered and sparkled. Lady Colefax joined them for coffee. The evening was a triumph; the King did not leave until 1.45 a.m., so much did he apparently enjoy the company and the exquisite setting.

At Cliveden on Tuesday 16 June Nancy Astor held a ball that was the envy of society, with more than a thousand guests gathered in the enormous ballroom. Joyce Grenfell, her niece, wrote that she had never enjoyed a party so much. The house was festooned with flowers from the gardens. Nancy was in pale blue satin and wearing a tiara to greet her guests. Dinner was served beforehand, the orchestra struck up at 10.30 p.m. and the guests danced till 4 a.m., when eggs and bacon were served. But such rampant hedonism grated on some that summer; one house party guest, Harold Nicolson, wrote to his wife, Vita Sackville-West:

> Cliveden, I admit, is looking lovely. The party also is lavish and enormous. How glad I am that we are not rich. I simply do not want a house like this where nothing is really yours, but belongs to servants and gardeners. There is a ghastly unreality about it all. Its beauty is purely scenic. I enjoy seeing it. But to own it, to live here, would be like living on the stage of the Scala theatre in Milan.

Others similarly disapproved of opulent display; Beverley Nichols wrote that nobody who attended a glittering reception at Londonderry House ever forgot it, because of the atmosphere of power, stability and permanence. He also sounded a warning about the 'hint of the tumbril in the roll of the drum', implying that overt privilege could spark social revolution. Stanley Baldwin remarked in 1936 that the Marchioness's lavish hospitality was 'very magnificent and beautifully done, but to me it was out of date and at times in dubious taste'.

At a grand ceremony for the Presentation of the Colours to three regiments of the Brigade of Guards on 16 July 1936, the schism between the new King's circle and the traditionalist 'old guard' was made apparent. The parade was held in Hyde Park, and two temporary stands had been erected to provide seating for the spectators. The first stand was appropriated by the royal family, their retainers and functionaries, including Queen Mary, her daughter-in-law the Duchess of York, and her two small daughters, Elizabeth and Margaret Rose, wearing identical outfits. The other stand was occupied by the King's fashionable and sophisticated friends, many of them American in origin, and was graced by the immaculately turned-out Wallis Simpson, sitting next to Emerald Cunard. The King and the Duke of York were in uniform and on horseback to take the salute. The two groups of spectators eyed each other warily; the gap between the two sets of bleachers graphically demonstrated the rift between them. Immediately after the ceremony an Irish journalist pointed a loaded revolver at the King but was disarmed by a special constable, and narrowly escaped a lynching from the crowd. Edward saw the altercation, and the gun fell under his horse's hoofs, but he kept his nerve and was subsequently praised for his bravery. The assassination of Archduke Franz Ferdinand and his wife in 1914 by a fervent nationalist with a cause, a revolver and an unexpected opportunity had occurred only twenty-two years earlier. The repercussions then had been dire, and kings and heads of state were aware they took a calculated risk when they appeared as figureheads at public events.

The Berlin Olympics began on 1 August 1936. The event was an international showcase for the city and an unparalleled propaganda opportunity for the Third Reich. Berlin was bedecked with swastika flags and banners, and loudspeakers barracked the populace and visitors alike with stirring martial music and hectoring announcements. Pickpockets and petty criminals had been rounded up and interned, though prostitutes were allowed to practise their trade as potential customers arrived. The *Juden Verboten* signs had been put into storage until the festival was over. Designed in every detail by Albert Speer, the Olympics were Wagnerian in atmosphere; the vast Olympic stadium held 100,000 people, and the rapturous crowds cheered the small man in the brown uniform whose apotheosis this was. The games attracted athletes from fifty-three nations, and the many British visitors included Lord Rothermere, Lord Beaverbrook and Sir Robert Vansittart. Some were seduced by the spectacle, including 'Chips' Channon, who thrilled at being 'received by Ribbentrop, [and] Hitler and escorted everywhere by Storm Troopers'. When he was presented to the Führer, 'Chips' claimed he was more excited than when he had met either Mussolini or the Pope. Beverley Nichols, who attended as a journalist, was more caustic: 'There were Rolls Royces, white as milk, bearing the pudding-faced aristocracy of England, murmuring to each other that really the Hitler Jugend [Hitler Youth] were rather wonderful, almost like gods [...] and they didn't look as if they wanted a war, did they?'

Having spent most of the summer in Germany, von Ribbentrop finally returned to London as official Ambassador, arriving by train on 26 October 1936. He attracted ridicule before he had even left Victoria Station, by insisting on holding the 'Hitlergrüss', the distinctive Nazi salute, for more than thirty seconds. He then read out a statement to the press, denouncing Communism as the 'most terrible of diseases'. This was undiplomatic language, an unprovoked attack on the Soviet Union that defied protocol, as new ambassadors must refrain from public remarks until they have presented their credentials to the head of state. Even the pro-German *Daily Mail* concluded that von Ribbentrop seemed oblivious to British tolerance for differing political ideologies.

Von Ribbentrop attempted to intimidate the unfortunate staff at the German Embassy, inspecting them in a parody of a military review and insisting they return his 'Heil Hitler' salutes. They were professional civil servants in the diplomatic corps, with no particular allegiance to any party, and had been shaken by the unexpected death of the former ambassador. The Embassy was undergoing a massive refurbishment, ordered by Hitler and directed by Albert Speer, so the von Ribbentrops were obliged to find a temporary residence while the work was completed. They rented a suitably grand house in Eaton Square; by a strange quirk of fate it belonged to Neville Chamberlain, soon to be Prime Minister.

Tactless von Ribbentrop visited Anthony Eden at the Foreign Office and attempted to impress him with his personal closeness to the Führer. He boasted to Eden that it would be a major advantage for Britain having him as Ambassador, as he could convey to the Foreign Secretary the Führer's thoughts. Eden pointed out that Britain had its own Ambassador in Berlin, whose job it was to relay the policies of the German government. He briskly stated that von Ribbentrop's role was to report back to Berlin the views of the British government. Given such an elementary lesson in the workings of international diplomacy, von Ribbentrop sulked.

On 30 October von Ribbentrop went to Buckingham Palace to present his credentials to Edward VIII, who described him as a 'polished but bombastic opportunist'. He presented a Nazi salute to the King; the Italian Ambassador Count Grandi later recalled how he would not be pressured by 'preposterous' von Ribbentrop into offering a similar Fascist salute to the monarch, and the Germans complained about him to the Italian Foreign Minister. On 31 October the von Ribbentrops attended a cocktail party given in their honour by Mrs

Greville at her London home; then they left to spend the weekend at Lord and Lady Londonderry's estate, Wynyard, near Durham. The von Ribbentrops were keen to cultivate the key hostesses whom they saw as the gate-keepers to British decision-makers.

As she operated in a different social milieu, Sibyl Colefax was able to avoid contact with the German Embassy, and she disapproved thoroughly of the Nazi regime. 1936 was a very difficult year for her. Her husband Arthur contracted pneumonia and died suddenly on 19 February, shortly after the death of her friend Rudyard Kipling, and she mourned him intensely. Aged sixty-two, Sibyl now faced a very uncertain future with characteristic courage. She took a short holiday, then returned to Colefax & Fowler, working ever harder to generate income. She continued to entertain her social circle, though in reduced circumstances; Virginia Woolf uncharitably complained that Sibyl was economising on the ingredients she served at dinner. Sibyl tried to maintain a façade of composure but confided in the American writer Thornton Wilder that she would prefer to retire from public life and live with her memories, but that she had no choice because she had no financial resources left and was forced to sell Argyll House.

One of her swan-song parties in Chelsea was very poignant; on 10 June 1936 Edward VIII and Mrs Simpson were her principal guests, with Harold Nicolson and Robert Bruce Lockhart, Kenneth and Jane Clark, Lord Berners, the socialite Daisy Fellowes and the heiress Princesse de Polignac. Two gifted and powerful men, Sir Robert Vansittart, Permanent Under-Secretary at the Foreign Office, and the American banker Tom Lamont, head of Wall Street behemoths J. P. Morgan, also attended. Lord Berners had been puzzled when

Sibyl had phoned him to say she wanted him to come and meet Arthur. 'But I thought Arthur was dead?' he queried, perhaps mindful of Mary Borden's portrayal of the delusional society hostess in *To Meet Jesus Christ*, allegedly based on Sibyl. 'Oh, not *my* Arthur, she replied, as though that were obvious, 'Artur Rubinstein', meaning the virtuoso pianist.

Dinner went smoothly; Robert Vansittart listened politely to the new King's enthusiasm for *rapprochement* with Nazi Germany, and his offer to help bring this about. (As monarch, Edward VIII was required to avoid involvement in and comment on the decisions taken by his democratically elected government.) It was after the meal that the evening started to unravel. Sibyl invited her guests to make themselves comfortable around the drawing room grand piano. Pushy Princesse de Polignac bagged a prime position on a stool right by the instrument; 'I have never seen a woman sit so firmly: there was determination in every line of her bum', wrote Harold Nicolson. Sibyl joined the younger guests on the rug, in an attitude of studied informality; Harold observed that she looked incongruous, as though someone had left an inkstand on the floor.

When everyone was settled, Rubinstein launched into Chopin's Barcarolle on the piano. The King was at first nonplussed, then irritated – he had expected the better-known Barcarolle from *The Tales of Hoffmann*. At the first opportunity he rose, thanked the great musician firmly and went to leave. It was only 10.15, a disaster for Sibyl, but just as Edward VIII reached the front door, Winston Churchill arrived, and they exchanged pleasantries in the hall. Meanwhile, Noel Coward leaped to the piano and embarked on his exuberant song, 'Mad Dogs and Englishmen'. Hearing music more to his taste, the King changed his mind and returned to the party, staying till 1 a.m., and the evening was salvaged.

With a heavy heart Sibyl put Argyll House and most of its contents up for sale. Virginia Woolf visited her there on 27 October 1936 and was horrified to find that every household item and piece of furniture had been ticketed by the auctioneers, and would-be buyers were picking over the material remains of Sibyl's former life. The two women sought refuge in the drawing room, and Woolf wrote of Sibyl: 'She looked old and ill and haggard lines were grooved as if with a chisel on either side of her nose. I felt extremely sorry for her. We were like two survivors clinging to a raft. This was the end of all her parties; we were sitting in the ruins of that magnificent structure which had borne so lately the royal crown on top.'

Sibyl moved into a more economical, much smaller house in Lord North Street in Westminster, where she continued to entertain. Now her guests were wedged tightly together on small gilt chairs in the pretty, *bijou* dining room, elbow to elbow, but the conversation continued to be fascinating, and Sibyl's ability to trawl for talent was unsurpassed. Most friends were sympathetic about her gallant struggle to keep going in reduced circumstances; at the end of 1936 Harold Nicolson organised a 'Sibyl fund' to provide her with an all-expenses-paid three-week trip to New York.

Wallis Simpson had faintly scandalised 'Chips' Channon when, shortly after the death of George V, while the nation was still in mourning, she remarked that the last time she had worn black stockings was while dancing the Can-Can. Lady Astor's footman Gordon Grimmett recalled the sycophantic crowd who hung on her every word; he offered Wallis a choice of cocktails – one called Paradise, the other a White Lady – at a party. '"Huh," she said, "whoever heard of a white lady being in Paradise?" It was not, I think you'll agree, the funniest remark of the year, yet the circle around her screamed with laughter and clapped their hands as though she was the greatest wit since Oscar Wilde,' he recalled.

Emerald and Sibyl competed fiercely to be Wallis's main confidante between 1935 and 1936. Mrs Simpson and the King alternated between the rival hostesses. Very shortly after the death of George V, in February 1936, Wallis wrote to her Aunt Bessie, describing a weekend at the home of the new King; she mentioned in passing Emerald Cunard, 'who thinks she is the Prime Minister'. Early in April, Wallis held a dinner party at the Simpsons' apartment at Bryanston Court, and the hostesses' egos clashed in the confined, enclosed space. Naturally, Wallis's guest of honour was the King, and she had also invited Margot Asquith (Lady Oxford), Sibyl Colefax and Emerald Cunard, each of whom had apparently anticipated spending a cosy and intimate evening with the monarch and his lady friend, without competition, according to a fellow guest, Harold Nicolson: 'It is evident that Lady Cunard is incensed by the presence of Lady Colefax, and that Lady Colefax is furious that Lady Cunard should also have been asked. Lady Oxford appears astonished to find either of them at what was to have been a quite intimate party. The King passes brightly from group to group.'

In the summer of 1936 Mrs Simpson acted as the King's hostess at an official dinner, which irritated the guests of honour, the Duke and Duchess of York. Winston Churchill, a guest on this occasion, raised the thorny conversational topic of the mistresses of former kings, and then embarked on a lecture about the Wars of the Roses in the fifteenth century, between the royal houses of York and Lancaster. 'That was a long time ago!' snapped the Duchess, but Winston's point struck home; Elizabeth's brother-in-law often used the title of the Duke of Lancaster when hoping to pass incognito – in fact, he had chartered the use of a magnificent yacht, the *Nahlin*, to sail the Mediterranean later that summer, using that name as a disguise.

The Yorks retreated to Scotland for their summer holiday; meanwhile the King and Mrs Simpson, Emerald Cunard and the Duff Coopers sailed in luxury along the Dalmatian coast, around the Greek islands and to Istanbul; the cruise lasted from 10 August till 6 September. The King even invited a surprised Ernest Simpson to accompany the trip, though he tactfully declined, once again pleading pressure of work. The shipmates spent their time exploring, sunbathing and swimming. They lunched with Edward's cousin King George of Greece and his British-born lover, Rosemary Brittain-Jones. They were both divorced, and after lunch Wallis asked why they did not marry. She was told that, as Rosemary was a commoner and was still seen as a married woman, because her former husband was still alive, she could not marry the monarch. Rosemary's situation was not unlike that of Wallis herself.

The traditional royal visit to Balmoral could not be postponed indefinitely, and the new King arrived there in September. Wallis joined him, and the stoutly conservative royal household was horrified by her proprietorial approach. 'All this tartan's gotta go', she allegedly said, and Edward economised by sacking many of the elderly retainers. The Yorks came over for dinner, and when Wallis approached Elizabeth to welcome her, the Duchess swept past her, announcing loudly, 'I came to dine with the King'.

Relations reached a new low between the 'Yorkists' and the 'new Edwardians'. Influential people sided with one faction or the other. The Yorks were not invited to Emerald Cunard's or Sibyl Colefax's lunches and dinners, and those who supported them had no expectation of mixing socially with the King. Emerald scoffed at the idea of the Yorks having a 'set' of their own to rival those brilliant creatures around the King and Mrs Simpson. However, she was not immune to criticism; 'Chips' was shocked when Emerald showed him an anonymous note she had received in the post, which began: 'You old bitch, trying to make up to Mrs Simpson, in order to curry favour with the King.'

Lady Londonderry had no personal animosity against Wallis Simpson, but as a member of the British aristocracy and the wife of a senior politician she felt she had to intervene. She had often invited the Duke and Duchess of York to her receptions, and the Prince of Wales, but had ignored the rumours she heard about Wallis and left the Simpsons off her guest list. It was 3 November 1936 before she received a message from Buckingham Palace asking if Mrs Simpson could be invited to her customary Eve-of-Parliament reception, which was to be held that evening at Londonderry House. She complied, as it was impossible to refuse a direct request that obviously came from the King. A few days later, at a party at Emerald Cunard's home on 6 November 1936, Edith explained to Wallis that the British public would never accept a divorced woman as the wife of their king. Wallis wrote to her the next day, thanking her for her advice, and promised to speak to 'a certain person' along the lines she had suggested. Of course, Edith may have had moral objections too; she was a firm believer in the indissoluble sanctity of marriage, so in 1934, when her daughter Margaret had announced that she intended to marry Alan Muntz, a divorced man, she was appalled; 'He offers her a soiled life', she complained.

Lady Astor also knew the Prince of Wales socially; he appreciated her irreverent, lively style and had admired her resilience and loyalty in dealing with the imprisonment for homosexual offences of her son Bobbie in 1931. In 1933 they publicly competed in a round of golf at a charity event, and she tactfully let him win. At a dull fundraising dinner she livened proceedings and raised a laugh by telling the startled assembly that, if they did not give generously enough to meet that evening's target, HRH had authorised all the preceding speeches to be repeated. In 1936 she was indignant that for his first official dinner as King, he had invited Lady Cunard and Mr and Mrs Simpson, who she saw as 'disintegrating influences', and felt that only the best Virginian families (such as her own) were worthy of being received in the highest circles. She was particularly keen to have Mrs Simpson's name kept out of the Court Circular, in order to protect the dignity of both the United States and the British Empire. Her maid, Rose, found her attitude surprising; after all, Nancy (like Wallis) had divorced her first husband because he had been a volatile alcoholic, and had subsequently married a titled millionaire. Perhaps she feared British public opinion might turn against 'pushy' American divorcées, and so regarded Wallis as a threat to her own standing. Whatever her motives, Nancy Astor was adamant that Mrs Simpson should not become queen.

By the autumn of 1936 the society photographer Cecil Beaton, who had dismissed Wallis as 'brawny and raw-boned' when he met her in 1930, had been engaged to photograph her at his studio. This time he found her 'bright and witty, improved in looks and chic'. The reason for his change in attitude was transparent: 'Today she is sought after as the probable wife of the King. Even the old Edwardians receive her, if she happens to be free to accept their invitations. American newspapers have already announced the engagement and in the highest court circles there is great consternation. It is said that Queen Mary weeps constantly.'

Most British people were blissfully ignorant of the drama unfolding around the king, but in certain circles gossip was rife. The Simpsons separated, and Wallis sued Ernest for divorce, ironically on the grounds of his infidelity. Her decree nisi was discreetly granted in Ipswich on 27 October; 'King's Moll Reno'd in Wolsey's Home Town' trumpeted the *Chicago Sun–Times*. Edith Londonderry and Sibyl Colefax wrote Wallis letters of support. Meanwhile the British press maintained a tight-lipped silence on the topic of the monarch's love life. One magazine, *Cavalcade*, profiled Mrs Simpson without mentioning the King. The same publication claimed that an (unnamed) London hostess had imposed a fine of five shillings on any guest discussing the King's 'non-state activities' in front of the servants. Censors excised any articles and photographs in foreign publications destined for Britain if they mentioned the romance. Political pressure was put on the King by Stanley Baldwin to renounce Mrs Simpson; he warned that the government would resign and the press would no longer be restrained from attacking them both. The King refused, saying he was determined to marry her. The King installed Wallis in a decorous mansion in Regent's Park, where her friends such as 'Chips', Sibyl and Emerald would visit for tea. Sibyl tried to persuade Wallis to recommend Colefax & Fowler to the King, as decorators for Fort Belvedere. Wallis, with admirable restraint, was non-committal; both she and the King had other, more pressing, priorities.

The constitutional position was complicated; in essence, the wife of the King automatically became the Queen on marriage. But could the King, as Defender of the Faith (nominal head of the Church of England), marry a twice-divorced woman? Winston Churchill, whose own mother was the American-born veteran of a number of marriages, wondered aloud why the King could not have his 'cutie'. Noel Coward succinctly replied: 'Because the British people will not stand for a Queen Cutie.'

The American journalist H. L. Mencken described the romance as 'the greatest story since the Crucifixion', and inevitably the truth finally erupted. On 1 December the Bishop of Bradford, a Dr Blunt, mildly criticised the King for neglecting his Christian duty. The cleric had meant that the monarch should attend church more often, but that detail was lost in the cacophony, and 'The Blunt Instrument', as it was known at the time, opened the floodgates. Baldwin met the King on 2 December, giving him a stark choice: either to renounce Wallis, or else to abdicate. The Duke and Duchess of York returned to London from Scotland early on the morning of 3 December. As they stepped from the train at Euston, they could not miss the newspaper posters trumpeting 'The King's Marriage' in letters 12 inches high. Wallis fled to France the same afternoon, seeking refuge with her old friends Herman and Katherine Rogers in Cannes.

The startled British public read about their King's

all-consuming love for someone of whom they had never heard. On 5 December the *Evening Standard* published an article by George Bernard Shaw, who whimsically opined that a twice-married lady would make an excellent wife for a previously unmarried king. So gripping was the crisis that on 5 December the Londonderrys cancelled their weekend house party in County Durham to stay in London. Edith wrote to the Duchess of York, suggesting Queen Mary should make known her opinion on the situation. Elizabeth replied on 7 December thanking her, and admitting she and Bertie felt 'miserable', but stating that Queen Mary had to stay calm and impartial.

The crisis provoked two contrasting reactions in British society, according to Harold Nicolson. The upper classes were unhappy that Mrs Simpson was American, but they tended not to object to her being a divorcée. By contrast the middle and lower classes cared little for her nationality but couldn't accept the fact she had two husbands still living. The general public response was summed up by that season's alternative Christmas carol:

> *Hark, the herald angels sing,*
> *Mrs Simpson's pinched our King*

December 1936 was the lowest point of what had been a turbulent year for the House of Windsor. The Cabinet and Baldwin met on the morning of Friday 4 December and rejected Edward VIII's proposals to broadcast to the nation announcing his desire for a morganatic marriage to Wallis, which would make her his wife but not the nation's queen, with the circular argument that, as his advisers, they were obliged to counsel him against making such a speech. The King was now left with two alternatives: renunciation or abdication.

The same day Duff Cooper lunched with Emerald Cunard, who was excited but had no grasp of the constitutional issues at stake and did not comprehend why Edward and Wallis could not now marry and reign together. However, within days Emerald started to have doubts, and tried to cover up her role in fostering the affair between Edward and Wallis. On 9 December 1936 Harold Nicolson wrote to Vita Sackville-West:

> I forget whether I told you of Emerald's great betrayal?
> She came to Maggie Greville and said, 'Maggie darling,
> do tell me about this Mrs Simpson – I have only just met
> her'. That has torn Emerald for me. I would not believe
> the story if I had not heard it at first hand.

Emerald was one of the guests who joined Mrs Greville for lunch at Charles Street on 10 December, along with Lord Berners and the Duchess of Westminster. They must have had plenty to discuss.

On 9 December 1936 the Cabinet agreed that the King must go; the following day he signed the Instrument of Abdication and Baldwin presented it to a hushed House of Commons. The Abdication Bill was rushed through both Houses of Parliament on 11 December, and the ex-King broadcast live to the nation the same evening, explaining that he could not continue without the woman he loved, and acclaiming his successor, who had the benefit of a happy marriage and children. In an adjacent tower at Windsor Castle, listening to the radio as her brother-in-law justified his decisions, was Elizabeth, the new Queen. She was in bed with flu, and livid at having her family's life overturned by 'that woman'. She had twice refused Bertie's marriage proposals because she did not want to be a member of the royal family; she had accepted him believing that they and their children would be able to lead largely private lives. Now she was faced with a role that neither she nor her husband wanted, or had been trained for, and their futures were no longer their own.

The former King Edward VIII shook hands with his aghast brother, the new King George VI, and left immediately for Portsmouth, embarking on the appropriately named HMS *Fury* with twenty-six suitcases and a Cairn terrier, going into exile. The lovers were obliged to spend the next months apart until Wallis's divorce became final in April 1937, to avoid any question of collusion in the divorce process, which could threaten her decree absolute. Sibyl Colefax wrote presciently: 'From being the beloved Prince Charming and the real demo-crat who could and did understand the people, he goes to live out a life which must become a tragedy, among the gad-abouts of the Riviera and Rio de Janeiro.'

Mrs Greville concentrated on encouraging the Yorks, who were now *de facto* King and Queen. On the evening of Edward VIII's abdication broadcast she wrote a letter of support and encouragement to his younger brother:

> We all acclaim your Majesty [...] I feel a special sense of joy as I know so well your greatness, modesty, unswerving sense of duty and everything that represents the best in English life. I know that I will not have the same privilege of seeing you as before Sir but I will always stand aside and rejoice in your success and the beloved consort she who radiates peace and happiness.

Though appalled by developments, Queen Mary took the long view, writing, 'In any other country there wd. have been riots. Thank God people did not lose their heads.' In fact, public opinion was divided within Britain and its Dominions. As Sir Alan Lascelles later wrote:

> The attitude of the vast majority of the King's subjects was pragmatical [*sic*]; they did not regard the problem as a moral one; they did not condemn the King as a fornicator and an adulterer – they did not set up to judge him, or Mrs S., on these counts. What they *did* feel, overwhelmingly, was that, since they were called on to support a monarchy, they would not tolerate their Monarch taking as his wife, and their Queen, a shop-soiled American, with two living husbands and a voice like a rusty saw.

The Archbishop of Canterbury, Cosmo Lang, still smarting from not having been invited to Balmoral in the summer by Edward VIII, as was customary, revealed a somewhat unchristian desire to highlight the failings of the former monarch and those who had encouraged him in a BBC radio broadcast on 13 December 1936. He criticised 'a social circle whose standard and way of life are alien to all the best instincts and traditions of his people. Let those who belong in this circle know that today they stand rebuked by the judgement of the nation which had loved King Edward.' Both Elizabeth and Queen Mary endorsed Lang's criticisms of many of Edward VIII's friends. There had already been an undignified scramble by some who now pretended they had barely known the King or his mistress, and this rather ugly aspect of the whole business was seized on by Osbert Sitwell, the great friend of both Mrs Greville and the new Queen.

'Rat Week' was written on Sunday 13 December 1936, the

same night as Cosmo Lang's diatribe was broadcast to the world. Sitwell poured into his poem his distaste for those who had fawned upon the King and Mrs Simpson and encouraged their relationship, yet abandoned them as soon as it was expedient:

> Where are the friends of yesterday
> That fawned on Him,
> That flattered Her;
> Where are the friends of yesterday,
> Submitting to His every whim,
> Offering praise of Her as myrrh To Him?
>
> They found Her conversation good,
> They called Him 'Majesty Divine'
> (Consuming all the drink and food,
> 'they burrow and they undermine'),
> And even the most musical
> Admired the bagpipes' horrid skirl
> When played with royal cheeks outblown
> And royal feet tramping up and down.

Osbert distributed copies privately to his friends, including Mrs Greville, and the new King and Queen gave a copy to Queen Mary too. Visiting Polesden Lacey on New Year's Day 1937, Osbert's brother Sachie was annoyed to discover that Mrs Greville had received a copy of the poem, while he hadn't.

Lady Astor blamed Emerald for encouraging both the romance and the pro-Nazi leanings of the future King. Certainly Emerald had fostered the relationship, providing the settings and the flattery ('Majesty Divine' was how she addressed the King) and creating the social ambience. Noel

Coward had complained: 'I am sick to *death* of having "quiet suppers" with the King and Mrs Simpson.' Emerald also encouraged the *folie à deux* between them, seeing herself as Mistress of the Robes, the senior lady at court, as well as Wallis's confidante. However, it was Sibyl to whom Wallis was more likely to confide her thoughts, though Sibyl remained convinced that Wallis did not want to be Queen, had no intention of marrying the King and had no idea he would abdicate.

Emerald Cunard was immediately dropped by the royal family, and by those loyal to them. Mrs Greville, whose guest books show that Emerald dined with her seventeen times between June 1927 and 10 December 1936, did not host her again until November 1939; presumably she was rehabilitated by the coming of war. Emerald was the principal scapegoat, and Queen Mary was adamant. In a letter to Prince Paul of Yugoslavia (including the instruction that he should burn the missive), Queen Mary wrote:

> The other day in my presence, Bertie told George [the Duke of Kent] he wished him and Marina never to see Lady Cunard again, and George said he would not do so [...] I fear she has done David a great deal of harm as there is no doubt that she was great friends with Mrs Simpson at one time and gave parties for her. Under the circumstances I feel none of us, in fact people in society, should meet her [...] as you may imagine I feel very strongly on the subject.

Of all the hostesses it was Emerald who suffered most when Edward VIII abdicated. 'How could he do this to me?' she wailed. Emerald's main fault was her fondness for royalty, but her desire to manipulate her characters as though they were figures on a stage was thwarted when she found she could not control the narrative. She lost status, being very publicly blackballed by royal and court circles. She attempted to brazen it out, holding a party for Sir Thomas Beecham, but most of the women attending wore black, as though the former king had died rather than abdicated. Emerald was horrified at being publicly vilified by the Archbishop of Canterbury, and sat up till the early hours talking about it with the Sitwells. The seasoned Conservative politician and Scottish Earl, Lord Crawford, described Edward's American friends as 'all the touts and toadies who revolved around Mrs Simpson and whose influence of society was so corrupting', meaning in particular Emerald Cunard.

Others were deeply affected by the abdication. Lady Astor and her maid were in New York when the story erupted. Rose remembered: 'She was very upset when I broke the news to her: I'd heard the paperboy shouting it in the streets. She cried bitterly.' Nancy was vitriolic about Wallis: 'Really, she seems to have turned out an arch adventuress of the worst type', she wrote on 16 December 1936. Nancy blamed her fellow MP 'Chips' Channon for encouraging the romance, and on 11 December she remarked in his direction, 'People who have been licking Mrs Simpson's boots should be shot.' Nancy was commissioned by the BBC to broadcast a radio programme to the States about the abdication, explaining that Wallis Simpson's unsuitability was due to her marital history, rather than her American origins or non-aristocratic background. True-blue Tory Lady Londonderry took a different view of the nationality issue, wondering if the whole affair had been planned in America to undermine the Prince of Wales.

In America public reactions were understandably different.

Noel Coward, that veteran of 'quiet little suppers' with all the main dramatis personae, was also in New York that December. At first he was deeply shocked and upset that the King had decided to go. At a cocktail party he encountered Harold Ross, the editor of the humorous magazine the *New Yorker*, who found the whole business hilarious. Coward remonstrated with him in crisp tones, saying 'In England we're all terribly, *terribly* distressed. It is absolutely no occasion for levity.' Ross replied, 'You mean, the King of England runs away with an old American floosie, and *that* ain't funny?'

However, Coward had an ambivalent relationship with Edward VIII, who had once cut him dead the day after the songwriter had spent the evening playing the piano for him. Once the dust had settled, Coward suggested that statues of Wallis Simpson should be erected throughout the country by a grateful nation. Worldly Mrs Greville shared his view; she had been appalled by Edward's flaunting of Wallis, because of her personal loyalty to the Yorks, King George and Queen Mary. She had long held a low personal opinion of the Prince, as he was then, since visiting India with him more than a decade before, writing to her great friend Lord Reading the Viceroy in 1922: 'HRH is wearing his nerves out in a fruitless life and it is altogether very sad and as [Lord Birkenhead] said last night he cannot maintain his popularity under existing circumstances.'

By contrast, she had become genuinely fond of Bertie since becoming first his 'fairy godmother' and then his mentor. Being childless had left her with a nurturing instinct for the young; she had encouraged his romance with Elizabeth even when it had seemed hopeless, and had hosted the young couple for their honeymoon. She had even promised to leave her beloved home, huge estate and an enormous bequest to the Yorks so that they could live there with their two delightful daughters. Through an unimaginable twist of fate she was now the 'favourite aunt' of the King and Queen. It was all a long way from running a boarding house in Edinburgh.

Sibyl Colefax had cultivated royalty for her own ends, but she also genuinely liked both Edward VIII and Mrs Simpson, and wished to smooth the path of their romance. Just two weeks after Wallis fled to France, she wrote an emotional letter to her trusted old friend Sibyl, promising to tell her everything if they ever met again. After the abdication, unlike most of their former friends, Sibyl loyally continued to see the Windsors for many years; indeed she stayed with Somerset Maugham at the Villa Mauresque over Christmas in 1936, so she could console the lonely and shell-shocked Wallis Simpson. They spent much of their time playing cards. After one game of bridge Wallis was asked why she had not used her king of hearts. 'My kings don't take tricks, they only abdicate,' she replied.

1936 had been a dreadful year for Sibyl; in less than twelve months she had lost her friend Rudyard Kipling, her husband Arthur, her beloved Argyll House and her status as confidante of the King and his lover. In time she came to agree with the general view that the abdication at least saved Britain from the prospect of King Edward VIII, but she remained genuinely fond of them both. Because she proved to be a true friend to the Windsors, Sibyl was not dropped from court circles to the same extent as her vilified rival Emerald. However, she was still the unfortunate butt of practical jokes. As the momentous year drew to a close, as light relief, an advertisement appeared in the Personal column of *The Times* on 21 December:

> Lord Berners wishes to dispose of two elephants and one small rhinoceros (latter house-trained). Would make delightful Christmas presents. Apply R. Heber Percy, Faringdon House, Berkshire.

The press fell on the story like wolves; a spoof was a boost to the national mood before Christmas. The *Daily Sketch,* the *Daily Mail,* the *Daily Mirror* and the *Evening News* ran various versions of the story. Those journalists who rang Faringdon House were informed by Lord Berners, masquerading as his own secretary, 'Actually, I haven't seen the rhino myself, sir, but it is often about the house. It's quite gentle, I'm told. The weather is getting so cold for the poor things.' He also told the journalists that one elephant had been sent to Harold Nicolson and the other to Lady Colefax.

Harold Nicolson, through gritted teeth, responded to all media enquiries by commenting, 'I have known him for twenty-five years but I do not feel too friendly towards him today. I do not want an elephant, have never wanted one, and I have not bought one.' Blameless Sibyl's official response is not recorded; presumably she was already *en route* to the south of France to spend an anguished Christmas with Somerset Maugham and the exiled Wallis Simpson.

However, when Berners wrote to Gertrude Stein in February 1937 he reported 'Lady Colefax is in America. I had a row with her about an elephant [...] she was besieged by press photographers asking her if they could photograph her with the elephant. She was very angry. And now I see that she was knocked down by a pig at one of Elsa Maxwell's parties.'

His friend Lady Harris delighted in the joke too, writing to him:

> I have no intention of inviting SC to the film. You ought to know [...] that anyone who can be so cruel to animals as SC was to that poor elephant could never again join the crush beneath my glittering chandeliers. How could she have kept that poor noble beast squeezed in and shut up in that small antique Normandy *armoire* in the back part of her shop for weeks and weeks never letting it even see what was going on in the front part of the shop and giving it nothing to play with but the old school ties that had belonged to her late husband.

1936 was a year Sibyl was to remember with horror for many reasons.

9

The Coronation, the Cliveden Set and the Munich Crisis

The royal family were very aware that 1936 had been 'the year of three kings', and felt that the very image of a constitutional monarchy had been severely tarnished by the abdication. The 'heir' had abandoned his post, and the public was coming to terms with 'the spare'. The last coronation had been that of George V and Queen Mary in 1911. Twenty-six years later, the plans to crown Edward VIII had been radically overturned with just five months' notice. Pottery manufacturers agonised over their stocks of commemorative mugs, now overtaken by events; cast-iron post boxes embossed with the insignia ER VIII had been manufactured for use in towns all over Britain, and commercial artists scrabbled to redesign biscuit boxes and book jackets with pictures of King George VI and Queen Elizabeth. The iconography of the coronation was as fundamentally changed as the central figures.

Nevertheless, the ceremony held in Westminster Abbey on 12 May 1937 provided Britons of all classes with a welcome opportunity to celebrate, after the considerable shocks of the previous year. The King and Queen's great friend Mrs Greville had prime seats in the Abbey with her friend Osbert Sitwell, and Ladies Londonderry and Astor were in attendance as peeresses. Emerald Cunard busied herself organising concerts; Noel Coward had a new musical on stage, *Victoria Regina*;

and London was teeming with visitors. There were a great many parties. Mrs Ronnie delighted in sitting next to the grandson of the Kaiser, 'Fritzy of Prussia', at the Channons' dinner party; and in return she gave a spectacular dinner party at her home for forty guests, including the King of Egypt, the Mountbattens, Lord and Lady Willingdon and the ubiquitous 'Chips'.

The Windsors' wedding took place on 3 June 1937 at the Château de Candé, owned by their new friend Charles Bedaux. Their honeymoon began in Venice and Milan, then they moved to Schloss Wasserleonburg, a fifteenth-century castle in Austria that they had rented from the Countess of Munster, Peggy Ward, Sibyl Colefax's business partner. The Countess welcomed them on arrival, saying, 'Wallis, how well you are looking.' Ice formed on the Duke's upper slopes: 'The Duchess, you mean ...', he corrected their hostess.

Typically the Windsors did not query the motivation of Charles Bedaux, a wealthy, naturalised American, in cultivating them. He was an entrepreneur who had developed a mechanistic 'efficiency system' of mass production; it was the basis for Chaplin's satire in the film *Modern Times*. Bedaux wanted to smooth the path of his business endeavours within the Third Reich, so he delivered the former British King and his new wife as prestigious visitors. The Windsors were fêted in Germany and followed everywhere by the press; they met the Nazi high command and, of course, Hitler at his mountain retreat, Berchtesgaden. It was a PR coup for the Third Reich; the Duke was even filmed and photographed giving a modified Nazi salute. The Duke of Windsor was generally pro-German, but it seems he was simply too naive and inexperienced to make strategic decisions without professional advisors. After forty years of automatic deference, cap-doffing and seamless international travel organised and paid for by professionals, he had been lured by the controversial idea of making an all-expenses paid 'state visit' to the New Germany with his new wife.

Immediately after the triumph of the Berlin Olympics, the Third Reich once again clamped down on those of its citizens it wished to repress. At the instigation of Emerald Cunard and von Ribbentrop, in November 1936 Sir Thomas Beecham took the newly founded London Philharmonic Orchestra to Berlin. They played to a full house, and the guest of honour, Adolf Hitler, summoned the conductor to his box during the interval to congratulate him. At the end of the concert, Beecham spotted that the Führer was applauding too. He turned to his orchestra and said, 'The old bugger seems to like it!' The remark was picked up by the microphones and broadcast by radio across Europe.

Sir Thomas refused to be intimidated by the Nazis. His newly appointed secretary was Dr Berta Geissmar, who had been personal assistant to conductor Wilhelm Furtwängler. She was Jewish and had been forced to leave Nazi Germany for London. Beecham employed her and took her with him to Berlin, knowing that his hosts would not dare to menace her while she was under his protection. Beecham had long admired German culture, having visited Bayreuth first as a youth. Between 1929 and 1938 he made annual trips to Germany to conduct major music festivals, meeting many Nazi leaders, including Hess and Hitler. But not everyone approved; at a luncheon party at Sibyl Colefax's, Emerald asked Sir Austen Chamberlain to accompany her to the opera, a season of which was currently being conducted by her lover. Sir Austen said he would, but not if they were playing Wagner, whose music was 'typical of the bestiality and brutality of the modern Hun'.

To mark the coronation in May 1937, Hitler's representative, Blomberg, was the guest of honour at the lavishly refurbished German Embassy. Von Ribbentrop organised two very select lunches in his honour with those guests considered most important to German interests in London. The first lunch included the Archbishop of Canterbury, the Baldwins (whose Cabinet had just resigned), the Edens and Vansittarts, Lord and Lady Londonderry, Lord Lothian and Lord Derby, the press barons Lord Rothermere and Lord Kelmsley, and Mrs Greville.

The second lunch consisted of the Neville Chamberlains (he was the new Prime Minister), Duff and Lady Diana Cooper, the Samuel Hoares, Lord and Lady Halifax, Sir Thomas Inskip, Winston and Clementine Churchill, and Emerald Cunard. There was also a very grand reception at the embassy, with 1,400 attending and the Duke and Duchess of Kent as guests of honour. This party was fraught with problems; von Ribbentrop had insisted on issuing the invitations in German, rather than the normal ambassadorial *lingua franca* of French, or the language of the host country, in this case English. His arrogance irritated the diplomatic community, so the Turkish Embassy replied in Turkish, the Japanese responded in their own language, and Peter Rodd, husband of Nancy Mitford, RSVPed in Yiddish.

By 1937 von Ribbentrop was no longer an ardent Anglophile. His wife disliked the London posting, objecting to the damp and foggy climate, and resenting having to curtsy to royalty at formal occasions. Her husband was now frequently ridiculed for his gaffes; he had been christened 'Herr Brickendrop' by the cartoonist David Low. The final straw occurred during the lengthy preamble to the coronation service in Westminster Abbey. The von Ribbentrops had been told that any prestigious guest needing the loo should raise a hand and attract the attention of the Westminster school-boys acting as ushers, to be escorted to the facilities. But the boys enacted a subtle revenge on their classmate Rudolf von Ribbentrop (who, like his father, was also notorious for giving the 'Hitlergrüss' on inappropriate occasions) by responding to any hand gestures from his parents with Nazi salutes, and otherwise ignoring them.

Von Ribbentrop was recalled to Germany by Hitler to become Foreign Minister in February 1938, and left London in March, just as Hitler annexed Austria. He had spent at least ten months of his twenty-month ambassadorship in Germany, and was returning to his beloved Führer's inner circle. He was now anxious to have revenge on a country that he felt had humiliated him. Von Ribbentrop reported back to Hitler on Anglo-German relations; he was smarting from his less than successful mission to London, but he nevertheless reported that Lord Lothian and the 'Astorgruppe' still desired a positive relationship with Germany.

The 'Astorgruppe' was Ribbentrop's term for the loose agglomeration of British politicians who were broadly pro-appeasement, and Cliveden was seen as their spiritual home.

The 1930s was the last decade in which country house politics were to have a major influence on national and inter-national events. Cliveden had always been a forum where politicians and power-brokers discussed the issues of the day, and the subject of a resurgent Germany was much on the guests' minds. Nancy Astor had always advocated peace, urging the governments of Britain and America to support the League of Nations, to advance international understanding and so avoid another disastrous European war. Many of Nancy's circle were keen to appease the various demands of Nazi Germany, especially her great friend Philip Kerr, Lord Lothian. Important British politicians were frequent visitors to Cliveden, where the issue of appeasing Germany was hotly debated by politicians such as Lord Halifax, Sir John Simon and Neville Chamberlain. Joachim von Ribbentrop visited Cliveden and St James's Place to try to impress opinion-formers, though Nancy had limited tolerance for his more bombastic moments; when he greeted her with the Nazi salute, she told him, 'Stop that nonsense with me.' But it was at Rest Harrow, the Astors' seaside holiday home, that secret discussions had been conducted over the possibility of Prime Minister Baldwin meeting Hitler. Lord Lothian claimed that Hitler 'left me cold', but as late as 1937 he was willing to go to Germany to talk to the Führer and Goebbels. By contrast, Nancy's son David Astor was repelled by the Third Reich and wanted nothing to do with the new regime, having witnessed a Nazi parade when he visited Heidelberg.

The Astor-owned newspapers, *The Times* and the *Observer*, tended to concur with the general British view that German demands should be accommodated. In May 1937 Neville Chamberlain replaced Baldwin as Prime Minister, and the appeasement of Germany became government policy. Some sections of the media questioned Chamberlain's assumption that Hitler was sincere in his stated desire for peace. There was also growing disquiet that wealthy and privileged people might be making decisions to appease the Third Reich without using the official diplomatic channels and professional civil service expertise.

The type of power cluster that alarmed commentators occurred at Cliveden on the weekend of 24 and 25 October 1937. The Astors had invited, among others, the newly appointed British Ambassador to Berlin, Sir Nevile Henderson, Geoffrey Dawson, the editor of *The Times*, the Foreign Secretary Anthony Eden and Lord Lothian, as well as Alec Cadogan, a senior official at the Foreign Office. The international situation was debated, along with Hitler's behaviour and the need for Britain's rapid rearmament. Details were leaked to Claud Cockburn, editor of *The Week*. His magazine, small in circulation but widely read in Parliamentary and press circles, focused on the group around the Astors, though it was another publication, the left-wing *Reynolds News*, which first coined the phrase the 'Cliveden set'. The Astors and their supporters, as well as other powerful people like the Londonderrys, were thought to be operating clandestinely to allow Nazi Germany a free hand in Europe so that it could act as a bulwark against Communism. A cartoon by David Low appeared in the *Evening Standard* in 1938 satirising the 'Cliveden set' for their apparent pro-appeasement stance. Nancy Astor in a military uniform, her right arm raised in a 'Hitlergrüss' salute, is standing on the steps of Cliveden, backed by a banner bearing a portrait of Ribbentrop and the slogan 'To Nancy, sweet memories from Joe Ribbentrop'.

The so-called 'Cliveden set' did not operate secretly; they had no need to, as they were the establishment, but they were in favour of accommodating Hitler in order to avoid a future conflict. Nancy saw Chamberlain's personal approach to

Hitler and the Munich Agreement as a triumph, as did many people. Winston Churchill described Munich as a defeat, but Nancy responded 'Nonsense!' When she went to America shortly after Munich, she pronounced, 'I abhor Hitler and Hitlerism', but she still believed that war could be avoided by negotiating with Hitler.

Despite his wife's support of the pro-appeasers, Waldorf seems to have been more prescient about the way in which events in Europe were going. In September 1938, just as Chamberlain was trumpeting the Munich Agreement, Waldorf moved his most important paintings from their London house in St James's Square to Cliveden in leafy Buckinghamshire.

The *Anschluss* (annexation) of Austria by Germany on 12 March 1938 gave many observers pause for thought, but they saw it as Hitler's desire to reunite the German-speaking peoples, and therefore not as a *causus belli*. However, when Germany began to menace Czechoslovakia, alarm bells rang.

In September 1938, Hitler claimed that the people in part of Czechoslovakia, the Sudetenland, were ethnically German and that the land should be seceded to the Fatherland. Chamberlain was anxious to avoid conflict with Germany and so pressured Czechoslovakia to comply. The situation was tense; Czech troops massed on the border with Germany, and the British fleet was put on alert. On 28 September Hitler invited Prime Minister Daladier of France, Signor Mussolini of Italy and Neville Chamberlain of Britain to meet him to discuss the situation, and Chamberlain flew to Germany for close negotiations at Berchtesgaden. He returned with a signed agreement that seemed to end the crisis by agreeing to the peaceful acquisition by Germany of the Sudetenland. It included the phrase: 'We regard the agreement signed last night and the Anglo–German Naval Agreement as symbolic of the desire of our two peoples never to go to war with one another again.'

A few British people saw the Munich Agreement as a betrayal of the Czechs, and as acquiescence in the face of Hitler; most were relieved that the threat of war seemed to have been averted. It was only twenty years since the end of the Great War, and even those who had been too young to fight in it were aware of the devastation it had wrought on a generation. There were also other vested interests in 'coming to an arrangement' with Germany; politicians were wary, the Liberals recalling how they had lost credibility during the last conflict, and the Tories resentful about the consequent rise of Labour. For the wealthy, the Great War had been a financial disaster. Top rate taxes had risen to 50 per cent, the pound dropped to half its value in just four years, and families lost land and estates through paying death duties.

The spectre of Bolshevism continued to haunt the upper classes in the late 1930s; Communism might overturn the existing order, wipe out the ruling families, seize and collectivise all assets. Stalin the Bogeyman, with his purges, his five-year plans and his famines, seemed far more threatening than one of those new dictators busy reviving their moribund economies, getting their populace back to work and making the trains run on time. In addition, the new totalitarian regimes were represented in seductive and stirring propaganda coups, such as the Berlin Olympics, with floodlights, neo-classical backdrops and endless high-stepping extras.

In short, the pro-appeasement lobby in Britain wanted to

believe that the expansionist aims of Hitler were reasonable, and need not encroach on the interests of the home islands or the Empire. They were therefore inclined to accept successive initiatives and assurances, colluding in obscurantism, until it was almost too late.

During the first half of the 1930s the Londonderrys had political influence and a sense of mission; in the latter half they were increasingly out of step. The couple had made their first visits to Nazi Germany in December 1935 and January 1936, had met Hitler and Goering and been very impressed. Charley wrote, 'I discussed many political questions with Herr Hitler and found him most forthcoming and agreeable, and most anxious to make me fully acquainted with his political opinions. We had a conversation of nearly two hours, and on many points I found myself in agreement with him. I was much impressed, too, by his popularity.'

However, the Londonderrys' next visit to Nazi Germany was in September 1937, by which time relations between Britain and Germany had deteriorated notably; following the Berlin Olympics, repressive measures were once again introduced against Jews in Germany, ham-fisted von Ribbentrop had succeeded von Hoesch as ambassador in London, and Germany had become involved in the Spanish Civil War. General and Frau Goering had been invited to stay with the Londonderrys to attend the coronation in May 1937 but had declined, claiming in a letter to have received offensive messages and insults that deterred them. Nevertheless the Londonderrys went to stay with the Goerings in Germany again. This time Charley noticed a marked decline in the

German high command's welcome, and a mood of impatience. His host impressed upon him that Germany was looking elsewhere for allies, hence the *rapprochement* with Japan and Italy.

When Ramsay MacDonald was Prime Minister, he had appointed Charley to the Air Ministry in 1931, probably because of his regard for Edith. Charley's efforts to try to influence Nazi Germany had started with his experience as the Secretary of State for Air. His old mentor, who had been forced into retirement in 1935, was ailing. MacDonald had a breakdown in 1936 and saw a lot less of Lady Londonderry. Disillusioned, out of office, in poor health and lovesick, in November 1937 MacDonald set off on a cruise to South America with his daughter in the hopes that a holiday might help him recuperate. He wrote to Edith just before he left, asking her not to forget him entirely. Two days into the voyage, he died of heart failure, aged seventy-one.

Charley Londonderry's final visit to Germany was in late June 1938, and this time he had no quasi-official status; he was merely the Vice-President of the Fédération Aéronautique Internationale. On this visit he attempted to raise the issue of the treatment of Jews in Germany with people he met, not on humanitarian grounds but because it was doing 'untold harm and prejudicing the case which Germany is seeking to present as to their peaceful intentions and the desire to co-operate in harmony with other nations'.

Alarmed by the deteriorating relationship between Britain and Germany, Charley wrote a book entitled *Ourselves and Germany*. Just before it was due to be published, in March 1938, Germany annexed Austria. Charley updated the manuscript, adding a swift postscript, defending the *Anschluss* on the grounds that the majority of Austrians had wanted it. The book was then republished by Penguin in October 1938, incorporating further comments on the Munich Agreement. The publishers described it as 'the clearest exposition so far of the policy of rapprochement with Nazi Germany and a plea for a more sympathetic understanding of Herr Hitler's point of view'. Londonderry called for Britain to 'extend the hand of true friendship to the Third Reich [...] on our mutual goodwill, I am convinced, depends the assurance of peace in the years that lie ahead'. Rather naively, in the book Charley related part of Hitler's 1936 conversation with him. The Führer had condemned Russia's admission to the League of Nations, comparing it to a German folk tale about cunning Reynard the Fox, who acted humble to fool the other creatures of the Animals League. The animals let the fox into their circle, and once admitted, Reynard was able to murder them one after another, because they had abandoned their previous unanimous decision to exclude him. This is a telling moral tale, because Reynard's tactics were those adopted by the Third Reich to divide and dominate Europe, picking off smaller countries through guile and lies.

At the same time as Charley, in October 1938, just after Munich, Edith Londonderry published her own book, *Retrospect,* which is rather more biographical in tone. In a sweeping statement that came back to haunt her, she reiterated her suspicion of the left: 'The more positive "isms" are taboo, like Nazi-ism or Fascism, because they imply doing something; but a pink form of Communism finds a great deal of support.' She also commended the Munich Agreement, and expressed the view that any Socialist tendencies in Britain would be transient: 'in less than a decade [England] will mostly likely be laughing at herself for her pink thoughts and her pink boys; and all will be marching along, armed to the teeth, in the cause of peace [...] on this note I end these reflections, in the month of October, 1938.'

Within weeks of their books' publication dates, both Lord and Lady Londonderry were proved to have been wholly misguided. Those who had previously believed in Germany's good intentions were shaken to the core on the night of 9–10 November 1938. Across Germany, 20,000 Jews were arrested, businesses looted and 191 synagogues burned down by the Nazis in what came to be known as Kristallnacht. Lord Londonderry immediately wrote an angry letter to Goering, demanding an explanation:

> I am completely at a loss to understand your policy towards the Jews [...] I profoundly disagree with your claim that this is a matter of internal politics [...] I do not want to dwell on the grievous disappointment which I have had to undergo. I was able for so long to reply to any arguments put forward by those who have never had any belief that Germany had any desire to become a helpful partner in the comity of nations, but in relation to your treatment of the Jews I have no reply whatsoever, and all I can do is remain silent and take no further part in these matters, in which most people in this country are thinking my opinions have been wrong from the beginning.

Goering did not reply, and this was Charley's last correspondence with Germany's leaders. When German forces occupied Prague in March 1939, Charley's disillusionment was complete. He had attempted for years to bring about Anglo–German understanding but it was all a chimera, and they had been duped. Galvanised, he now threw himself into running the Civil Air Guard, training men and women to fly so they could support the RAF in case of war.

On 14 March 1939 the German army invaded Czechoslovakia, despite the Munich Agreement, and this was the turning point for many who had tried to accommodate Germany. Nancy Astor and her fellow appeasers finally changed their minds, but it was too late for her reputation. She spoke in the House of Commons on 16 March, asking 'Will the Prime Minister lose no time in letting the German Government know with what horror the whole of this country regards Germany's action?' A fellow Tory MP, Vyvyan Adams, interjected, 'You caused it yourself.' In hindsight, it is easy to criticise the pro-appeasement lobby for their naivety, but they were taken in by successive declarations of sincerity issued by various members of the Nazi high command. It seems not to have occurred to them that the people they were dealing with could lie.

These were difficult years for Nancy personally; her brother Buck had died in 1937, and her favourite sister Phyllis in 1938. She was starting to lose her debating abilities, and her speeches tended to become repetitive and poorly structured. Nevertheless she continued to entertain the great and the good of the era, the aristocrats, politicians and celebrities. In April 1938, at the age of fifty-nine, she gave a grand and glittering dinner party at her London house in honour of the new Foreign Secretary, Lord Halifax; the guest list included the Duke of Kent, the American Ambassador, Joseph Kennedy, the Archbishop of Canterbury and the Italian Ambassador,

Count Grandi. All of them were broadly in favour of Britain's continuing appeasement of the dictators.

Nancy was also inclined to take a characteristically high-minded attitude to issues of personal morality; she had lent a villa in Deauville to Lloyd George and Frances Stevenson, his secretary, unaware that the pair were lovers. When she discovered the truth, she tackled him about it. Lloyd George said, 'What were you doing with my secretary Philip Kerr?' 'Absolutely nothing!' blazed back Lady Astor. 'Then,' said Lloyd George, 'you ought to be ashamed of yourself.'

Mrs Greville had abandoned her early enthusiasm for Nazi Germany; her final visit to the country was in August 1937, when she set out again for Munich, planning to spend three weeks visiting various friends. She had also quickly tired of von Ribbentrop as a personality; her records show that she only hosted him for two dinners, in London, in 1932 and 1934. She asked Frau von Ribbentrop to dine on 26 November 1936 and 23 June 1937, but they were never invited to her country house, where she entertained the people she genuinely liked. By contrast, the German ambassadors who preceded von Ribbentrop, von Neurath and von Hoesch, appear on thirteen occasions in her visitors' books. The French Ambassador features on fourteen occasions between 1928 and 1940; the Belgian eleven times and the Italian Ambassador fifteen times. The Spanish Ambassador managed thirty-six social occasions, and the Brazilian Ambassador, H. E. De Oliveira, and his family clocked up an impressive forty-one appearances in a decade, including Christmases with her at Polesden Lacey. The meagre two occasions she hosted von

Ribbentrop are indicative of what she thought of his company, although she was a regular guest at German Embassy receptions, and inevitably encountered him at other social events.

Nevertheless she continued to dabble in international politics, having been charmed by Count Grandi, the Italian Ambassador. Like him, she desired good relations between Italy and Great Britain. She had met Mussolini, and through Lord Berners, who owned a beautiful house in Rome, she had visited the city many times. Now Mrs Greville was becoming too infirm to travel extensively, but her friend Ivy Chamberlain was willing and able to campaign for appeasement with Italy, by lobbying the Italian Senate. Ivy was the widow of Austen Chamberlain and the sister-in-law of his half-brother Neville, who was now Prime Minister. In January 1938 Chamberlain was irritated by 'meddling' letters from both Mrs Greville and Mrs Chamberlain. The ladies also tackled Anthony Eden, calling for *rapprochement* with Italy. On 18 February 1938 Ivy telegraphed her brother-in-law from Rome with unwanted pro-appeasement encouragement just as he was entering crucial negotiations with Count Grandi. In March intriguing diplomatic gossip was noted by Lord Killearn in Cairo that Lady Chamberlain had been entertaining Italian opinion-formers in high style in Rome, with large and sumptuous banquets. This was puzzling; it was generally known that Ivy Chamberlain had very little money after Austen had died, so the source of her entertainment budget was as mysterious as her motivation. It seems likely that Ivy's Roman charm offensive was bankrolled by someone with ample funds, a belief in appeasement, and a proven record of wielding 'soft power' through entertaining the political elite. Mrs Greville's *modus operandi* makes her a likely candidate; she was certainly close to Ivy, a frequent guest at

Polesden Lacey, though Mrs Ronnie was often slighting about her intelligence. One such verbal demolition occurred over dinner, with Mrs Ronnie alluding to the legend of the city of Ancient Rome being saved from enemy invasion when the alarm was raised by a flock of geese: '*Dear* Ivy Chamberlain [...] How well she is looking tonight!' And she kissed her hand in the direction of Lady Chamberlain, who was sitting at the other end of the table.

This was, of course, as we all knew, the signal for a frontal attack. When Maggie called any of her female friends 'dear' in that tone of voice, one could be sure that the sword was already half-way out of its sheath.

'I hear great things of her recent trip to Rome,' continued Maggie in dulcet tones. 'Mussolini, it seems, was quite *épris*. They were constantly together, and dear Ivy assures me that the Duce will do practically anything she tells him. She sighed, to give greater effect to her final thrust. *"Well ... it would not be the first time that Rome had been saved by a goose!"* It was cruel; it was unjust; it was delicious.'

She could certainly be vitriolic. Over lunch in July 1937 Harold Nicolson found himself next to Mrs Greville, who proceeded to demolish the reputations of her friends. He recorded his encounter with her in his diary with a mixture of disapproval, scorn and horrified pleasure, 'she is nothing more than a fat slug filled with venom'.

Mrs Greville had variable views on Jews; like many of her class, she mixed socially with clever high-achievers such as Philip Sassoon and the Rothschild family. For twenty years she was close to Rufus Isaacs, the former Viceroy of India, and after his first wife died she nurtured hopes of romance, but he married his secretary. Mrs Ronnie was also an enthusiastic patron of the architectural firm of Mewès and Davis, who had transformed Polesden Lacey and 16 Charles Street; the two eponymous partners were Jewish. But like many Britons of the time, she was convinced that there were anonymous hordes of observant Jews in Europe and Russia very different from her wealthy and distinguished Jewish friends. She was concerned that the European Jews might become refugees and 'invade' Britain. In her case, snobbery had the edge over the anti-Semitism unfortunately prevalent among people of all classes. Margot Asquith was typical of the type. In the mid-1930s she wrote: 'I have had, and still have, devoted friends among the Jews, but have often been painfully reminded of the saying, "A Jew is round your neck, at your feet, but never at your side."' Of course, in the 1930s no one predicted the wholesale genocide being planned in Germany, and very few would have endorsed it if they had been aware. As American Ambassador Dodd acutely remarked in Berlin as early as 1933, 'The Nazis did not invent anti-Semitism. They were simply the first to organise it so that it could be used as an effective weapon of the state.'

Mrs Greville thrived on debate and dissent, and Winston Churchill was often one of her guests. In the mid- and late 1930s he would transfix his fellow diners, issuing dire prophecies about Germany that eventually came true. It was through Mrs Greville that he met Professor Lindemann, a brilliant academic who she had cultivated and who was to become Churchill's scientific advisor and close ally throughout the war. At Polesden Lacey the men's discussions would go on into the night over port and cigars, to the chagrin of the ladies, who were waiting for them in the drawing room, in the traditional manner. In a less formal age Margaret Greville and her female guests would have stayed at the dining table and actively participated in the debate.

Mrs Greville once remarked that if she had had a daughter she would have liked her to be like Queen Elizabeth, and the two women were friends. Although her marriage to Ronnie was happy, it had been childless. George Keppel believed that if only the Grevilles had had children, her life would have been fulfilled. Margaret's request to adopt Sonia Keppel was gently deflected by Alice, who asked her to be Sonia's godmother instead, and she took a keen interest in Sonia's welfare throughout her life, as she did with many younger women, from her maid Gertie Hulton to the heiress Edwina Ashley, if she felt their interests needed protection.

Elizabeth Bowes-Lyon was born in 1900, a similar age to any daughter Mrs Greville might have had; she was pretty, accomplished, popular, a great dancer, full of fun and, best of all, she was Scottish. Like Margaret, she was patriotic, but unlike her, Elizabeth's ancestors were an ancient, wealthy family of aristocratic lineage, and she grew up in Glamis Castle, the setting of Shakespeare's *Macbeth*. Charming Elizabeth, much adored by her many, well-connected relatives, had the type of idyllic childhood that appealed to Margaret, whose own more modest upbringing was full of secrets. In addition, both women were fiercely loyal to Bertie, Prince Albert. The Yorks and their two little girls had many happy weekends at Polesden as well as parties at Mrs Greville's London home; Princess Elizabeth was apparently fond of exploring the subterranean servants' quarters of 16 Charles Street, in pursuit of the housekeeper's cat. In return, Maggie was invited to formal Palace receptions, as well as intimate little dinners and numerous family celebrations.

In the late 1930s, now that 'Bertie' and Elizabeth were the

King and Queen, Mrs Greville anticipated sadly that she would see them less frequently, and she spoke nostalgically of the past: 'I was so happy in the days when they used to run in and out of my house as if they were my own children.' However, even though their free time was more restricted, the King and Queen still saw their old friend regularly. They also communicated by letter; Mrs Greville amused the Queen in September 1937 by sending her a joke she had heard about a fashionable hat called the Wallis, because it was 'shady, with no crown'.

They still enjoyed the informality of weekends at Polesden; Beverley Nichols recalled one occasion early on a Sunday morning when he could not resist the lure of Mrs Greville's grand piano in the empty drawing room, and launched into playing improvisations on the theme of 'God Save the King', first as a funeral march, then as a mazurka and finally as a Bach fugue. The door opened, and there was Queen Elizabeth, looking puzzled and asking what he had been playing as it sounded 'faintly familiar'.

An example of the close friendship between Mrs Greville and Elizabeth occurred in the summer of 1938, when Mrs Ronnie was seventy-five years old. The international situation was grave and the King and Queen had planned an important state visit to France, to strengthen the *entente cordiale* between the two countries. Just five days before they were due to leave, Queen Elizabeth's mother, the Countess of Strathmore, died at Glamis. The visit was postponed by a month, but despite her grief Elizabeth put duty first and was determined to go. She was obliged to observe a formal period of mourning, but she exercised the monarch's unique prerogative to wear white instead of black. Her entire wardrobe was remade by designer Norman Hartnell, from hats and gloves to ballgowns and fur wraps. Her dazzling appearance in Paris, City of Light, radiant in snowy white and decorated with jewels worth £7 million, was a triumph, both diplomatically and sartorially. The Duke of Windsor had asked if he and Wallis could meet the King and Queen in Paris during the State visit, but the request was refused, so they left town for the duration. Wallis had recently been voted the best-dressed woman in the world, but it was the sister-in-law she had nicknamed 'Cookie' for her dumpy figure who had captured the admiration of *tout Paris*.

Mrs Greville was ill the day the King and Queen returned to Buckingham Palace from France; hearing of her old friend's poor health, Elizabeth popped round to Charles Street the same afternoon and sat at her bedside telling her about the wonderful time they had had in Paris. While relating this story afterwards, Mrs Greville became uncharacteristically emotional, sobbing 'Oh, my dear [...] what it would be to have a daughter like that!' She recovered her equilibrium by ordering some champagne, and being brusque to the footman who brought it.

Another young woman whose interests she fostered was Dorothé Mabel Lewis, Charley Londonderry's illegitimate daughter by the American actress Fannie Ward. Dorothé was a beauty, and her early marriage to 'Babe' Barnato, a First World War ace, ended after only a year when he died in the great influenza epidemic, leaving her widowed at twenty and extraordinarily rich. In 1922 Dorothé married Terence Plunket, the sixth Baronet, and they had three boys. The Plunkets were much liked by the Duke and Duchess of York, and were also frequent and welcome visitors at Londonderry House and Mount Stewart, where Edith knew the truth of Dorothé's parentage but accepted her wholeheartedly. Dorothé was a gifted dancer, and excellent company, while Terence was a charming Anglo-Irish gentleman with few pretensions who liked a laugh. The whole family often visited Polesden Lacey in the 1930s, usually staying for the weekend, and several of Lord Plunket's improvised ditties survive in Mrs Greville's scrapbooks:

> *A visit made pleasant by an artist's touch*
> *A hostess whose genius is marked by a touch*
> *No one can equal*
> *Dear Mrs Ronnie we thank you so much*
> *A hostess de luxe with a masterly touch*
> *No one can equal – we thank you so much.*

In February 1938 British and American society was shocked to hear that Lord and Lady Plunket had both been killed in a tragic accident in the United States; William Randolph Hearst had invited them to a party he was giving at his home in California, but their plane crashed as it was coming in to land, killing them instantly and leaving their three children orphaned. Queen Elizabeth wrote to Lady Londonderry, a tactful letter, given the fact that Dorothé was known to be Charley's illegitimate daughter, and that the bereaved Plunket boys were therefore his grandchildren: 'We both felt so sad over the ghastly tragedy of Dorothé and Teddy, as you know what intimate friends of ours they had been for many years. They both gave so much happiness to so many people of all kinds and sorts; their going does leave a terrible blank indeed. Those dear little boys make one's heart *ache.*'

Within days of the Plunkets' funerals, attended by both Charley and Edith, a discreet notice appeared in *The Times* announcing that Lord Londonderry and Teddy's younger brother would be the boys' guardians. Mrs Greville was greatly upset by the deaths of the Plunkets, and it was at this point that her health started to give serious cause for concern; she was prone to chest infections, and for a number of years she had tended to go abroad during the winter months to avoid the worst of the British climate. But now she was suffering frequent bouts of pneumonia and bronchitis, and on occasion bad attacks of phlebitis forced her to use a wheelchair. Nevertheless she was determined to maintain her social life, and in July 1938 she disobeyed doctors' orders and rose from her bed to attend Ascot. To make things easier for her the King and Queen insisted that their old friend should use the Royal Entrance to the racecourse, a considerable privilege.

Such preferential treatment was not extended to all the London society hostesses. Following the abdication, Emerald remained something of a pariah among those close to the royal family for a number of years. On 18 May 1937 the King and Queen attended a ball given by the Duke and Duchess of Sutherland at Hampden House, Green Street. It was the first time since the Great War that the reigning King and Queen had attended a private dance. Crowds of well-wishers gathered outside the house to cheer them as they arrived and departed. Lady Cunard, intimate friend of the former King Edward VIII, postponed her own arrival at the party until after the monarchs had left. Emerald was only too aware that she was, in the memorable phrase from *1066 and All That*, 'left over from a previous reign'.

As a leader of society, Edith Londonderry was aware of every current, rapid and possible rock in the social stream. She planned to give a ball at Londonderry House three weeks after the coronation, in honour of the new King and Queen. At the end of May 1937 she wrote to Queen Elizabeth, proposing a guest list for her approval. Thanking her for consulting them, Queen Elizabeth replied: 'Lady Cunard is really the only one that we do not want to meet just now. The bitter months of last autumn & winter are still so fresh in our minds [... her presence ...] would inevitably bring so many sad thoughts that we would prefer not to meet her [...] there is nobody else on your little list, except possibly poor Mrs Corrigan, who one could take exception to, and I do appreciate your tact & kindness in writing.'

Meanwhile, Sibyl Colefax continued her demanding dual career as energetic society hostess and businesswomen, despite her age; she was already sixty-two years old when, in 1936, tragic personal circumstances forced her to sell her beloved home and to find new ways of increasing her income. Throughout the late 1930s she continued to entertain frenetically, though her time and funds were both in short supply. Witty but wicked Lord Berners liked to parody the people he knew, and he saw Sibyl as a legitimate target. He was acquainted with Gertrude Stein and Alice B. Toklas, an American couple who lived in Paris, and had written pastiches of their distinctive avant-garde literary endeavours, which owed much to Surrealism. In 1936 he wrote *Portrait of a Society Hostess*; the style mimics Stein's prose poems, but the subject of his satire was his old friend Sibyl Colefax:

> Give a canary champagne and it spins. Chandelier drops glitter and drops and are conversation. Bohemian glass is cracked in Mayfair. Mayfair-weather friends come and go come and go come and go. The house is always full full full.
>
> Are you there? Are you there? There! There! Are you not all there? Many are not quite all there but royalty are there and lots and lots and lots. Glitter is more than kind

hearts and coronets are more than comfort. She praises and embarrasses she praises and embarrasses she confuses cabinet ministers. Some will not go.

Pragmatic Lady Colefax was making major changes to her business. In 1938 her partner Peggy Ward, now the Countess of Munster, planned to retire from the firm, and she suggested John Fowler, a highly gifted decorator, as her replacement. He came from a modest background and was largely self-taught, having started as a restorer and painter of old furniture. Fowler's passion for French culture gave his interior design work a light and often witty touch, and he particularly liked *toile de Jouy* wallpaper and textiles. The new partnership of Colefax & Fowler gave them both fresh impetus; John Fowler was now working in traditional British country houses, where he appreciated the accretion of art and artefacts over centuries. In return Sibyl's decorating style became less conventional and more sophisticated due to his influence.

The Bruton Street premises operated both as a shop, selling fabrics, wallpapers, fitted carpets and rugs, and as an interior design practice. John Fowler provided bespoke designs to meet the client's brief. The firm offered a complete decorating service, and had a skilled freelance team of craftspeople, from upholsterers and gilders to plasterers and dyers. Increasingly the business stocked antique furniture and unusual *objets d'art*, acquired by both partners on buying trips to France and around rural Britain, which increased their retail sales and added atmosphere. Colefax & Fowler managed to capture and reinterpret the distinctive look of grand English country houses, with convivial groups of armchairs and sofas, large rugs in jewel colours, wooden panelling and well-polished traditional furniture. There was a subtle emphasis on comfort and convenience, with well-placed occasional tables and table lamps. Decoration was provided by touches of Oriental lacquer and blue and white Chinese vases, Imari porcelain or *famille rose* pots, and large arrangements of fresh garden flowers, or bulbs in pots. The mood was that of an interior that has grown naturally and gradually over many years, and the company appealed to people who wanted an 'instant inheritance'.

Meanwhile, Sibyl was still in touch with the Duke and Duchess of Windsor. In August 1938 Harold Nicolson and Sibyl were fellow guests at a formal dinner at the Villa Mauresque, Cap Ferrat, home of Somerset Maugham. There was a hurried chat about the Gordian knot of protocol before the Duke and Duchess arrived. It was tricky; Sibyl was looking forward to seeing her old friend Wallis, but refused to curtsy to her, just because the former king desired it. Nicolson was prepared to address him initially as 'Your Royal Highness', then 'Sir', as though he were still a prince, but not 'Your Majesty' then 'Sir', as would be appropriate for a king. They all agreed to call Wallis 'Duchess', but then were thrown by the Duke apologising for arriving late because 'Her Royal Highness' had been delayed. To confuse matters further, the Duke and Duchess spent the entire evening calling each other 'darling', laughing and chattering animatedly. The Windsors were happy living in France, and liked the culture, but were uncertain what the future might bring.

One important London figure who was a confirmed Francophile was Laura Corrigan. She divided much of her time in the late 1930s between London and Paris, flitting between the two capitals. She had been 'taken up' by fellow American Elsa Maxwell, professional party organiser for the rich, who helped her to establish herself in Parisian high society. With her own fortune and Elsa's contacts Laura was once again employing well-connected characters to hack a path for her to the sunny uplands of high society, throwing magnificent parties at which she liberally distributed exquisite and valuable gifts to her guests. Laura was neither an intellectual nor high-born, but she recognised that curiosity, greed and acquisitiveness are universal character traits. She played upon these human failings to draw people to her, using her great wealth. Elsa Maxwell remembered her fondly: 'A great London Hostess [...] the irrepressible Laura Corrigan, who established a formidable handicap in the American Cinderella Derby by covering the ground from switchboard operator to rich widow in a record six months.'

Even allowing for hyperbole (in fact Laura had married Jimmy Corrigan in 1916, and he had died in 1928), Elsa Maxwell genuinely admired Laura. She said her client 'was not beautiful, she was not educated or particularly clever – [and] her innocent blunders of speech provided almost as much amusement, behind her back, as her parties.'

But Elsa was adept at helping wealthy American *parvenus* get established in Parisian high society for a fee throughout the 1920s and 1930s. She was adept at garnering publicity for her clients and herself, skills that were appreciated by the venues where she organised their parties and receptions, such as the Ritz Hotel in Paris.

The magnificent Ritz in the Place Vendôme had been the home-from-home of rich Americans for many decades, and from 1938 onwards it was Laura Corrigan's main residence in France. She maintained the vast Imperial Suite on a permanent basis; unfortunately her grip of the French language was somewhat idiosyncratic, and she blithely called it her *'ventre-à-terre'*, a phrase that literally means 'belly to the ground' but which colloquially means 'flat out'.

Because of her linguistic tangles and her familiarity with the finest of luxury settings, Laura Corrigan appreciated the Ritz Hotel with its multilingual staff. However, in London she preferred to take a prestigious town house for the season, complete with experienced staff, in order to entertain under her own roof in great style. She needed large, historic houses, ideally belonging to an aristocratic owner, and money was no object. In June 1938 she was based at 11 Kensington Palace Gardens, which she had rented for the season from the Duke and Duchess of Marlborough. She gave a spectacular party, and of course details were reported in the newspapers. Lady Diana Cooper was in black, Lady Weymouth wore white and silver and Lady Cunard sported a topknot of roses. The Duke and Duchess of Kent led the dancing, and a cabaret was provided by Chinese jugglers and a xylophone player.

Throughout 1939 it became increasingly apparent that war was inevitable. Harold Nicolson expressed his frustration at what he saw as the past misguided attempts of Mrs Greville and Lady Astor to influence the foreign ambassadors and political classes for their own self-aggrandisement:

> I do not believe that any intelligent man such as Grandi could have left [Mussolini] under any illusion that the will-power of this country is concentrated in Mrs Ronald Greville. He must know that in the last resort our decision is embodied, not in Mayfair or Cliveden, but in the provinces. The harm which these silly, selfish hostesses do is

immense. They convey to foreign envoys the impression that policy is decided in their drawing-rooms. People [...] are impressed by the social efficiency of silly women such as Mrs Greville and Lady Astor. Anybody who knows the latter understands that she is a kindly but inordinately foolish woman. Yet these people have a subversive influence. They dine and wine our younger politicians and they create an atmosphere of authority and responsibility and grandeur, whereas the whole thing is a mere flatulence of spirit. That is what always happens with us. The silly people are regarded as representative of British opinion and the informed people are dismissed as 'intellectuals'. I should be most unhappy if I were Lady Astor. She must realise that her parrot cries have done much damage to what (to do her justice) she must dimly realise is the essence of her adopted class and country.

For some individuals, any notion of defeatism was to be stoutly challenged; in the middle of June 1939 Winston Churchill heard from an American journalist, Walter Lippmann, that American Ambassador Joseph Kennedy believed that war was inevitable and that Britain would be defeated. Winston refused to believe that was possible, but that if it happened then it would be up to the Americans to 'preserve and maintain the great heritage of the English-speaking peoples'.

On 3 June 1939 Philip Sassoon died from complications following influenza, aged only fifty. Bob Boothby, who had been a close friend between 1925 and 1935, said, 'War was not his element. His death, like everything else about him, was well timed.' Sassoon had been increasingly depressed by the news his international contacts provided about the

Germans' plans for subjugation of Europe, and some believed his death was self-willed.

Throughout the summer of 1939, the last season before the war, there was a flurry of social occasions and grand balls. A particularly glittering occasion was held at on 6 July at Holland House, the West London home of the sixth Earl of Ilchester, for the début of Sonia Cubitt's daughter Rosalind. (She was to become the mother of Camilla Parker Bowles, now HRH the Duchess of Cornwall.) The guests of honour were the King and Queen, and Noel Coward and the ubiquitous Queen Ena of Spain were also present. Naturally, Mrs Greville was determined to attend; the successful launch of her god-child's daughter to the cream of society, including her dear friends the monarchs, was unmissable. Still weak from a bout of pneumonia, the seventy-six-year-old was carried up the stairs in a wheelchair by two of her footmen. Around her neck was the astonishing five-strand diamond necklace that had once belonged to Marie Antoinette. It was not a night for half-measures.

In July 1939 Mrs Laura Corrigan took Dudley House in Park Lane for two months for a rumoured £5,000. Among other events, she gave a large dinner party at which the American Ambassador Joseph Kennedy and his wife were the principal guests. The party was the eve of the Kennedys' débutante daughter Eunice being presented at Buckingham Palace. Her young brothers Bobby and Teddy watched her leave from the balcony of their house in Grosvenor Square.

Nicolson had condemned the 'silly hostesses' earlier in the year, but their attitudes were certainly not unusual for their era. It was only gradually becoming apparent to the general public the true nature of life – and death – under totalitarian regimes, especially the Third Reich. On 30 August 1939

Nicolson had a lunch with Sibyl Colefax, Lady Cunard and Ivone Kirkpatrick, who had been First Secretary in Berlin between 1933 and 1938. Kirkpatrick chillingly described conditions in Germany, and the 'sense of evil arrogance' that emanated from the Führer.

At the beginning of August 1939 'Chips' Channon drove down to Polesden to see Mrs Greville. He described the house and grounds as magnificent, silent and spacious, well maintained by his hostess's long-established wealth. He found his hostess notably older, thinner and greyer than he remembered, but nevertheless they settled down for such a fulsome gossip that he nearly ran out of time to dress for dinner. Even 'Chips' was taken aback by Mrs Ronnie's vindictive opinion of her old friend Grace Vanderbilt. 'There is no one on earth quite so skilfully malicious as old Maggie [...] she was vituperative about almost everyone, for about 40 minutes.' In the middle of August 1939, just weeks before the outbreak of war, Mrs Greville was planning a recuperative holiday in Le Touquet and Deauville. As the gravity of the situation became clear, she cancelled her plans to go to France, and stayed at Polesden with friends to await developments.

With war looming, Waldorf Astor decided to remove all the Astors' valuables from their London home to Cliveden for safety. He asked Rose to collect from the bank the Sancy diamond too, forgetting that he had already been to the bank and absent-mindedly put the gem in his pocket. Rose was not pleased, but Waldorf was preoccupied. In August 1939 he reduced the number of staff at Cliveden, and once again he was planning to help open the Canadian Red Cross hospital on site.

As another war with Germany seemed imminent, 'Chips'

Channon likened the mood in the House of Commons to getting married for the second time: 'it is impossible to work up the same excitement. Certainly tonight London is quiet and almost indifferent to what may happen. There is a frightening calm.' In New York, on 1 September 1939, W. H. Auden recorded his creeping sense of doom as the last hours of peace of 'a low, dishonest decade' ebbed away.

War in Europe was unavoidable unless Germany drew back from the brink. Hostilities broke out between Germany and Poland, and on 1 September 1939 there was a special session of Parliament to discuss the crisis. It was a day of high emotion. Neville Chamberlain put the blame squarely on Hitler's shoulders; he listed the recent course of negotiations, and when he revealed that sixteen points that Hitler claimed had been rejected by the Poles had never been presented to them by the Germans, Nancy Astor was heard to exclaim, 'Well, I never did!' Even on the brink of war she was astonished to discover that the Nazis had lied. Chamberlain soberly read out the ultimatum he had sent to the German government, stating that unless they abandoned their aggression against Poland, Britain would fulfil its promise to go to war.

At 11.15 on the morning of Sunday 3 September, Prime Minister Neville Chamberlain, veteran of the Munich Agreement, broadcast live on the radio to a hushed and expectant nation. He announced that the British government had waited for a response to the ultimatum, but that no reply had come from Berlin as the deadline had expired, 'and consequently, this country is at war with Germany.'

10

'Bravery under fire': 1939–1945

Within minutes of Chamberlain's broadcast, air-raid sirens sounded throughout London. Although Margot Asquith had blithely informed Emerald Cunard that gas masks were unnecessary and air raids were not dangerous, the sinister wail was to become all too familiar to Britain's inhabitants, who now learned to live with the threat of bombs, the need to 'take cover' at a moment's notice, the exigencies of rationing and life in the blackout. Urban children were evacuated to the countryside; Mrs Greville's country house, Polesden Lacey, took in thirty schoolchildren from the East End on the very first day of the war, accommodating them in flats over the garages.

The King and Queen elected to stay in London for the duration of hostilities, but as the war became more intense they often slept at Windsor Castle. Queen Mary took up residence with the Duke and Duchess of Beaufort at Badminton, accompanied by a retinue of no fewer than sixty-three servants.

Many expats headed back to Britain; on 12 September the Windsors, 'Fruity' Metcalfe and three Cairn terriers were picked up from Cherbourg by the British destroyer HMS *Kelly*, commanded by the Duke's cousin Lord Louis Mountbatten, and deposited on the quayside in blacked-out Portsmouth. They stayed for two weeks; the Duke offered his services in support of his King and country and hoped to remain in Britain permanently. However, the royal family were implacably opposed to the idea, especially Queen Elizabeth. Another solution was required, and it was agreed that the Duke would act as liaison officer with the British Military Mission near Paris. He was wearing khaki uniform and his many medals when he and Wallis lunched at Lady Colefax's home on 27 September 1939.

In anticipation of the bombing campaign, which did not materialise for months, many wealthy Londoners closed up their town houses and moved into the big hotels. It had become increasingly difficult to staff and heat private homes, as fuel was rationed and servants were recruited for war service. Hotels were convenient and convivial alternatives, as all meals in restaurants were initially limited to three courses and had to cost 5 shillings a head or less. A hotel restaurant was no more expensive than a more modest establishment. As the American war correspondent Ed Murrow remarked, 'at least you would be bombed with the right sort of people.'

Many notable members of London society were on the move in the early days of the war. Lady Londonderry closed up most of her family's palatial house at the bottom of Park Lane and ate at the Dorchester Hotel. The best hotels were packed with celebrities, socialites and statesmen. London was full of servicemen and women, who filled the theatres, night clubs and dance floors. Some householders continued to entertain to the best of their abilities. Sibyl Colefax moved from Lord North Street early-eighteenth-century terraced house in Queen Anne's Gate, which Lady Diana Cooper described as 'frail as a pack of cards, and Queen Anne cards at that'. At first, during air raids, the servants would be sent down to the basement while 'Coalbox', as she was fondly known, and her guests would serve themselves the meal. Once the Blitz began in earnest in September 1940, Sibyl's guests refused to shelter in the kitchen, knowing they would be no safer there. 'Chips' Channon defied the bombs and held lavish dinner parties at his house in Belgrave Square until it was badly damaged by a bomb in November 1940.

The Dorchester Hotel on Park Lane had opened in 1932, and it became the focus of many Londoners' wartime social lives. It was believed that its reinforced concrete construction made it safe in air raids. When the Blitz began in September 1940, residents and visitors sought refuge nightly in the hotel's subterranean Turkish baths, where beds had been installed in cubicles for the VIP residents. However, 'the Dorm', as it was known, had been excavated laterally beyond the building's foundations, so a mere twelve inches of tarmac and gravel lay between the drive outside the hotel's entrance and the ceiling of the supposedly secure shelter. One stray bomb landing outside the main entrance could have wiped out what Mrs Corrigan called 'la cream de la cream' of London society.

The hotel attracted a mixed clientele, from Cabinet ministers to brigadiers, dowagers to diplomats, officers to actors. Some residents negotiated what was known as the 'duchess' rate, a reduced tariff because their presence added lustre to the hotel's reputation. Dorchester regulars included the Foreign Secretary, Lord Halifax, and his wife, and Oliver Stanley, Minister for War from 1940 onwards, who was married to Lady Maureen, daughter of Lord and Lady Londonderry. It also attracted a rather more louche clientele. Canadian diplomat Charles Ritchie wrote: 'In the Dorchester, the sweepings of the Riviera have been washed up – pot-bellied, sallow, sleek-haired nervous gentlemen with loose mouths and wobbly chins, wearing suede shoes and checked suits, and thin bony women with fox capes and long silk legs and small artificial curls clustering around their bony sheep-like heads.'

Mrs Greville closed up her exquisite eighteenth-century town home in Charles Street and decamped to the reinforced concrete Modernism of the Dorchester in July 1940. She used a discreet side entrance to avoid being seen crossing the crowded lobby in her wheelchair. The hotel was the nexus of government, the armed services and international intrigue, and while many rich septuagenarians with indifferent health might seek safety in the provinces, Mrs Greville chose a ringside seat in order to watch the Luftwaffe's concerted attempts to destroy London. From a vast upper-storey suite, with her faithful servants, and ablaze with magnificent jewellery, Maggie was determined to go out with a bang.

Between bombing raids she entertained her favourites by inviting them to exquisite meals in her suite, using fresh produce sent up from Polesden's Home Farm, such as milk, butter, newly laid eggs and cream, which were otherwise extremely difficult to obtain legitimately in rationed Britain. Resolute and defiant to the end, she refused to descend to the underground air-raid shelters during air raids; as bombs fell on London and anti-aircraft batteries in Hyde Park blasted into the sky, Mrs Greville would telephone VIPs sheltering in 'the Dorm', daring them to join her upstairs, and dismissing them as cowards if they felt discretion was the better part of valour.

Meanwhile, old friends and rivals also converged on London. The rapid advance of armies across Europe caught Mrs Keppel out once again (the first occasion had been in August 1914). Following their hurried retreat from Italy in July 1940, the Keppels sailed from St Jean de Luz in a Royal Navy troop ship crammed with British nationals and military personnel. In the confusion Violet Trefusis handed her jewellery to a man she assumed to be a porter, and never saw him (or it) again. The journey back to Britain was fraught and uncomfortable, and, as in 1914, Mrs Keppel decamped to the Ritz to recuperate. Mrs Greville rapidly tired of hearing tales about the Keppels' ordeal, and told Lady Londonderry: 'To hear Alice talk about her escape from France, one would think she had swum the Channel, with her maid between her teeth.'

Mrs Greville was aware of her tarnished image, due to her early enthusiasm for the Third Reich. Duff Cooper, the MP whose election she had tried to sabotage, had embarked on a lecture tour of the States at the beginning of the war, to persuade neutral America to support Britain. She complained about his 'dereliction of duty' in being overseas. Duff Cooper responded robustly, pointing out that she was probably harbouring resentment against those who, like him, had long warned of the dangers of the Nazis.

To redeem her reputation, she placed a feature in the *Evening Standard* (2 February 1940) claiming that, while the Nazis had attempted to cultivate important Englishwomen for propaganda purposes, she had regularly travelled to Germany primarily in order to take 'the cure' at Baden-Baden. She added that she was currently recovering from an (unspecified) illness, and her only dinner engagement that winter had been with Lord and Lady Halifax. (He was the Foreign Secretary, and therefore an unimpeachable reference.) Mrs Greville also donated nearly £6,000 to buy a Spitfire for the RAF. Any wealthy individual could, in principle, commission a plane, but only a true egotist with a great deal of ground to make up would have their own name painted on its fuselage. The P8643 *Margaret Helen* saw active service from April 1941 till December 1944; in fact, it outlived its sponsor.

After the fall of France in the summer of 1940 and the evacuation of Dunkirk, the invasion of Britain was expected imminently. During the Blitz, from September 1940, London was bombed from the air night after night. As the warning sirens began, the populace would take cover wherever they could, hiding in basements or Underground stations from screaming bombs and murderous incendiaries. The blackout made any nocturnal journey a hazardous procedure for pedestrians and motorists, but moonlit nights revealed the distinctive twists and turns of the Thames and provided a map to the Luftwaffe pilots. The bombers were met with anti-aircraft guns defending the capital, and the noise was ferocious. Charles Ritchie wrote:

> Dined at the Dorchester Hotel which is like a luxury liner on which the remnants of London Society have embarked in the midst of this storm. Through the thick walls and above the music of the band one could hear the noise of the barrage and at intervals the building shook like a vibrating ship with the shock of an exploding bomb falling nearby.

After virtually sleepless nights Londoners would emerge to assess the latest devastation. Mrs Greville, Sibyl Colefax and Emerald Cunard continued entertaining their guests on the upper floors of the Dorchester, studiously ignoring the crump of bombs and artillery fire outside. Many floors below, down in the basement a sixteen-year-old trainee chef was preparing their meals. Clement Freud was the grandson of Sigmund Freud, the pioneer of psychoanalysis, and in 1940 he started working in the Dorchester kitchens, peeling vegetables. Freud and some fellow workers rented a vacant eighteenth-century house in nearby Charles Street, where Mrs Greville had her grand house. It was a calculated risk, because their house was wooden-framed, and a risky place to be during air raids.

The kitchen staff were inventive in making up for the paucity of their wages; Freud paid his rent by smuggling out two cooked chickens a week for consumption by his flat-mates. By 1941 he had been promoted to be a waiter, and due to the paper shortage, the New Year's Eve dinner menu was patriotically printed on a single tiny piece of card, shared between each table of ten diners. The champagne flowed, the lights were dim; Lew Stone's famous band lifted the atmosphere. Freud served his table with the turtle soup, then the fillets of sole *bonne femme*, but he omitted the inter-vening course. At midnight, while the revellers sang 'Auld Lang Syne', Freud retired to a storeroom with ten portions of Beluga caviar, a freshly baked baguette and a bottle of Dom Pérignon. Almost sixty years later he fondly remem-bered the occasion as the best New Year's Eve meal he had ever consumed.

Nancy Astor had believed that conflict with Germany was avoidable until the eleventh hour, but once it was declared she and Waldorf threw their considerable energies into the war effort. She had been ridiculed by one fellow MP as 'The Member for Berlin'; now the couple focused on her constitu-ency of Plymouth, a vital port for the British war effort. In 1939 the Astors became mayor and mayoress, devoting them-selves to helping the inhabitants of the city throughout the long and dangerous years of bombardment and attack. Based at their combined home and constituency office at Elliott Terrace, they worked together organising the relief effort following terrible bombing. Nancy provided practical help and raised morale. 'I stuck to Plymouth. Plymouth stuck to me,' she said in later years.

Nancy divided her time between her constituency, Cliveden and the House of Commons. At the age of sixty-one she acquired a motorbike and learned to ride it to cover the miles between Cliveden and London quickly and independently. She had developed a taste for motorcycling, having ridden pillion with T. E. Lawrence on the Brough machine that led to his death. She was a fast, impatient and reckless rider, so it was some relief to her family when she started to spend more time in Plymouth, which she travelled to by sleeper train or chauffeur-driven car.

Most of the house at Cliveden was mothballed, and precious items from the London house, such as tapestries, art and furniture, were stored there in anticipation of bombing raids on the capital. Some of the staff left to join up, and the grounds were turned over to the production of vegetables. Mr Lee, a housekeeper and a few dailies kept Cliveden ticking over, and the chef used the garden produce, but it became difficult to entertain on any scale as the war progressed. In addition, the Red Cross hospital for Canadian wounded soldiers was reopened, and evacuees from London were housed all over the estate. The four Astor sons served in the armed forces. Nancy's first son, Bobbie Shaw, served in a barrage balloon unit, being unfit for active service because of his medical history.

Nancy was indefatigable after the fall of Dunkirk, touring the Plymouth hospitals, raising the morale of the exhausted soldiers who had been brought back. She also contacted her dear friend Philip Kerr, Lord Lothian, now British Ambassador to Washington, offering to help persuade the Americans of the threat to Britain from Germany. He returned to Britain briefly in October 1940, and stayed at Cliveden; but within two months she received the devastating news that he was dead. He had died of kidney failure, having refused medical treatment that might have saved him because of his Christian Scientist beliefs. Nancy was devastated at the loss of her great friend and ally. She hoped that Waldorf might be appointed British Ambassador to Washington in his place, but Winston Churchill dismissed the idea. Nancy's pro-appeasement stance in the past and her abrasive personality made her unsuitable for such a sensitive diplomatic role as the ambassador's wife, just as Britain was fighting for its very survival and was desperate for American assistance.

The Astors' London house in St James's Square was damaged in October 1940 by incendiary bombs. It was larger than they needed as a family home, so they turned it over to the Free French forces to use as their HQ. The family retreated to a small self-contained flat at the back of the house, with a front door giving onto Babmaes Street, a cul-de-sac where streetwalkers plied their trade. One night Nancy spotted a young, drunk American serviceman lying on the pavement. She helped him to his feet and told him he was coming home with her. 'Oh no I'm not, my mother warned me about women like you!' he protested, misunderstanding her intentions. Nevertheless she managed to get him into the flat, and he was allowed to sleep it off. The next morning he was given a lecture on the evils of alcohol and a £5 note, and shown the door. Nancy took a particular delight in showing drunks the errors of their ways.

The Astors sat out the Blitz in reduced circumstances, but, like many London households, they were suddenly overrun by rats ejected from their regular habitats by the bombing. The rodents invaded St James's Square and the adjacent flat in Babmaes Street, getting under the floorboards, infesting the gutters, scouring the dustbins. Largely nocturnal, they made a racket throughout the small hours. It was all very different from life before the war.

The Blitz in Plymouth was terrifying. The city was a vital strategic naval port and was ruthlessly targeted by the Luftwaffe. On the night of 20 March 1941 a massive air raid devastated the city. Earlier that day Nancy and Waldorf had hosted a visit by the King and Queen. The royal party's train left the station as the air-raid sirens sounded, and two hours later German bombers dropped thousands of incendiaries onto the city. They hit the maternity ward of the hospital, the commercial sector, department stores, boarding houses, churches, pubs, warehouses, factories and houses, and fires raged all over the city. Nancy had a narrow escape – she had been standing in the open in Elliott Street watching the aircraft when she was ordered to take cover by an air-raid warden. No sooner had she stepped inside her hall and closed the front door than a bomb landed outside the house, blowing in the windows. With her household she took refuge in the basement, where Rose picked fragments of glass out of her hair.

The Queen sent a heartfelt telegram to Nancy, anxiously asking what had become of the places and people the royal couple had visited just hours before the first raid. 'Oh, curse the Germans', she wrote. Nancy delivered an impassioned radio broadcast to the States, describing the devastation delivered by Hitler's New Order. She also addressed the shell-shocked inhabitants of her adopted city: 'Today Plymouth knows the meaning of total war. Mercifully we have suffered only half of what Hitler's other victims have suffered. At least we have not been driven out of our country. Our sailors, soldiers and airmen will see that we never are.'

Plymouth was targeted the following night, and again intermittently for months. As in many wartime cities, life for the inhabitants was grim, with unpredictable raids, power cuts, odd explosions, damaged sewerage systems and burned-out streets full of rubble, under which were dead bodies. Communications during wartime were often fractured and difficult. The Astors alleviated the situation by organising temporary housing, clothing and food distribution, and setting up canteens. They also sent impassioned letters to *The Times*, pleading for help in dealing with the devastation caused by the bombing.

As well as offering their practical and organisational skills, the Astors attempted to boost the morale of the battered populace of Plymouth. Nancy would cajole and encourage, and had a talent to amuse small children. Despite her age of sixty-two, she would even turn cartwheels, to the astonishment of onlookers. By contrast, Waldorf was a quiet, thoughtful tactician; to provide entertainment and as a relief from stress he arranged for military bands to play on Plymouth Hoe in the afternoons and early evenings, so that the citizens could dance. Day after day, hundreds people of all ages and backgrounds waltzed or foxtrotted in the open air, with a view over the English Channel, their worries temporarily suspended.

Winston and Clementine Churchill visited Plymouth in May 1941 to inspect the damage. A photograph of the time reflects the tension between Nancy and her former

Parliamentary sparring partner, now the nation's personification of hope for victory. Picking their way through mountains of rubble, Winston and Clemmie were resoundingly cheered by the citizens of Plymouth, and tears ran down the Prime Minister's face. Nancy, wearing a fur coat and a fixed smile, followed in their wake.

Waldorf was now in his sixties, and his health was poor. He had a suspected stroke, brought on by a fierce row with Nancy, who insisted he give her some American sweets that were intended for the children of the city. He refused, and she threw a fearful tantrum in front of their lunch guests. He became ill, his breathing was erratic and his colour high, alarming symptoms in a man with a heart condition. Waldorf spent six weeks recuperating in Cornwall without Nancy, and this was the beginning of a growing estrangement between them. Nancy was irritated by his incapacity, her conviction in the precepts of Christian Science leading her to believe that with enough faith he could overcome any ailment. In August 1941 she reluctantly accompanied him to their house on the island of Jura. Travel was immensely difficult during wartime, and 10 days of enforced relaxation on a Scottish island with her ailing husband was now Nancy's idea of hell.

While Nancy barely tolerated her afflicted but adoring husband, Emerald Cunard's relationship with her fickle lover of three decades finally foundered. When war broke out in 1939, Emerald Cunard was in Mexico selling some silver mines that had been left to her by her mother decades before; she was gradually liquidating all her assets to support her lifestyle. She was still out of favour with the royal family – it was exactly three years since the abdication, but in a letter to Prince Paul of Yugoslavia in December 1939, Queen Elizabeth wondered whether von Ribbentrop's erroneous impression of the British spirit had been Lady Cunard's fault.

Emerald was keen to escape London, and in January 1940 she closed up her exquisite house in Grosvenor Square, sold many of her belongings, leaving others in storage, and moved into a suite at the Ritz. She helped to organise the Sunday Club for Officers in the ballroom at the Dorchester, offering young officers tea and sandwiches, and a chance to dance with well-bred young ladies. Later that year came a welcome opportunity to travel. Sir Thomas Beecham had long-standing conducting commitments in America. Emerald was at a loose end, and she could afford to travel with him. She still resented his relationship with Dora Labbette, and their young son Paul, but this was a chance to get him to herself.

In the autumn of 1940 Emerald and Sir Thomas moved into a suite in the Ritz-Carlton Hotel in New York. He was sixty-one and she was sixty-eight; they had been involved for three decades, though Sir Thomas later insisted that for they had been 'just friends' for ten years, and Lady Cunard believed that he was impotent, an implausible story as his son, Paul, had been born in 1933. Together they set out in mid-December for a leisurely rail journey to St Louis, where he conducted two concerts, before spending Christmas in Tucson, Arizona. In Los Angeles they took tea with the Woolworth heiress Barbara Hutton, and dined with the film star Gary Cooper. Emerald was determined to keep Beecham amused and away from Dora and Paul, back in war-torn London, through the winter of 1940 to 1941. What she could not foresee was that her serially unfaithful lover would fall in love yet again – but this time in America.

Beecham first met the gifted British pianist Betty Humby in London in 1938. She was unhappily married to a London vicar, and she went to America in May 1940 with her young son Jeremy, in order to obtain a divorce. In 1941 she joined Sir Thomas's musical entourage, and their friendship developed. Emerald began to hear hints about the conductor and his pianist, both away on tour. She tackled Sir Thomas, but he laughingly dismissed her concerns, saying that Betty was 'descended from a long line of dentists', implying such mundane origins barred her from consorting with a grandee like himself.

On 9 February 1942 Sir Thomas and his musicians left Emerald in New York for a conducting engagement in Seattle. The same day, the gossip columnist Maury Paul, whose pen name was Cholly Knickerbocker, published a story that was automatically syndicated to the sixty Hearst-owned papers throughout the United States:

> Excitement is i-n-t-e-n-s-e over the manner in which comely Betty Humby, a young and very talented English pianist, reportedly has injected herself, and a bit of a crescendo, into the never-too-tantalizing Cunard-Beecham symphony. That Sir Thomas appreciates Betty – musically – is borne out by his statement that she can 'play Beethoven better than I can direct it.' […] naturally, all this has sent 'Dear Emerald's' blood pressure up like Vesuvius in an angry mood.

Sir Thomas was cornered by a clutch of reporters on the train shortly before he arrived at his destination. He would not be drawn, saying 'My dear fellow, there are two ladies' names mentioned here. It's a private matter. It's not the sort of thing the people of Seattle are interested in.' However, they were very interested, and not only in Seattle. While Emerald fumed in her New York hotel, Beecham conducted Betty's performance at Carnegie Hall. Beecham returned with her to Sun Valley, Idaho, and Betty's divorce was granted on 3 July 1942. Utica, Sir Thomas's wife of nearly forty years, still refused to divorce him through the British courts; this time Beecham sought a legal solution in America.

Emerald remained in New York throughout the autumn of 1942, hoping that her lover's latest romance would founder. While she was staying with Mona Harrison Williams, the wife of a Wall Street financier, her hostess invited some friends for lunch. One of them, an English film actress, Leonora Corbett, blithely mentioned that she had just received a letter from an old schoolfriend, Betty Humby, containing the startling news that Betty was about to marry Sir Thomas Beecham, the famous conductor. Emerald struggled through lunch, but confided to her hostess afterwards that she wanted to die.

Emerald booked the first available ticket back to Europe, sailing from Baltimore to Lisbon on a Portuguese ship, the *Serpa Pinto*. It was hazardous to cross the Atlantic, even in a supposedly neutral ship, and they picked up survivors from another vessel, which had been torpedoed by a German U-boat. After a tense three-week delay in Lisbon, Emerald flew back to London. Her close friends were aware of her humiliation, despite her resolute determination to pretend that all was well. Chips Channon wrote: 'Emerald was gay, exquisite, full of life and fun and we sat enthralled for three hours [...] She kissed me affectionately goodnight, and I admired her courage, for I know her heart is broken over Thomas Beecham's desertion. She loved him for 34 years.'

In December 1942 Sir Thomas finally divorced the wife he

had wed in 1903, and he married Betty Humby in January 1943 in New York. Betty was twenty-nine years younger than him. Emerald, six years older than him, was broken-hearted by his betrayal after more than three decades of devotion. Dora Labbette was also stricken by Beecham's desertion. She first heard of his marriage through a notification from his lawyer in London. Making a huge bonfire in the garden of everything that reminded her of Sir Thomas, Dora put a match to it.

Back in London, Emerald moved into a compact seventh-floor suite at the Dorchester. Her new home comprised a sitting room with a small dining table, eight dining chairs, a bedroom, maid's room and bathroom. She stuffed the suite with oversized buhl cabinets, looming ormolu furniture, marble statues and fine porcelain from her former London home, creating an obstacle course for the staff. With great determination Emerald returned to what she knew best, surrounding herself with chatter and glitter, and intimate little dinner parties with creative tyros, such as Ernest Hemingway, Cecil Beaton and Isaiah Berlin.

A lifelong insomniac, she now re-read Balzac novels through her sleepless nights as bombs fell on London, telephoning her patient friends in the small hours to discuss plot details or fictional characters' motivations. Her devoted maid Mary Gordon asked her if it was wise to telephone a friend so late; Emerald replied, 'At two o'clock? Do you think he goes to roost with the chickens?'

The menace of war had depressed demand for Colefax & Fowler's decorating services, and in 1938–9 Sibyl's income from the company dropped to £500. When hostilities started, Sibyl threw her considerable energies into running a Women's Voluntary Service canteen in Belgravia while her business partner John Fowler, who was exempt from military service because of his poor health and myopia, enlisted as a fire warden in Chelsea and drove ambulances. Colefax & Fowler's premises remained at Bruton Street, run by assistants, and Sibyl and John worked there whenever their other duties allowed. As the war progressed, the strict rationing of materials and a shortage of skilled craftspeople were a handicap. Nevertheless, Sibyl and John used their considerable ingenuity; army blankets were dyed, cut into strips and re-stitched to make striped curtains. Surplus silk parachutes became voile drapes, and pyjama fabrics, calicos, bookbinding linens and striped cotton nurses' uniforms served as furnishing fabrics. The firm's customers resourcefully plundered their own stocks to supply old bedspreads, sheets and tablecloths which were dyed and turned into slip-covers. John Fowler even converted one client's discarded frock into cushion covers for her sitting room.

Sibyl's wartime mania for socialising led Noel Coward to remark that she hadn't been known to finish a sentence since September 1939. She clung on in Queen Anne's Gate, but rationing drove her to organising 'ordinaries', dinner parties held at the Dorchester on Thursdays, after which each participant would receive a discreet bill for their share of the meal and beverages. Over the course of the war, the cost gradually rose from 10 to 15 shillings a head, and wine and sherry became scarce, but the 'ordinaries' were a great success because of Sibyl's unerring ability to attract the most interesting people to her table. She was so well informed that in May 1940 she told Harold Nicolson that Churchill was about to appoint him as Parliamentary Secretary to Duff Cooper, Minister for Information; Harold was amazed, but Sibyl was correct.

Invitations to her social events were now even more illegible; Noel Coward joked that the war censors were compelling Lady Colefax to use a typewriter. When Churchill became Prime Minister in May 1940, Lord Berners played yet another subtle but savage trick on poor Sibyl. He sent her a hand-written note:

> *Dear Sibyl,*
>
> *I wonder if by any chance you are free to dine tomorrow night? It is only a tiny party for Winston and GBS. I think it important they should get together at this moment. There will be nobody else except for Toscanini and myself. Do please try and forgive this terribly short notice. Yours ever,*
>
> *Eight o'clock here and – of course – any old clothes.*

This was the perfect bait for Sibyl – an intimate little supper with Churchill, Shaw and Toscanini – but who was the host, and where was the party? The signature was illegible, the address looked like Berkeley Square, or maybe Belgrave Square, but the house number was a Gordian knot of digits. Sibyl rang everyone she knew in increasing desperation, as the hours ticked by, determined to grasp the glittering prize that remained tantalisingly out of reach.

Gerald Berners also satirised Sibyl in a light comedy called *The Furies*, which was staged in the summer of 1942 in Oxford. It features a female character called Adelaide Pyrex, a socially ambitious woman who claims 'houses are my passion' and who cannot refrain from suggesting improvements to the homes of others. Adelaide Pyrex bears a marked resemblance to interior decorator Sybil Colefax. Not everyone was so heartless; Sibyl's finances were in a dire state, and on 8 March 1943 there was a well-attended benefit evening held for her at the Dorchester, with a pianist and a quartet. Perhaps surprisingly, it was Lady Cunard who organised the evening to raise funds for her former rival.

The most formidable of the great hostesses, Margaret Greville, finally passed away at the Dorchester in September 1942. Now in her late seventies, she had been in increasingly poor health, partially losing her eyesight and confined to a wheelchair, claiming that she had 'everything wrong with her except leprosy'. Although she was regarded by some as an 'Edwardian period piece', she socialised with the great and the good till the very end.

She was on devilish form for one dinner party in her suite; as the bombs fell outside and sirens wailed, the great hostess was ablaze with the Greville emeralds because, she claimed, if one was going to be blown up, one should go out in style. As the food was served, she challenged her guests to guess the special ingredient in the savoury mousse they were eating. 'Rabbit!' she hissed, and gave a long, appraising glance at the wife of the Chilean ambassador, who was wearing a modest fur cape that definitely was not mink.

Charles Ritchie, the Canadian diplomat, left a vivid account of her in her final months:

Dined with the Masseys off salmon-trout and asparagus.
Mrs Ronnie Greville was there – sitting in a bath-chair

with her feet dangling onto a footstool, her small hand covered in diamonds, and with her painted face – she looked like a monstrous baby – something in *grand guignol*. This was also the impression given by her only having one eye – the other is dead and blind – and that one raked the table round – illuminated by intelligent malice. The conversation was on a royal plane during a great deal of dinner, highly aristocratic tit-bits of scandal (Lady Y who has run away with the groom. Lord X who had eloped with his stepmother.) [...] the old girl is kept alive by her sleepless snobbery, her still unquenchable zest for the great world. She is a Lowland Scot, and the Lowland Scot from Boswell on is the most insatiable animal on earth when it comes to worldly glitter and bustle. I should know – I am one.

Despite her disabilities, Mrs Greville was still scheming to the end. She informed Victor Cazalet MP that the King and Queen felt that Winston Churchill was hogging the limelight by delivering stirring messages to the populace that should come from the King. On 28 June 1942 she insisted to the Canadian High Commissioner that Prime Minister Churchill should go. 'I have known him for fifty years and he has never been right yet.' She was still close to the royal family, and made the lengthy and uncomfortable journey to Scotland, joining the King and Queen for afternoon tea at Balmoral on Sunday 16 August 1942. Alan Lascelles, who pushed her wheelchair, noted in his diary that Mrs Greville 'has been a constant mischief-maker for twenty-five years, but I don't think she will make much more now'. Queen Elizabeth was taken aback by her old friend's appearance. She wrote to Osbert Sitwell on 13 September 1942: 'it was too pathetic to

see this little bundle of unquenchable courage and determination, quite helpless except for one bright eye. I had not seen
her for a couple of months, and was very shocked and sad
at the change. But with all her weakness there was just the
same tenacity of purpose, and I felt full of admiration for
such a wonderful exhibition of "never give in".'

On 25 August 1942 the Duke of Kent, younger brother of
the King, was killed in a plane crash in Scotland while on
active service. He had been a friend of Laura Corrigan, Mrs
Greville and Lady Astor, and he visited Plymouth with the
Astors just two days before his death. Noel Coward, who had
known him for nineteen years, his brother King George VI
and his cousin Dickie Mountbatten wept inconsolably at the
funeral at St George's Chapel, Windsor. One can only imagine
the thoughts of widowed Queen Mary; she had lost one son,
John, who died in adolescence; her eldest, David, was estranged
from her by the abdication; and now Prince George had been
killed as the result of a ferocious war between her country of
origin and the nation where she was Queen.

The Duke of Kent's death and the arduous journey back
from Scotland may have exacerbated Mrs Greville's final
illness. Back at the Dorchester she took to her bed, and her
devoted maid Adeline Liron and butler Bole cared for her as
her vitality ebbed away. Old friends visited; Beverley Nichols
recorded that her final words to him were: 'That damned
Ribbentrop. Thank God I told him what I thought of him
when he came to Polesden [...] I told him that if ever there
was a war, he might beat the English, but he would never
beat the Scots.'

Osbert Sitwell wrote a moving account of her final hours
in a letter to Queen Elizabeth. He described how Mrs Ronnie
had stopped eating, and had told him that she was in pain

and wished to die. Then she had a cerebral thrombosis, which left her in a coma. Osbert stayed with her, but she did not regain consciousness. Osbert attended the doctors' conference on Monday evening, but there was nothing more they could do. Mrs Greville died peacefully at 2 a.m. on 15 September 1942, with the faithful Bole at her bedside.

Till the very end she managed to deceive; her own doctor, Alexander McCall, signed her death certificate giving her age as seventy-five, but in fact she was three months short of her seventy-ninth birthday. However, one important truth did emerge immediately; the Londoner's Diary gossip column in the *Evening Standard* for 15 September, the day of her death, stated baldly that 'Her fortune came to her from her father, William McEwan', confirming in print what many had long suspected.

Following her funeral at Polesden Lacey and a memorial service in London, which was packed with ambassadors, the participants gossiped about her life and legacy in a way that would have delighted her. But Mrs Ronnie had one more card to play. In a lifetime packed with manipulation and duplicity her most daring ploy had been her offer to bequeath her property and a substantial fortune to Prince Albert. Between 1914 and 1942 she enjoyed twenty-eight years of ample hospitality from the royal family. She could not have foreseen that her protégé and his Scottish wife would become King and Queen in 1936; nevertheless at some point she changed her will, deciding instead to leave the bulk of her estate to the National Trust in memory of her father. Crucially, she did not tell the royal family about her change of heart; Queen Elizabeth found out during a visit from Gerald Russell, Mrs Greville's solicitor, a few weeks after her death, and wrote to her husband, the King, with the disappointing news.

However, there was a consolation prize; a small black tin trunk, which contained some sixty pieces of the most spectacular jewellery in existence. 'With my loving thoughts', Mrs Greville left the Queen her diamond and platinum Boucheron tiara, the five-strand diamond necklace that had once belonged to Marie Antoinette, the Empress Josephine's emeralds and a diamond ring that had belonged to Catherine the Great. The provenance of these jewels, their ownership by historic women of international influence, mattered to Mrs Greville; now they were the property of Queen Elizabeth, the daughter she never had.

Laura Mae Corrigan's war record amazed those who had previously sniggered at her malapropisms and misunderstandings. She had been based in Paris since 1938, retaining the Ritz Hotel's Imperial Suite. It occupied a large section of the first floor, and was furnished with Laura's exquisite tapestries and Louis Quinze furniture. On occasions she obligingly moved out to allow VIPs to stay there instead, such as Winston Churchill in the spring of 1940, before the fall of France. With the onset of war she used her fortune and her contacts to organise a charity, the Bienvenue au Soldat, a relief effort that sent packages of essentials to wounded soldiers and civilians and supplied hospitals. Although she was a civilian, Laura Mae Corrigan adopted a uniform, a rather chic one of her own devising, which gave her a certain undefinable authority in Paris.

Occupied Paris was a tense city, but Mrs Corrigan, as an American national, was a neutral, and a phenomenally wealthy one. When the German High Command requested the Imperial Suite for the use of Reichsmarschall Hermann Goering, head of the German Air Force, Mrs Corrigan helpfully moved into a less palatial suite, but stayed on at the Ritz, rightly seeing it as the nexus of power. The high-ranking Nazi officers who took over the hotel approved of the pleasant, middle-aged American widow in couture fashions and assorted wigs. She had positive pro-Nazi credentials: she had known von Ribbentrop, now Hitler's Foreign Minister, when he was German Ambassador in London, and was an acquaintance of the Duke of Windsor, who was fondly believed to be pro-German.

The American Ambassador had advised all US nationals to leave France before the inevitable German takeover, but there were some who resolved to stay, among them the interior designer Elsie de Wolfe. However, unwelcome news reached Laura Corrigan. She had invested her husband's fortune wisely, and her annual income in 1940 was $800,000, worth about $12 million nowadays. Now that France had fallen to the Nazis, the American government was anxious to prevent the Germans sequestering vast fortunes and using them for their own ends. Consequently Laura was informed by the US State Department that her American assets were frozen while she remained in France and her income would be restricted to just $500 a month.

With her cash supply effectively cut off, Laura reviewed her options. If she tried to leave France, her magnificent possessions might well be confiscated. It dawned on her that perhaps the best course of action was to stay, and to use her belongings as bargaining chips. She planned to sell her luxury possessions clandestinely to finance her activities in support of the war effort.

For ten weeks workmen had laboured to transform the

Imperial Suite. Goering required a vast bathtub; lengthy wallows in the tub were part of his ongoing treatment for morphine addiction, as immersion in hot water for hours helped minimise the withdrawal symptoms while doctors administered injections of methadone. Goering's compulsive acquisitiveness was legendary; he collected art, antiques and jewellery. His great girth and time-consuming therapy meant he was delighted to acquire more without having to leave the Imperial Suite. But it was a dangerous game to play: the Nazis were now the law enforcers in Paris, and if Laura showed her complete hand, Goering might order all her assets seized, and she might find herself interned on some trumped-up charge.

First, she hid her magnificent fur collection; the Ritz Hotel had a number of discreet built-in cupboards and she secreted her sables and minks in one of these, then arranged for a massive armoire to be placed in front of the cupboard. Her furs lay safe and undiscovered throughout the war. Then she sought a meeting with Goering. He was as wealthy as Croesus, mercurial and capable of acts of great violence; he was also obsessed by gems and jewellery, and was rumoured to keep a bowl full of precious and semi-precious stones next to his bed. Taking a calculated risk, Laura first offered him an emerald ring; perhaps surprisingly, he paid her £50,000 for it. She then sold him a gold dressing case, which he sent to Hitler. He also paid handsomely for Laura's magnificent Renaissance tapestries and her antique French furniture, as well as a number of her gem-studded bracelets which he wore under his uniforms, according to Elsa Maxwell.

Superficially, it seemed as though she was actively collaborating with the Nazis, but in the autumn of 1941 she sold all her belongings except for two dresses and a small selection of clothes, two wedding rings, a wristwatch and a string of pearls. Laura gathered up her cash and her remaining portable belongings and headed for Vichy, the spa town that was the headquarters of the collaborationist French government, and consequently a nest of spies, Germans, French Resistance operatives and displaced expatriates. Laura took a room in a modest hotel and used her cash to continue funding her charity for war wounded. She also assisted Americans who were trapped in France because they lacked the funds to arrange safe passage out of the country, and she acquired the nickname of 'The Dollar Queen' among those she helped. She used her neutral status to flit between occupied and free France, assisting French soldiers, the Resistance and civilians, a dangerous business.

Following the Japanese attack on Pearl Harbor in December 1941, Hitler followed suit by declaring war on the United States. Now that Americans were considered enemy aliens in German-occupied Europe, the attitude towards them changed. About a hundred American women were interned by ·the Germans at a camp at Vittel, which was crowded and uncomfortable. Laura Corrigan arranged for packages containing warm clothing, soap, cigarettes, toiletries and food to be sent in to them. Eventually even she ran out of money; on 5 October 1942 *Time* magazine reported:

> Laura Mae Corrigan, 60, [sic – she was nearly 64] wealthy expatriate who became known as 'the American Angel' for her war relief in France, finally had to abandon her work for lack of funds. A Cleveland steelmaker's widow who had been one of London's most spectacular hostesses for more than two decades, she plunged into the job of helping feed, clothe, doctor and amuse soldiers and war

prisoners in France three years ago, sent aid to thousands of men in French prisons and camps, took to selling her jewels and clothing when her money began to run out. Last week she had sold the last of her jewels, the last of her furs, [and] prepared to return to London.

She escaped through neutral Portugal, and once back in Britain, Mrs Corrigan took a suite at Claridge's and threw a party on Christmas Eve 1942; one of her guests was her fellow society hostess Emerald Cunard. In March 1943 Mrs Corrigan was presented to King George VI at a glittering reception held by the Overseas League, a reflection of her valuable war work. She continued to help wounded soldiers for the duration of hostilities, and leased 11 Grosvenor Place to create a club for young Allied Air Force officers. The house belonged to Lord Moyne, director of his family's brewing firm, Guinness, and Leader of the House of Lords. The Wings Club opened in August 1943; her old friends were happy to lend their names to this venture, with the ubiquitous 'Chips' Channon serving on the club committee and the widowed Princess Marina, Duchess of Kent, as chief patroness. It seems as though Laura's wartime activities impressed many when they came to light; during a row about who was *parvenu* and who inherently bourgeois, 'Chips' Channon stoutly defended Mrs Corrigan to Emerald Cunard, saying that Laura was in the best society, and that anyone in Paris who was not received by her was 'beneath consideration'.

For her war efforts she was given the Légion d'Honneur by Marshal Pétain, and the Croix du Combattant, which is rarely awarded to women because it is only given for acts of bravery in the front lines. She also received the King's Medal from George VI. Elsa Maxwell said of Laura, 'she was honest, she had vitality, and she had a heart as big as a bank'. Nevertheless, she remained the butt of jokes to war-hardened Londoners; V2 rockets were known colloquially as buzz-bombs, but Laura blithely referred to them as 'bugger bombs'. In addition, Evelyn Waugh wrote to Nancy Mitford alleging that the newly liberated French had suspected Mrs Corrigan of collaboration and attempted to shave her head as a punishment, but received a rude shock.

As soon as possible after the city was liberated, Laura Corrigan returned to Paris and her old haunts; in September 1944 Duff Cooper, who had just been appointed British Ambassador to France, spotted her occupying her favourite corner of the restaurant at the Ritz Hotel, exactly as she had in the late 1930s. As before, she divided her time between her two favourite capitals. Noel Coward spotted her in London on New Year's Eve 1944 at Loelia Westminster's party: 'Everyone was there, from Laura Corrigan to Laura Corrigan.'

Nancy Astor was delighted when the country of her birth came to the aid of her adopted homeland in December 1941, following the Japanese attack on Pearl Harbor. She had known Franklin D. Roosevelt since 1918, and had successfully lobbied him to send warships to Plymouth to augment the Royal Navy's campaign before America formally entered the war. Nancy made every effort to ensure the American servicemen arriving in Britain were made welcome.

Her dedication to serving the people of Plymouth was remarkable, but as the war ground on, her abrasive nature affected her personal relationships. Her long-standing lack of reverence for Churchill was well known; on one occasion years before the war Nancy had yelled, 'If I were your wife I would put poison in your coffee!' Winston replied, 'And if I were your husband I would drink it.' More recently she had speculated aloud about what disguise might suit him for a masquerade ball. 'Why don't you come sober, Prime Minister?' Just two weeks after the Churchills visited Plymouth, her critical remarks in Parliament about 'doddering old politicians in all parties who ought to have been buried long ago', actually aimed at Herbert Morrison, the Minister for Home Security, were taken to include Churchill.

To compound her offences, in August 1942 Nancy publicly questioned the Soviet Union's volte-face to support the Allies against Germany, counter to the previous Nazi–Soviet Pact. While most British politicians were welcoming Uncle Joe's change of heart, Nancy (who, unlike them, had met and locked antlers with Stalin in 1931) stated: 'I am grateful to the Russians, but they are not fighting for us. They are fighting for themselves [...] the Russians were allies of Germany. It is only now that they are facing German invasion that they have come into the fight.'

Churchill privately agreed with her logic, but being right does not always make one popular. Nancy's constant, audible commentary on her fellow MPs as they spoke in the House had long irritated many, but now she seriously misjudged the urgent, staccato national mood. In a Parliamentary debate on 18 March 1943 Nancy spoke in favour of women being employed in the Diplomatic Service, but drifted into condemning the historic immorality of France and attempted to blame all the ills of the current world on men, which was not well received by a House of Commons at the height of the struggle for the nation's survival.

Meanwhile Waldorf's health was deteriorating, and he spent more time at Cliveden, where he was involved in the hospital and its 250 patients. He was worried about the future of Cliveden. When the Astors' great friend Philip Kerr, Lord Lothian, had died in 1940, he had left Blickling Hall, his seventeenth-century stately home in Norfolk, and its contents to the National Trust under the innovative Country House scheme, which he had devised. In 1942 Waldorf decided on a similar plan to conserve Cliveden, leaving the house, contents, estate and an endowment to the National Trust. The mansion and grounds were to be opened to the public on designated days, an arrangement that would have infuriated his father, 'Walled-off' Astor. It was agreed that the Astor family should stay in occupation as long as they wanted to remain.

Their London house, 4 St James's Square, became progressively more damaged by bombs until it was almost uninhabitable and was requisitioned for use as a services canteen. The four Astor boys served in the armed forces, and Major Jacob Astor was awarded both the Légion d'Honneur and the Croix de Guerre. In 1944 'Jakie' married the daughter of the Argentinian Ambassador. Nancy was horrified that he was marrying a Catholic, and this led to a *froideur* with her favourite son. When she suggested that her sons should come to Cliveden for a family weekend without their wives, they all refused.

By 1944 Nancy's family were convinced that her political career had to end. She was now sixty-five years old, and her reputation was still compromised by her association with the appeasement movement. Her behaviour in Parliament, always unorthodox, had recently become quite erratic. In addition, the political mood in the country was changing; the electorate were turning against the patrician classes who had led them before the war, and Socialism was on the rise. Waldorf was convinced that Nancy would not be returned at the next General Election, and therefore she should resign in advance. Bravely, he persuaded her to announce her forthcoming retirement; she agreed, but was outraged. Typically, Nancy chose a party at Grosvenor House on 1 December 1944, held to celebrate the twenty-fifth anniversary of the entry of women into Parliament, to announce that she was retiring at the next General Election.

Sadly, agreeing to leave public life led to a bitter estrangement between Nancy and Waldorf. He was patient with her, but she was furious at being asked to give up her political career. When the war ended, she mourned the closure of the most exciting, productive and worthwhile era of her life. She said, 'Only I and Mr Churchill enjoy the war, but only I admit it.'

The Londonderrys were also still tainted by their attempts to appease the Germans before the war, but they both made sterling efforts to defeat the enemy once war was inevitable. Edith had written in 1938 of the duties that she felt incumbent on her because of her social position:

> There is still [...] an Upper Class, its ranks diminished and impoverished by the war, who still wield a certain influence behind the scenes, and, in times of crisis, their presence will still be felt, something solid and very British, and, above all, they are people who were born and bred to the old tradition – that possessions carry duties with them, before pleasure.

Lady Londonderry divided her time between Mount Stewart in Northern Ireland and Londonderry House. She was President of the County Down and Durham branches of the Red Cross, and was greatly involved in the war work of the Women's Legion, training non-combatants to produce their own food on allotments, and she helped organise the Woman's Legion, once again supplying women to vital war work such as delivering planes and running mobile canteens.

She piled mattresses in the basement of Londonderry House and offered shelter to anyone caught by the Blitz. However, Londonderry House was damaged by successive bombing raids over London; by the middle of September 1940 Irene Curzon, sister-in-law of Oswald Mosley and friend of Nancy Astor, noticed that many of its windows had been smashed. The Londonderrys were also struck by the accumulation of financial worries; by 1939 Lord Londonderry's annual expenditure exceeded his income by £106,000.

Because of his prominent position as a figurehead in Northern Ireland and his extensive air experience, Lord Londonderry was appointed as the Regional Commandant of Northern Ireland's Air Training Corps. At the end of 1940 Charley Londonderry tried to persuade Winston Churchill to give him a ministerial job in Whitehall, or in Northern Ireland, but his cousin declined; just before the war, over dinner at Emerald Cunard's, they had rowed over the likely response of France in the event of a German invasion. It was a supreme irony that during Lord Londonderry's four years at the Air Ministry he had been far-sighted enough to authorise the development of the first all-metal monoplane fighter aircraft, which led to the Hurricane and the Spitfire, even though Prime Minister Ramsay MacDonald had been reluctant to fund the initiative to rearm the Air Force on the grounds of cost. As the RAF fought the Luftwaffe through the skies over the Home Counties during the summer of 1940, few were aware that the British planes so vital to the country's survival had been brought into being by a career politician who had once described Hitler as 'kindly'.

The Londonderrys were struck by personal tragedies: their eldest daughter Maureen, who had married Oliver Stanley, Minister for War, died of TB on 20 June 1942, and the controversial marriage of another daughter, Margaret, to Alan Muntz, which her parents had so bitterly contested, ended in divorce. While Edith kept busy with her war work in order to keep sorrow at bay, Charley was under-occupied, depressed and in poor health; in 1945 he wrote to his old friend Ettie Desborough: 'the war, the crisis of our lives, finds me completely isolated and under a sort of shadow which I cannot get away from [...] I want you to know that I have no illusions about it and that I am bitterly disappointed. I had great chances and I have missed them by not being good enough and that really sums up the whole thing.'

The last years of the war were, if anything, more difficult than the first for the hostesses. In 1944 Sibyl fell in the blackout, breaking an arm and injuring her back. She was now seventy years old, and her frenetic lifestyle and intense workload had taken its toll. She decided it was time to retire from the firm of Colefax & Fowler, and she sold her share of the business to Nancy Lancaster, the American niece of Lady Astor. Mrs Lancaster was a beauty, well connected, an ardent enthusiast for British country house life and a decorator of great flair; both Syrie Maugham and Sibyl Colefax had approached her in the past with proposals for a professional partnership, but she had demurred.

The relationship between Nancy Lancaster and John

Fowler was not always smooth – Lady Astor described them as 'the unhappiest unmarried couple in England' – but creatively it was very successful. She was a perfectionist, familiar with American standards of comfort and convenience, and Fowler designed coherent decorative schemes that distilled traditional English taste while discreetly indicating the social status of the client. Wisely Nancy Lancaster retained the name of the company, as by now it had established a reputation for quality and originality. Sibyl found it hard to let go of Colefax & Fowler, and continued to use the London premises as her office, frequently dropping in to write letters and make phone calls in pursuit of her social life. Meanwhile, her relentless namedropping and claims that she knew everyone irritated Margot Asquith, who commented that one could not even discuss the birth of Christ without Sibyl insisting that she had been there in the manger.

Forthright Margot Asquith also clashed with Emerald Cunard, who gave a candlelit dinner party in her Dorchester suite on 7 January 1944. The two women crossed swords when Margot accused her of having 'done a bunk' to avoid the bombing earlier in the war; Emerald's real reason for going to America had been to try to win back the waning affections of Sir Thomas Beecham, but she could hardly say so.

Emerald's cosy and antique-cluttered drawing room at the Dorchester now became a bolthole for many as the war dragged on. James Lees-Milne, a sensitive and perceptive Old Etonian working for the National Trust, frequently dropped in for tea or dinner, and spent part of Christmas Day 1943 alone with her. On 15 June 1944 Lady Cunard was hosting a dinner party at the hotel. It was the first night of the V2 rockets, pilotless flying bombs whose engines could cut out at any moment; they were a new form of terrorism for battle-weary Londoners. Emerald vigorously refused to believe such technological developments were possible, and told Duff Cooper, Minister for Information, that stupid people would believe anything in wartime.

Emerald loathed the war and described it as 'vulgar'; throughout fearsome air raids she resolutely ignored the sound of explosions and artillery fire outside, and any dinner guest cowardly enough to flinch over his caviar would be shot a look of scorn. While Emerald kept calm and carried on in her cluttered hotel suite, occasionally taking cover during air raids under her dining table with the telephone and a Shakespeare play, her estranged daughter Nancy was leading a rickety existence in rooms in Half Moon Street, less than a mile from the Dorchester. Nancy had arrived in Liverpool on 22 August 1941, on a ship from New York, and stayed in London for the next three and a half years, with occasional trips to France as soon as it was liberated. Mother and daughter had many London friends in common, some of whom were keen to try to mend the rift between them, but the gulf was too great, and even the Second World War could not reunite them.

As the war ground to its conclusion, the surviving Queen Bees resolutely continued their work and personal commitments in the face of various privations: food and petrol rationing, the shortage of servants, a lack of money, the demise of friends and family members, and in some cases personal betrayal, bitter disappointments and family tragedies. However, during the Second World War many in Britain were in a similar position and there was a sense of solidarity, as most were engaged either in vital war work or some other form of active service. For six years the population of Britain dedicated themselves solely to surviving and then to winning the war. In the face of bombing and the threat of invasion, the desire for occasional entertainment, recreation, mental stimulation and psychological escape had been stronger than ever, and the hostesses, now in their sixties and seventies, had acquitted themselves with honour. With the return of peace the indomitable old ladies hoped to resume some aspect of their previous lives. Five of them had survived the war; now that peace had been achieved, each of them, adaptable and resilient as they were, faced the challenge of devising new roles for themselves, and new strategies to cope with an uncertain future.

11

Peace and Austerity

___

In 1945 Britain was depleted, nearly bankrupt, and its infra-
structure had been pulverised. Most people were shabbily
dressed, thin and poorly housed. Families were sundered;
many had lost their homes, their incomes, their friends and
loved ones. People of all classes and backgrounds had taken
on enormous responsibilities, and coped with unfamiliar
threats and privations. For formerly wealthy women, fending
for themselves without servants had been a revelation.
Mistresses suddenly found themselves in the previously
unknown realms of their own basements, first sheltering from
bombardment, and then gradually getting to grips with recal-
citrant ovens, poor lighting, iron rations, mystifying cookery
books and inadequate cleaning materials. Class distinctions
had eroded, and there could be little doubt that the adjective
'pre-war' would come to have a nostalgic aura, but meanwhile
there was immense cause for celebration.

On 8 May 1945, VE Day marked the end to hostilities
in Europe; in London an exhausted but jubilant populace
flooded into Trafalgar Square, and crowds cheered MPs as
they left the House of Commons; Nancy Astor was slightly
hurt that the cheers for her were less effusive than for her
colleagues. That evening Sibyl Colefax and Ivor Novello
went to a party at 'Chips' Channon's house, which had
been damaged by bombs, but the candelight still flickered
in the exquisite Amalienburg room. Outside, London was

jubilant; searchlights had been turned on, and the city was lit up, the streets awash with people dancing and celebrating. On VJ Day, 15 August 1945, the end of the war was announced. James Lees-Milne dined at one of Sibyl's ordinaries, and hordes of people flocked to Buckingham Palace.

In the aftermath Nancy Astor was jubilant to find that her name was included in the *Sonderfahndungsliste GB*, the Germans' 'Black Book', which listed 2,820 prominent names considered the enemies of the Nazis, who were to be arrested immediately after the planned invasion of Britain in the autumn of 1940. The opponents of the Third Reich included Vera Brittain, Winston Churchill, Harold Nicolson, Virginia Woolf and Charles de Gaulle. It was a considerable source of pride to find one's name on the list; Rebecca West sent a telegram to Noel Coward, saying: 'My dear – the people we should have been seen dead with'. Nancy commented, 'It is the complete answer to the terrible lie that the so-called "Cliveden Set" was pro-Fascist.'

Nancy reluctantly stood down as an MP on 5 July 1945, at the age of sixty-six. Announcing her retirement, she remarked that the decision had been forced upon her, and that it should please the men of Britain. 'I am an extinct volcano,' she seethed. Waiting for the storm to pass, patient Waldorf went to stay with his stepson, Bobbie, and then with his own son David, but when he returned to Cliveden, Nancy decamped to their holiday house in Kent.

Waldorf persevered, and they agreed to travel together to the United States in 1946. Nancy was desperate to see her family after the long years of war, but it was difficult to get a passage. They obtained passenger tickets on a Fyffes' banana boat, the utilitarian *Eros* (a far cry from the *Queen*

Mary, the *Aquitania* and her other pre-war modes of transport). It took fourteen days to reach New York from Tilbury instead of the usual seven because of the weather. The chef had been unenthusiastic to find Nancy's name on the manifest as she was the MP who had attempted to abolish rum rations for merchant seamen, but so effective was her charm campaign that the entire crew lined up to sing 'For she's a jolly good fellow' as the Astors disembarked in New York, their first homecoming since the start of the war. They stayed in the luxurious Ritz Carlton, a world away from grey, austere and gritty Britain. Waldorf gave a lunch party at the Hotel Astor for the crew of the *Eros*, and the chef asked Rose out on a date, an evening that involved energetic dancing fuelled by rum and Coca-Cola.

The Astors toured the States, accompanied by Rose and Arthur Bushell. Nancy even rode a performing horse, hanging on with great aplomb as it reared and bucked, a feat impressive at any age, but especially for one approaching seventy. She was treated in America as an international media celebrity, but following their return to Britain, Nancy and Waldorf returned to their separate lives. Waldorf showed tenacity and forbearance in the face of all her tirades, and rarely complained.

Matters might have gone more smoothly if Nancy Astor had achieved the recognition she undoubtedly deserved after all those years as an MP, by elevation to the House of Lords. But women were barred, and it was not until 1958 that they were accepted. The first woman to take her seat in the House of Commons was denied the reward deemed suitable for so many male MPs after decades of public service. It is a savage irony that the same constitutional protocols that drove her husband, Waldorf (and, following his death, their eldest son,

William), unwillingly into the House of Lords were to curtail her pioneering career, because of her gender.

As had been the case after the Great War, there was a great pent-up desire to travel once peace was restored. Alice Keppel, the last and best-loved mistress of Edward VII, returned to her Italian home L'Ombrellino, outside Florence, after the war, but she died on 11 September 1947, five years after her great friend and fellow Edwardian hostess Mrs Greville. She was buried under the cypress trees in the Protestant cemetery in Florence. A memorial service for 'La Favorita' was held in St Mark's, Audley Square, where Mrs Ronnie had been both married and commemorated. It was the end of an era, and Lady Colefax was among the notables who attended.

The return of peace meant that people who had success-fully avoided each other no longer had excuses. Sir Thomas Beecham and his wife, Betty, had spent the war years in the States. They returned to Britain on 2 June 1945, and bought a house near Petworth in Surrey. The American journalist Virgil Thomson arranged to interview the Beechams, but first he went to visit his old friend Emerald Cunard. She asked him to bring her news of her old lover, but Thomson spared Emerald his true impressions, which were that Beecham was perfectly happy with his new life. The famous conductor was now sixty-six, and Betty was thirty-seven, a wife-secretary-housekeeper-companion who, like him, was a musician and devoted to his career. He no longer had to spend his evenings with cabinet ministers, money men and aristocrats to satiate the socially acquisitive instincts of Lady Cunard, now aged seventy-three. Bob Boothby was sympathetic:

He took most of her money for his operas, and then married Betty Humby without telling her. She never recovered from the shock. Few people who knew her would regard her as a pathetic figure but, in her final years, she was. Whenever I saw her she came up to me with tears in her eyes and said, 'Have you seen Thomas lately? Tell me how he is.' She loved him.

Cecil Beaton described Beecham's marriage as the 'bombshell that shattered her', but she was adept at hiding her feelings. She also did not talk about her estranged daughter Nancy. Emerald caught a brief glimpse of Nancy one evening in London shortly after the end of the war as she was being driven through London in a car. The vehicle swerved suddenly to avoid a woman who had stepped out into the road; the headlights picked out the distinctive, whippet-thin figure of Nancy, and Emerald gasped, but said nothing. It was the last time Emerald saw her daughter.

Lady Cunard threw herself into post-war London social life with gusto, though it was uncertain what was keeping her afloat beyond her natural buoyancy. According to Cecil Beaton, she claimed to be in love with a charming young man called Nicholas Lawford, and he went along with the conceit, leaving bunches of flowers on the handle of her bedroom door before setting out for the Foreign Office every morning. But the romance was not serious, merely a diversion that allowed her gamely to hoist her tattered flag once again over the ruins of her love life.

Not all her contemporaries were keen on Emerald. Max Beerbohm was staying with Lord Berners shortly after the Second World War. Beerbohm had known Lady Cunard in the Edwardian era: 'I haven't seen her for years, has she changed at all?' he asked his host. Berners replied, 'No, it's wonderful, she's exactly the same.' There was a measured pause, then Beerbohm said, 'I am very sorry to hear that.'

She subsumed her passions into her social life; Evelyn Waugh complained about her relentless pursuit of him throughout the summer of 1945. Tiny, pastel-hued and over-painted, Lady Cunard was instantly recognisable, and much in demand. In January 1946 Emerald was a guest at a ball at the Argentinian Embassy; 'Chips' Channon surveyed the glamorous throng, which recalled the pre-war era, and announced portentously, 'This is what we have been fighting for.' Emerald acerbically replied, 'Why, dear, are they all Poles?' She was still capable of startling her listeners; aged seventy-four, she scandalised conventional Lord Esher by telling him how she had spontaneously taken off her shoes to show her still beautiful feet to a young admirer.

In February 1948 she was a guest at Georgia Sitwell's party in honour of the wise-cracking Hollywood actress Mae West. The Duchesses of Kent and Buccleuch were there, as was the ubiquitous 'Chips' Channon, resplendent with his ruby and diamond shirt studs. The party didn't end until 5 a.m.; it was almost like the old days. But one element had changed; Emerald's famous vivacity and energy were fading at last. At one dinner party she unexpectedly proposed a macabre toast, 'To death!' She had started to suffer from a persistent sore throat, and an attack of pneumonia and pleurisy left her weak. She consulted her doctors and received a terminal diagnosis, of cancer of the throat. It was time to get in touch with her daughter, Nancy, and her old friend Tony Gandarillas, Chilean playboy and opium addict, was the go-between.

Nancy Cunard had become increasingly troubled and eccentric. In February 1945 she had returned to newly liberated France to find her house in Normandy had been comprehensively looted by both German troops and local people. Horrified, she salvaged what she could and put the house on the market. For the next few years she flitted restlessly around the world, finally returning to Paris in 1948. Nancy had always been highly strung, and now she was prone to bouts of paranoia. She feared police surveillance, and her behaviour became increasingly irrational, veering from alcohol-fuelled reckless promiscuity to assaulting hotel porters. Skeletally thin, she was once discovered attempting to wash all her clothes at the same time as herself in the bath at the London flat of her bohemian friend, Viva King, and she would rip up hundreds of pounds worth of banknotes if left in charge of them.

During June 1948 Nancy Cunard was in Giverny when she was told that her mother was dangerously ill. Their old friend Diana Cooper tried to persuade Nancy to go to London to be reconciled with her mother. Nancy asked if Emerald had specifically asked for her, and because she hadn't, Nancy refused to go. On 6 July, Tony Gandarillas warned Nancy that her mother was sinking fast, but still she still refused to make the trip to London.

Emerald had been drifting in and out of consciousness for days, but inexplicably she rallied. She kept whispering a word that sounded like 'pain.' Her maid, Mary Gordon, gave her a pencil and she scrawled the word 'champagne'. When the bottle arrived, Emerald indicated that Mary, the nurse and the doctor should each have a glass; she was determined to be hospitable till the very end.

Emerald died on 10 July in her suite at the Dorchester, aged seventy-five. Tony broke the news to Nancy, who cried, predominantly out of pity for her mother's loss of Sir Thomas to a younger woman, but she would not go to London for Emerald's cremation. Emerald had said she wanted no memorial service, but had left no instructions as to the disposal of her ashes. Sir Robert Abdy, the art connoisseur, and a great friend, organised the *ad hoc* ceremony, dispersing Emerald's mortal remains to the elements in Grosvenor Square, scene of so many of her social triumphs. This solemn gesture did not go entirely to plan; it was a breezy day, and Sir Robert found himself liberally sprinkled with the appropriately tenacious ashes of Lady Cunard.

In her will Emerald left Mary Gordon her wardrobe, furs, monogrammed silk sheets, linens, silver plate and cash of £1,500, worth about £35,000 in today's values. The rest of her possessions were divided equally between her friends Lady Diana Cooper, Sir Robert Abdy and Nancy. Nancy justified accepting Emerald's bequest because she believed her mother had attempted to curb her behaviour by controlling her allowance in the 1930s. Nancy tried to meet Mary Gordon, the maid, but the latter wanted nothing to do with her mistress's rogue daughter. In fact, Lady Cunard had left far less than anyone expected. It appeared that during Emerald's last year she had come close to the end of her financial resources. In addition, the Inland Revenue claimed arrears of income tax and super tax against her estate. Her possessions, including antique furniture and pictures from the Dorchester suite, were held in store while the tax issue was resolved. With impeccable timing, she had died not long before she would have run out of money.

The remaining American capital brought Nancy Cunard a useful £350 income a year, and by selling most of the paintings and furniture she was able to buy an old house in the Dordogne. But Emerald's famous gems and pearls, left to Diana Cooper, turned out to be false – at some point Lady Cunard had quietly sold her real jewellery and had exact replicas made, in order to continue funding her lifestyle.

The *Daily Mail* obituary described her as 'an extraordinary and dynamic woman. She was among the last – and the equal of the grandest of the social hostesses of the Great Capital at its peak.' Interestingly, the newspapers reported that she was seventy-one at death; born in 1872, and dying in 1948, she was in fact a month away from her seventy-sixth birthday. Like her rival Mrs Ronnie, Emerald shaved a few years off her age for cosmetic purposes.

She was much missed by her friends. Lady Diana Cooper mourned her for years, and thought of her every time she visited the Dorchester. James Lees-Milne also admired her for her dazzling wit and brilliant repartee. Sachie Sitwell eloquently wrote in *The Times*: 'Those who loved her will miss her wit and subtlety and nuance and will mourn her company, and think of her at concerts, in theatres, above all at the opera. This was what she loved most, and perhaps it took the place, for her, of religion.' Tellingly, for years afterwards, her maid Mary Gordon would return to Grosvenor Square to leave flowers on the anniversary of Emerald's death. Ticked off by an officious jobsworth on one occasion, in later years she would cross the square bearing a bouquet, and let drop a single bloom, as if by accident.

Sibyl Colefax had dreamed throughout the war of returning to her beloved Italy, but the years of peace were hard, and she was dogged by both money worries and ill-health. Although in straitened circumstances, she continued to entertain at her home, regularly attracting guests of the calibre of Harold Macmillan, T. S. Eliot, Cyril Connolly, the Mountbattens and the Kenneth Clarks. But in August 1946 she slipped and fell getting out of a taxi, and was taken to hospital with a broken thigh and hip. Her accident ruined her long-cherished plans; she had been on the point of going to Florence to stay with Bernard Berenson when she was incapacitated. She spent frustrating months in a hospital bed, visited by friends such as Noel Coward. In May 1947 her old friends the Duke and Duchess of Windsor were in London, and while they seemed more reconciled to their titles, others were still uncertain how to address them. Nigel Nicolson, the son of Harold and Vita, visited Sibyl in her nursing home:

> When I arrived, Somerset Maugham and Peter Quennell were already there. [Sibyl] told us that she was expecting a fourth guest, the Duchess of Windsor, and that she had warned the nurse to meet the Duchess and escort her upstairs. She must not announce her as Mrs Simpson, but as the Duchess. The girl met her as instructed, and as she guided her along the corridors, she muttered to herself, like the White Rabbit in Alice, 'I mustn't say Mrs Simpson. I must say the Duchess. Not Mrs Simpson.' She opened the door of the room where we were sitting, and announced with a flourish, 'Mrs Simpson, m'lady.'

Despite her slow recovery, Sibyl still enjoyed the company of actors and performers such as John Gielgud and Noel Coward; in the middle of a heatwave in July 1948 she held a first-night party for the cast and friends celebrating the opening of *The Glass Menagerie*, by Tennessee Williams. James Lees-Milne had become a good friend, and he was very grateful for Sibyl's influence in persuading reclusive eccentric Lawrence Johnston to give his remarkable garden Hidcote to the National Trust in August 1948, in order to ensure its preservation after his death. She had cultivated

'Laurie J' for four decades, immersing herself in the study of horticulture, and Sibyl was one of the few people he trusted. Lees-Milne recorded an interesting remark of Sibyl's in September 1948. She stated, 'No, I am not happy. Old people are never happy. But I *was* happy. Now I am only interested in the young.'

Sibyl certainly liked the company of the young. In June 1948 Nigel Nicolson took her to the cinema to watch the newsreel coverage of the departure of the Mountbattens from Delhi at the end of his Viceroyalty. London had been alive with gossip that Edwina had been having a passionate affair with Nehru. As Sibyl and Nigel sat in the dark watching the flickering screen, Sibyl said: 'What they didn't show was Edwina kissing goodbye to Nehru at the airport. That deeply shocked Indian opinion and undid all the good that Dickie had done.' The woman in the seat in front of them turned round and said coolly: 'Hello, Sibyl. I thought I recognised your voice.' It was Edwina Mountbatten, and sitting next to her was her husband, the former Viceroy. It was an awkward moment. When the lights went down for the feature film, Nigel and Sibyl crept out quietly.

By January 1949 it was apparent that Sibyl was ill, painfully thin with curvature of the spine and a racking cough. Diana Cooper saw her at a wedding and described her as 'poor little Coalbox, bent double in silver fox. She can only see now a dreary circle of ground beneath her eyes.' Nevertheless she was full of plans for the future and rarely complained. She continued to entertain at home and at the Dorchester, and still sent her guests discreet bills afterwards. This was the only way she could fund civilised parties, and the participants appreciated this pragmatic arrangement.

Despite her declining health, she was still bright-eyed and

alert almost to the end. On her last night alive Sibyl Colefax was convinced that her husband Arthur was outside in the street and was waiting to be let in. She died in her sleep early on the morning of 22 September 1950, aged seventy-five. By chance, Harold Nicholson was in Florence and arrived at Bernard Berenson's home shortly after the telegram that announced her death. By a strange irony, he was in the very place where his old friend had so wanted to return, but had been denied by the war and bad luck. Sibyl was mourned by the many who had benefited from her passion for collecting and mixing together those she thought would enjoy each other's stimulating company. As one of her former 'young people', Kenneth Clark, remarked: 'Sibyl genuinely loved people and bringing them together was her life's work. One should have loved her more than one did.'

It was following her return to America for Christmas 1948–9 that Laura Mae Corrigan died. She had arrived in New York from Paris on Christmas Eve, to spend the holiday with her sister Mrs David Armstrong-Taylor, of San Francisco. The two women were staying in the Plaza Hotel in Manhattan when Laura was taken ill and rushed to hospital, where she died the following day, 22 January 1948, exactly twenty years after the death of her husband. The *New York Times* obituary (24 January 1948) noted uncensoriously that she had once been a waitress in Chicago, that her father had been an 'odd jobs' man and that she had never been accepted by Cleveland society after her marriage to the heir to the Corrigan-McKinney Steel Company. The paper frankly stated that New York was similarly unwelcoming, though she subsequently achieved great success in London society, and had her revenge by excluding the 'Knickerbocker crowd', the American Astors and Vanderbilts, from her parties. In addition, the Cleveland set played no part in the Corrigans' social life, although Laura donated $5,000 annually to the Cleveland Fund for the benefit of the city. She also gave $25,000 to the Cleveland Museum of Art to purchase great works by Cézanne and others, and paid for the care and feeding of the animals she had personally provided for the Cleveland Zoo. Her body was returned to the city that had snubbed her; she was interred in Lake View Cemetery in Cleveland, where a simple but massive polished monument marks the joint grave of James and Laura with the single name 'Corrigan'.

In London a memorial service was held in her name at that favourite church of the Mayfair hostesses, St Mark's, North Audley Street. Laura would have been gratified to know that it was attended by so many of her old friends, including the Duchess of Kent, the Duke and Duchess of Buccleuch, the Duke and Duchess of Marlborough and her great rival Lady Cunard.

Although she gamely attended the first state opening of Parliament after the war, on 26 October 1945, Edith Londonderry's priorities had now changed. In the years after the Second World War Lady Londonderry largely dropped out of public life, concentrating on caring for her family and restoring Mount Stewart. Mrs Keppel stayed there in 1946 and was horrified that Edith dined in trousers, managed with no maid and had placed children in bedrooms adjacent to her own. As 'La Favorita' snorted at the time of the abdication, 'Things were done differently in my day.'

On 20 June 1946 it was reported that the Royal Aero Club would take over Londonderry House in Park Lane, which had been damaged by wartime bombs. As part of the lease, the Londonderrys retained the use of a twenty-two-room flat in the house. They also rented the house out for high-end receptions, such as followed the wedding of Raine McCorquodale, the daughter of novelist Barbara Cartland, and Gerald Legge, on 21 July 1948. On 25 May 1950 there was a dance in honour of seventeen-year-old Lady Jane Vane-Tempest-Stewart, Edith's grand-daughter, but such grand occasions were rare for the Londonderry family in an era of national austerity.

Edith's beloved husband, Charley, had become an increasing cause for concern. His passion for flying had led him to take up gliding, and in November 1945 he had a bad accident when the towing cable snapped. Although he broke no bones, it was the start of a period of ill-health, and in 1947 he began to have small strokes, which rendered him incapable of movement and speech. He died at Mount Stewart on 10 February 1949, aged seventy, and was buried at Tír-n'an Óg (Gaelic for 'Land of the Ever Young'), the Vane-Tempest-Stewarts' burial ground. Edith was bereft after fifty years of marriage.

Her new title was the Dowager Lady Londonderry, and she was now seventy years old. Charley's political career had been irreparably damaged by his association with Nazi Germany. Opinion on his motivation is still divided. His patriotism was not in doubt, and he always advocated that all dealings with Germany should be negotiated from a position of well-armed strength, but it was his judgement that gave cause for concern. He told Bob Boothby, 'There were really only two things I could do. Build an Air Force, or try to make friends with the Germans.' His intentions were honourable, but his personal reputation had suffered because of his pro-German stance between 1935 and 1938. His former guest von Ribbentrop had been captured by the Allies at the end of the Second World War and faced justice at the Nuremberg War Trials. Von Ribbentrop boasted of his pre-war friendships with the Duke of Windsor and Lady Astor, and he asked that they and Lord Londonderry be called as character witnesses in his defence. Unsurprisingly, his request was denied; after a lengthy trial he was found guilty and executed in 1947.

The Londonderrys' son Edward, always known as Robin, became the eighth Marquess, but he too died, on 17 October 1955. Robin was the second of Edith and Charley's children to die; her eldest, Maureen, had died in June 1942. Lady Londonderry was concerned about the future of her beloved family home, Mount Stewart. She gave the gardens to the National Trust in 1957, and her last surviving daughter, Lady Mairi Bury (*née* Vane-Tempest-Stewart, Dowager Viscountess Bury), handed over the house and most of its contents to the Trust in 1977.

Despite the vicissitudes and tragedies of her final years, Edith still felt she had a role to play as an important hostess. Her last great political reception at Londonderry House was in 1958, more than four decades after she had presided at her first, and her last Prime Minister to act as guest of honour was Harold Macmillan. Edith was already ill with the cancer that was to kill her, but even in her final months she maintained the determination, practical common sense and humour that had governed her life, as Beverley Nichols recalled:

When I last entered Londonderry House [Edith] had only a short time left to live. Most of the place had been shut up, never to be reopened, and one had the feeling that the great staircase was thronged with ghosts. We lunched upstairs in a room brimming with flowers sent over from Mount Stewart, the estate in Ireland. She was in considerable pain, with a broken hip, but she was still the life and soul of the party, which included Jack Profumo. Somebody mentioned an unfortunate member of Parliament who had been arrested in Hyde Park for indecent behaviour with a guardsman. Apparently he had led the young man into a shrubbery, where his improprieties were clearly visible to the police. This was not the sort of topic which in those days was considered suitable for discussion with octogenarian dowagers, but Circe was more than equal to the occasion. 'What a *silly* man!' she exclaimed. 'There are plenty of laurels in Hyde Park. Why did he have to choose a *deciduous* shrub?'

Edith died on 23 April 1959, aged eighty. Her body was also buried at Tír-n'an Óg, the family plot she created at Mount Stewart. She is interred next to her much-loved husband, and their graves are surrounded by statues of Irish saints.

Nancy Astor in her old age was physically vigorous, white-haired and beautiful, with an excellent complexion. She now lived in Hill Street in London, as there was no longer the pre-war need to entertain lavishly. Practical problems, such as rationing and the shortages of servants and fuel, irritated her. Deprived of the chance to express her scorn in the House of Commons, she had developed a habit of berating and intimidating younger men on her twin passions, Catholicism and Communism. Waldorf spent the last years of his life at Cliveden, managing the estate and his business affairs, taking the opportunity to explain everything to Billie, his eldest son, who would succeed him. His health had declined, and he used a wheelchair. In August 1952 Waldorf had a massive heart attack while staying with David. He was determined to return to Cliveden because 'It would distress your mother if I die anywhere else'. They had been estranged for seven years; now Nancy came back for his final days, and the couple were reconciled. Before dying he told each of his children, 'Look after your mother'. After his death Nancy bitterly regretted the years wasted. She felt she couldn't remain at Cliveden, and so spent most of her time in London, moving in 1958 into an apartment at 100 Eaton Square. Her eldest son instructed that Nancy was to want for nothing, so she had Charles Dean as her butler, a housekeeper, an Austrian chef, a chauffeur and Rose Harrison as her maid.

A determined teetotaller to the last, Lady Astor did not know that her staff added a tot of Dubonnet to her mid-morning Ribena, on the instructions of her niece Nancy Lancaster. She also acquired a dog, a burly and self-willed corgi called Madam, who was taken out for a walk every evening by William, the odd-job man. The Belgravia back-streets housed a number of small pubs frequented by servants, where William and Madam became well known. The other regulars habitually fed the greedy dog with snacks, while William tackled the thirst for which odd-job men were famous. But one evening, energetic and restless Lady Astor snapped a lead onto the collar of a surprised Madam before anyone could intervene, and the mis-matched pair set out together into the dusk. At the first corner, the corgi dragged her horrified mistress down a cobbled mews and into the 'snug' of a pub, where they were greeted, appropriately enough, with genial cries of 'Evening, Madam!' As an internationally recognisable public figure and lifelong teetotaller, Nancy was horrified that Madam had betrayed the standards of behaviour normally expected of her household.

In 1953 she visited the States again, and once more made headlines. At one of the many parties she attended, she watched as influential Senator Joseph R. McCarthy, the scourge of the Liberal Left, sipped a cocktail. 'Too bad it isn't poison,' she hissed, torn between her hatred for alcohol and the loathing of Communism she shared with McCarthy. Throughout the 1950s Nancy Astor travelled extensively, exploring Rhodesia, America and Europe, wintering in Nassau, Casablanca and Marrakesh. Lady Astor remained fit and healthy, celebrating her eightieth birthday with a game of golf. However, she lacked purpose now that her career had ended and Waldorf had died. At the end of April 1955 Noel Coward found her 'still full of vitality but sad at heart, obsessed with the idea that her life is over. In spite of her tiresome Christian Science and temperance tirades, I have a great affection for her. She is a remarkable character, frequently wrong-headed but I don't think wrong-hearted, and undoubtedly a tremendous personality.'

There were some compensations: in 1959 she was given the freedom of the city of Plymouth, and in return she donated a magnificent set of jewellery, to be worn by Lady Mayoresses in the future. It comprised a platinum necklace nearly four feet long, set with diamonds and sapphires, with matching ear-rings. It was valued at around £600,000 in 2015, and was an extraordinarily generous gift to the city from the woman who had done so much for its people.

Nancy Astor survived to see (but, perhaps fortunately, not comprehend) the Profumo affair, which had erupted at her old home Cliveden, and which implicated her eldest son, Billie. He and Nancy had been the first mother-and-son partnership in the House of Commons. Following Waldorf's death, Bill inherited his title, and entertained his friends and contacts at Cliveden. He knew Stephen Ward, society osteopath, who had treated him following a riding accident. Ward became a tenant of Spring Cottage on the Cliveden estate, and occasionally used the open-air swimming pool in the walled garden, which Bill had installed. It was in these glamorous surroundings, in July 1961, that a pool party organised by Ward led to the Profumo affair, which brought down a government. It occurred during the Cold War, shocking the establishment with the revelation that a Soviet Embassy official and the British Minister for War had shared the affections of the same beautiful *demi-mondaine,* Christine Keeler.

The scandal broke in 1963, two years after the pool party. Stephen Ward took a fatal overdose and died during the trial. Bill Astor's reputation suffered too – he was given a tough time by the press, who assumed he had abandoned his friend Stephen, though in fact he had funded Ward's legal and day-to-day expenses. Although Bill had not been charged with any wrongdoing, his name was also dragged through the mud. One of the witnesses, Mandy Rice-Davies, was quizzed over her allegation that Bill Astor had been one of her lovers, something that he had denied. 'He would, wouldn't he?' she replied, a short but pithy phrase that has since entered the *Oxford Dictionary of Modern Quotations.*

Nancy Astor was now eighty-two years old, and her grip

on reality was fading. Her friends and family agreed that it would be better to keep the Profumo affair from her. They arranged a rota to telephone her daily at her London apartment just before the 1 p.m. and 6 p.m. radio news. The newspapers were censored, and the television at Eaton Square mysteriously no longer functioned. Visitors were warned not to tell her, but Bobbie Shaw showed up one evening drunk, insisting that 'mother ought to know', keen to prove that he wasn't the only black sheep of the family. Nancy was agitated and ordered Charles her butler to phone Cliveden; instead he rang the servants' quarters at Eaton Square, having first taken the receiver off the hook, so that all evening it appeared to be impossible to contact Cliveden. Nancy insisted they should go to Cliveden the following morning to be at her son's side, but Rose managed to distract her that night, and by the following day she had forgotten about it.

Lady Astor's memory, always so sharp, began to fail. Her sleep habits became erratic, and Rose had to put her to bed, tucking her in like a child to ensure that she slept. She worried about money, but she also became a 'soft touch' for scroungers. Her family gave her a magnificent diamond solitaire ring for her birthday – diamonds were always her favourite gems. 'What do I look like, Rose?' she asked. 'Cartier's, my lady', came the loyal reply.

Nancy's long and passionately led life finally ended on 2 May 1964. She was staying at her daughter Wissie's home, Grimsthorpe Castle, in Lincolnshire, when she had a severe stroke. Her final days were attended by her family and her long-suffering maid Rose. 'Jakie, is it my birthday, or am I dying?' she asked with typical frankness, on waking to find all her relatives around her bed. She spent a week in a coma, but revived a little on the evening of 1 May and uttered a single word, 'Waldorf'. She died the next day. Rose remembered: 'I went into the bedroom. She looked so beautiful and so very peaceful. She had suffered so little. It was a good picture to take away with me. I had one other thing to take as well, a link with the past, "Madam", my lady's dog. Together we slipped out of the house.'

Nancy Astor's body was cremated and her ashes interred at the Octagon Temple at Cliveden, next to Waldorf's. At her request, her casket was draped with a Confederate flag given to her in Virginia.

12

Legacies

'Giving parties is a trivial avocation, but it pays
the dues for my union card in humanity.'

Elsa Maxwell

Between the wars these six singular women chose to collect,
to cultivate and to influence prominent people in the
diverse fields of British society where they hoped to make an
impact. It is important to assess their legacy, their achievements and their failures, to understand how they changed
society and to appreciate the motivations that drove them.

In an era where it was still very unusual for respectable
women to have any sort of public role, or even acceptable
for them to work outside the home, each of the Queen Bees
created her own social milieu and populated her receptions
and dinner parties with those she wished to encourage, to
promote and to bring into contact with like-minded individuals. It is notable that each of the Big Six was already mature
in years before she established herself as a hostess of note.
These exceptional women saw their social role as a vocation,
a career or a calling.

Had they been born in the twentieth century rather than
the nineteenth, they might well have had satisfying professions
of their own, becoming political leaders, theatrical or musical
impresarios, social reformers, businesswomen, diplomats,

advocates or full-blown celebrities. As it was, they worked within the parameters of what was achievable at the time to change British society for the better in a number of different ways. It is perhaps difficult to appreciate nowadays just how radical these women were, born and brought up in the Victorian era, when male supremacy was assumed and assured as a matter of course.

These individuals were self-motivated, and often largely self-educated. The three Americans, Nancy Astor, Emerald Cunard and Laura Corrigan, came from very different backgrounds, but each benefited from being largely unplaceable in terms of her class when she arrived in British society. The three Britons similarly exemplified the changing nature of the English scene; while Lady Londonderry was a blue-blooded aristocrat who grew up in a castle, Sibyl Colefax was the overlooked child of an unhappy middle-class marriage, and Margaret Greville was the illegitimate daughter of a millionaire brewer from Edinburgh and his servant.

The 'ladies of influence' were able to take advantage of the increasingly permeable nature of British society after the Great War. The rigid hierarchy of class, stratified by the landowning aristocracy grouped around the court and much involved in the political life of the nation, where everyone knew their place, was overturned by the seismic social upheaval caused by four years of war and the financial ramifications that followed. With the return of peace, many of the aristocratic families withdrew from professional entertaining, and the wealthy and well-connected new host-esses filled the gap, despite their often humble origins. Through the deliberate courting and acquisition of those people who in former times might have cut them dead, the Queen Bees demonstrated that, in a more democratic era, aptitude and determination could achieve more than high birth could alone.

These were symbiotic relationships; each hostess provided a forum for the ambitious, the curious and those who wanted to climb the greasy pole. To be taken up by a well-connected society lady, to be invited to her soirées, her dinner parties and receptions greatly helped people with ambitions, because it was at such occasions that they could be introduced to power-brokers and king-makers, in surroundings of seductive luxury.

The hostesses exerted 'soft power' over their guests, providing them with a forum where they might find allies, explore arguments, make useful contacts, expand their views, share information and form friendships, even romances. In addition, the sense of 'exclusivity' in being one of the 'chosen few' was inherently flattering to the participants. In the political realm such opportunities were in marked contrast to the combative cockpit that was the House of Commons, where formal protocols and a strict pecking order governed the business of Parliament. In addition, proceedings in Parliament were recorded in Hansard, and reported in the press; for a young and inexperienced MP an invitation to Mrs Ronnie Greville's evening reception in Charles Street or Lady Astor's weekend house party at Cliveden was a valuable opportunity to side-step the competition, to get the ear of a senior party grandee in a convivial and informal setting.

The 'clubbable' nature of the hostesses' opulent homes, both in London and in the country, is often overlooked as an important factor in their charm offensives. The effect of candlelight glittering on old silver, the smooth deference of liveried servants, comfort, luxury and the provision of excellent food and wine were also appealing, and each of the

Queen Bees competed to provide the perfect setting for her guests. Of course, almost any woman of substantial means could arrange dinner parties and receptions; it took a hostess of genius to exert 'soft power' sufficient to change society.

Two of them were trailblazers for generations of women who followed. Nancy Astor was a lone female MP in the largely hostile House of Commons for a number of years after her first election in 1919, but she was determined to champion the valuable contribution that women could make to public life, advocating their employment in the police force, the judiciary, the diplomatic corps and social work. A more reticent character might have been cowed by the ostracism she faced from fellow back-benchers, but Nancy single-mindedly pursued the causes to which she was committed. By using the Astors' fortunes to host receptions and social events in London she provided a much-needed forum for men and women to be able to meet and lobby lawmakers and opinion-formers to whom they had previously had little access. She described her motivation:

> What I really like to have in my house is a party which contains thoroughly opposing elements – pacifists and fire-eaters, reformers and die-hards, rich and poor, old and young. When they meet each other, they generally make friends, and when they make friends, they can find some of the solutions to their problems.

While Nancy had not been an active supporter of the pre-war suffrage movement, she saw no reason why a woman should be barred from an active and fulfilling life merely because of her gender.

Despite animosity, ridicule and occasional personal attacks, Nancy Astor became a role model for many ambitious and committed women who didn't start with her advantages. She proved that a woman could represent a geographical community, her beloved constituency of Plymouth, as well as representing and defending the interests of a specific sector of society, namely women and children. Undoubtedly it was the Astors' wealth that allowed her to embark on a political career, and she would not have been successful without a phalanx of staff and an acquiescent husband, but it was her own stamina and determination that drove her as an MP throughout her twenty-six-year career. She sustained her marriage, helped to run a number of complex houses and a huge estate and brought up six children.

The manner in which Nancy Astor's contemporary Edith Lady Londonderry expressed her commitment to politics was fundamentally different, but the results were even more far-reaching. She had been brought up as a blue-blooded daughter of the aristocracy and married into a High Tory family. Nevertheless, Edith Castlereagh, as she was at the start of the Great War, had the foresight to identify British women of all classes as the disregarded workforce who had the potential to help win the war. She also had the persuasive powers and organisational abilities to tackle and overcome reactionary views, creating the Women's Legion as a body that could harness the knowledge, expertise and willpower of women, freeing up their menfolk to fight overseas. She campaigned for her cause through the press and garnered support from the influential to mobilise wives, mothers, daughters and girl-friends of all classes. It was an immense achievement; by the end of the First World War many of the jobs previously monopolised by men were being filled by women. Such a social transformation in the space of less than four years was instrumental in convincing the British government that women should have the vote. In addition, the Sexual Disqualification Act, which followed in 1919, lifted the restrictions that had previously denied them access to many of the professions. Without Edith's motivating force, persuasive abilities and excellent political contacts the campaign for women's suffrage might have foundered once again.

In 1958 Edith wrote a thoughtful biography of one of her predecessors, Frances Anne Londonderry, who had been an influential political hostess in the nineteenth century. She expressed the view that, had the earlier Lady Londonderry been born a man, she would certainly have been a statesman, perhaps even Prime Minister. Perhaps Edith secretly thought the same about her own career; she had been an astute and able political hostess with considerable influence, and she had exerted 'soft power' for decades.

Like Edith, all the Queen Bees were past the first flush of youth by the time they were best able to exercise their influence, in the decades between the wars. They were middle-aged, established figures who used their status to achieve their aims. In 1918 Mrs Margaret Greville was fifty-five years old, and one of the wealthiest and best-connected women in the country, before she was able to vote for the first time. As a consummate businesswoman she exerted considerable power in the running of the brewery left to her by her father, but she also used her funds to bankroll a luxurious lifestyle that brought her proximity to political power, in Britain and overseas. She was an *éminence grise* behind the scenes of British society in the 1920s and 1930s, an intimate of men such as Sir John Simon, Austen and Neville Chamberlain, and keen to advance her protégés Oswald Mosley and Bob Boothby. She recognised the extraordinary potential of Winston Churchill, and even though they often disagreed politically, he was always welcome at her table, even throughout his 'wilderness years'. Many of the alliances and friendships on which he came to rely during the Second World War were with people he had met through the auspices of Mrs Greville.

Proximity to power was Mrs Greville's prime motivation, but she was also adept at spotting potential in young people and helping them get established through her contacts. She was dismissed by Harold Nicolson as a 'common, waspish woman who got where she did through persistence and money.' Although she revelled in being rich, she also donated a great deal of her wealth to charity. Naturally, she also used her fortune to manipulate people and draw them to her. Her friend Beverley Nichols described her accurately as: 'A social Napoleon. They don't make women like that nowadays. She wasn't beautiful, she was brilliant, she was a fabulous snob. And yet, one had been genuinely fond of her.'

Perhaps Mrs Greville's greatest influence, however, was in acting as 'fairy godmother' in the personal relationships of the British royal family. Her role as potential benefactor to Prince Albert in offering to leave him her estate developed into genuine friendship, and she played a crucial part in advancing his courtship of Elizabeth Bowes-Lyon, who had twice turned down his proposals of marriage, when it seemed hopeless. If Bertie had not married Elizabeth, who was to be such a rock to him when he was forced onto the throne after his brother's abdication, it is debatable whether he would have made such a success of consolidating the Crown at a critical time in the nation's history. In addition, if George VI had not married Elizabeth, the key personnel of the British royal family would now be very different; there would be no

Queen Elizabeth II, for example, and no Prince Charles as the next in line to the throne.

By contrast, Lady Cunard's ambitions to shape the future of the royal family by furthering the romance of Edward VIII and Wallis Simpson eventually brought her vilification from the establishment and a degree of social ostracism, taking some of the lustre off her previous reputation as a cultural *salonnière* of brilliant wit and conversation. A happier legacy lies in the way in which she wholeheartedly championed the cause of opera, ballet and classical music in Britain between the wars, to the great benefit of the national cultural scene.

Without her loyalty, her own considerable financial support and her ability to wheedle substantial funds out of the wealthy it is unlikely that her faithless lover, Sir Thomas Beecham, would have achieved the many international accolades he won as impresario, conductor and leader of world-class orchestras. Emerald richly deserved the title of 'the Queen of Covent Garden', if only for her fundraising acumen and her genuine commitment to the arts in an era long before government subsidies or corporate sponsorship.

Money and its procurement in pursuit of one's aims were to be the driving factor in the later life of Emerald's great rival, Lady Colefax. It was in order to maintain her relentless performance as the ringmaster of her own cultural circus that Sibyl bravely tackled the financial shortfall between her income and her expenditure and set up her innovative and successful decorating firm eventually known as Colefax & Fowler. It was to become so influential on 1930s and 1940s interior design that some have likened it to the instantly recognisable appeal of the interior decoration firm of Laura Ashley in the 1980s. The firm provided employment and practical expertise for many, and inspired young people to take up interior design as a viable profession.

Sibyl was the most driven 'tuft-hunter' of all of the hostesses, but she also had a knack of blending the traditional upper classes, those whose status had traditionally come from the ownership of land, with a more open and eclectic elite. Around her table could be found members of the new, creative meritocracy, such as Cole Porter, Noel Coward, Charlie Chaplin, Laurence Olivier and Vivien Leigh as well as leading writers and academics, such as John Maynard Keynes and Virginia Woolf. She made it her life's work to bring together people she thought *should* know each other – writers and intellectuals, actors and art experts – to their mutual enjoyment.

It was clever, curious and well-connected Sibyl who first championed the integration of Anglo-American elites, thanks to her transatlantic contacts, and the other hostesses quickly followed suit. These informal connections 'across the pond' were to pay dividends when the Second World War came, with the hostesses bringing influential Americans to their tables and under their influence as part of their 'war effort'.

Laura Mae Corrigan's wartime career was perhaps the most surprising, because it appeared to be in complete contrast to the lifestyle that had made her famous. She had left behind her humble origins in rural Wisconsin to throw perpetual parties in London and Paris, peopled by the acquisitive and the curious. Throughout the 1920s and '30s she deliberately cultivated the Bright Young Things, the more decorative aristocrats and selected European royalty. Those who had patronised her as 'rich but dim' were forced to reappraise their opinions when she showed her real mettle, staying in Paris under the noses of the Nazi high command, selling her jewellery to Goering and helping those caught up in the hostilities in Vichy, playing a dangerous game of double-bluff in occupied France. She spent all her available fortune on assisting the war effort in dangerous circumstances, only returning to Britain when she ran out of money in 1942. Her great friend and mentor Elsa Maxwell wrote, 'Laura was a *parvenu*[sic] all right, but she had more character and social conscience in her little finger than all the phony patricians who sneered at her.'

Like most of their contemporaries, the great hostesses had been anxious to avoid another European war and used personal contacts, visits to Germany and arguments for greater harmony between opposing nations in their common cause. The Astors were accused of colluding with the Germans through their clique, the 'Cliveden set'. Mrs Greville was an early enthusiast for Hitler, and the Londonderrys made several trips to the Third Reich in the hopes of avoiding war. They believed that Germany's representatives were sincere, and so did not comprehend Hitler's aims until it was almost too late. But when war became inevitable, each of them demonstrated her inherent patriotism in the desperate fight against Fascism, and the Allies eventually triumphed after six long years of conflict. Although the late 1940s and 1950s brought austerity, financial hardship and ill-health, which curtailed the great hostesses' activities, they had a considerable benign influence on many aspects of Western society during a critical period of world history.

The six great hostesses had succeeded in overcoming, variously, the stigma of illegitimacy, the taint of having grown up in poverty, the sadness of an unloved childhood, the deaths of much-loved parents, discrimination on the grounds of class and gender, the humiliation of divorce, the sting of a husband's infidelities, the numbing loneliness of widowhood and the estrangement or loss of one's own children. In place of these personal tragedies, each one had devoted considerable energy to embarking on a career and creating a social circle of her own, using charm and ingenuity to attract those whom she wished to court, and nurturing those she wished to foster. Shortly before her death, Laura Corrigan remarked, 'As a little girl I often dreamed of knowing all the kings and queens in the world. And I have had my wish.' It was an achievement shared by all the Queen Bees.

Source notes and acknowledgements

Introduction

p.6 *it was enormous fun* . . . Oswald Mosley, *My Life*, Thomas Nelson and Sons Ltd, 1968, p75-6

Chapter one

p.10-11 *Mr Mackay struck* . . . Lewiston Daily Sun, 20 January 1891

p.12 *a sort of honeyed poison* . . . Patrick Balfour, *Society's Racket*, John Long Ltd, 1933

p13 *In any generation* . . . Sonia Keppel, *Edwardian Daughter,* Hamish Hamilton, 1958, p170

p.13 *my father worked* . . . Sibyl Colefax, unpublished autobiography, quoted in Kirsty MacLeod, *A Passion for Friendship: Sibyl Colefax and her circle*, Michael Joseph, 1991, p17. Reproduced by kind permission of Penguin Random House, UK.

p.15 *as the train moved out* . . . ibid. p21-22

p.16 *Once I had fallen in* . . . ibid. p28

p.20 *Myself, I don't care* . . . Lady Londonderry, from Anne De Courcy, *Society's Queen: The Life of Edith, Marchioness of Londonderry*, Phonix, 1992

p.21 *You might send the enclosed* . . . ibid.

p.21 *I don't blame you* . . . ibid.

p.26 *I suppose you've come over* . . . Edith Cunard and Nancy Astor quoted in Adrian Forth, *Nancy: The Story of Lady Astor,* Vintage, 2013, p55-6

p.29 *she had a course* . . . George Moore, from Rupert Hart-Davis, *George Moore: Letters to Lady Cunard 1895-1933,* Rupert Hart-Davis Ltd

p.32 *You have come into this life* . . . ibid.

p.33 *dearest Maud* . . . ibid.

p34. *When my husband came back* . . . Lady Cunard, from Lois Gordon, *Nancy Cunard: Heiress, Muse, Political Idealist,* Columbia University Press, 2007, p14

p.35-6 *one of the finest streets* . . . Mark Twain, letter to the *San Francisco Alta California,* 15 November 1868

Chapter two

p.38 *Throughout most of Kingy's* . . . Sonia Keppel, *Edwardian Daughter,* Hamish Hamilton, 1958, p170

p.47 *henceforth my attitude* . . . The Marchioness of Londonderry, *Retrospect,* Frederick Muller Ltd, 1938, p97

p.53 *Why you should wish to hear* . . . George Moore, from Rupert Hart-Davis, *George Moore: Letters to Lady Cunard 1895-1933,* Rupert Hart-Davis Ltd

p.53 *I thought you might be coming to dine with me* . . . ibid.

p.54-5 *the fact is that I am alone* . . . Letter from Mrs Margaret Greville to King George V, 25 May 1914. Reproduced by kind permission of Her Majesty Queen Elizabeth II, from the Royal Archives at Windsor Castle.

p.55 *Mrs Ronny* . . . from the diary of King George V, 14 June 1914. Reproduced by kind permission of Her Majesty Queen Elizabeth II, from the Royal Archives at Windsor Castle.

Chapter three

p.60 *The whole of London* . . . Osbert Sitwell, *Great Morning*, Macmillan and Company Ltd, 1948, p282

p.67 *The effect of regular work* . . . The Marchioness of Londonderry, *Retrospect*, Frederick Muller Ltd, 1938, p118

p.68 *Women cooks* . . . ibid. p109

p.78 *took a house in London* . . . Consuelo Vanderbilt Balsan, *The Glitter and the Gold*, Heinemann Ltd, 1953, p160

p.81-2 *as numb as an old piano* . . . Margot Asquith, *Autobiography*, Penguin, 1920 (second ed. 1936), p224-5

p.82 *It was a wonderful sight* . . . ibid.

Chapter four

p.85 *The older aristocracy* . . . Patrick Balfour, *Society's Racket*, John Long Ltd, 1933, p77

p.87-8 *I feel you realise* . . . Letter from Lady Astor to Lady Londonderry, quoted in Anne De Courcy, *Society's Queen: The life of Edith, Marchioness of Londonderry*, Phoenix, 1992, p164

p.93 *I was vaguely aware* . . . Michael Astor, *Tribal Feeling*, John Murray Press, 1963, p92

p.103-4 *My dear Viceroy* . . . letter from Mrs Margaret Greville to the Marquess of Reading, circa 20 February 1922, held in the British Library

p.108 *to listen to clever talk* . . . Virginia Woolf, 'Am I a Snob'?, reproduced in Jeanne Shulkind, *Virginia Woolf: Moments of Being*, Pimlico, 2002

p.109 *Dear Gerald Berners* . . . Beverley Nichols, *The Sweet and Twenties*, Weidenfeld and Nicolson, 1958, p156 p.110-11 *In the world of opera* . . . Osbert Sitwell, *Great Morning,* Macmillan and Company Ltd, 1948, 249-50

p.112 *You brought into the world* . . . George Moore, from Rupert Hart-Davis, *George Moore: Letters to Lady Cunard 1895-1933,* Rupert Hart-Davis Ltd

p.115 *Nittie Vandercrump* . . . E. F. Benson, *Freaks of Mayfair,* originally published 1916 by T.N. Foulis, republished 2001 by Prion Books Ltd, p125

p.118 *Acrobats, jugglers* . . . Barbara Cartland, *The Isthmus Years: 1919-1939,* Hutchinson and Co, 1942, p94

p.119 *Europe in the 1920s* . . . Elsa Maxwell, *RSVP: Elsa Maxwell's Own Story,* Little, Brown and Company, p21. Reproduced by kind permission of the Permissions Company Inc.

Chapter five

p.125-6 *The dark shadows* . . . The Duchess of Westminster, *Grace and Favour,* Weidenfeld and Nicolson, 1961, p.123. Reproduced by kind permission of the Orion Publishing Group.

p.126 *Those were the days* . . . Lord Bob Boothby, *Recollections of a Rebel,* Hutchinson, 1978, p67

p.127 *The hostesses of the twenties* . . . Beverley Nichols, *The Sweet and Twenties,* Weidenfeld and Nicolson, 1958, p79

p.128 *short, five foot two* . . . Rosina Harrison, *Rose: My Life in Service,* Cassell, 1975, p142

p.131 *I've never heard* . . . Virginia Woolf, 'Am I a Snob?', from Jeanne Schulkin (ed.), *Virginia Woolf: Moments of Being,* Pimlico, 2002, p70

p.131-2 *conversation by brilliant men* . . . Oswald Mosley, *My Life,* Thomas Nelson and Sons Ltd, 1968, p75-6 p.132 *a bit of an old bag* . . . Lord Bob Boothby, *Recollections of a Rebel*, Hutchinson, 1978, p67

p.136 *the Americans* . . . John Foster Fraser, quoted in Stanley Walker, *Mrs Astor's Horse*, Frederick A. Stokes Company, 1935, p44

p.138 *In 1926 Lady Cunard* . . . Patrick Balfour, *Society's Racket*, John Lang Ltd, p139

p.141 *She is coming* . . . Alfred, Lord Tennyson, 'Come into the garden, Maud' from *Maud and other poems*, 1850

p.141 *He was generally* . . . Lord Bob Boothby, *Recollections of a Rebel*, Hutchinson, 1978, p67

p.144 *Her natural milieu* . . . Beverley Nichols, *All I Could Never Be*, Jonathan Cape, 1949, p188

p.145 *She appeared to dispense* . . . Consuelo Vanderbilt Balsan, *The Glitter and the Gold*, Heinemann Ltd 1953, p160

p.150 *When her husband died* . . . Stanley Walker, *Mrs Astor's Horse*, Frederick A. Stokes Company, 1935, p11-2

p.151 *She was once rebuffed* . . . ibid., p12

p.152 *to provide boxing matches* . . . *Daily Mirror*, 29 November, 1929

p.154 *Mrs Greville is rich* . . . *Daily Express*, 13 July, 1927

Chapter six

p.164 *I think I should leave* . . . Mrs Greville, quoted in Beverley Nichols, *Sweet and Twenties*, Weidenfeld and Nicolson, 1958, p82-3

p.165 *as pretty as* . . . Beverley Nichols, *All I Could Never Be*, Jonathan Cape, 1949, p50

p.167 *To go from* . . . Mary Borden, 'To Meet Jesus Christ' from *Four O'Clock and other stories*, Heinemann, 1926, p273 p.168 *if it had not been* . . . Beverley Nichols, *The Unforgiving Minute*, WH Allen, 1978, p152-3

p.169 *Lunch with Sibyl* . . . letter from Harold Nicolson, 1 October, 1931, printed in Nigel Nicolson, *Harold Nicolson: Diaries & Letters 1930-39*, Fontana Books, 1969, p95-6. Reproduced with the permission of the Harold Nicolson Estate.

p.170 *It has fallen out* . . . George Moore, *Heloise and Abelard*, Cumann Sean-eolais na héireann, 1921, republished 2003 by Kessinger Publishing

p.172 *Now, Mr Taylor* . . . Kenneth Clark, *Another Part of the Wood*, John Murray Press, p194

p.181 *A few only* . . . E. F. Benson, *As We Are: A modern review*, Longmans, Green and Co, 1932, republished by Hogarth Press, 1985, p191-2

p.187 *Cliveden struck me* . . . Beverley Nichols, *The Unforgiving Minute*, WH Allen, 1978, p198

p.187-8 *Entertaining for the Astors* . . . Rosina Harrison, *Rose: My Life in Service*, Cassell, 1975, p142

Chapter seven

p.197 *International society is not* . . . Stanley Walker, *Mrs Astor's Horse*, Frederick A. Stokes Company, 1935, p11-2

p.198 *a handsome young* . . . Barbara Cartland, *The Isthmus Years, 1919-1939*, Hutchinson and Co, 1942, p13

p.200 *The 1914-1918* . . . Noel Coward, 'Past Conditional', compiled in *Autobiography*, Methuen, 1986, p277. © The Estate of Noel Coward, 'Past Conditional', Bloomsbury Methuen Drama, an imprint of Bloomsbury Publishing Plc.

p.203 *It was difficult* . . . Geoffrey Harmsworth, 'I Meet Hitler', *The Daily Dispatch*, 1 October 1933, p11

p.203 *his dank complexion* . . . *a dreadful revelation* . . .

Diana Cooper, from Philip Zeigler, *Diana Cooper*, Hamish Hamilton, 1981, p186

p.208 *They only dine* . . . Sibyl Colefax, letter to Berensen, 1933, Colefax MS Eng c. 3176, held in the Bodleian Library

p.210 *I once heard* . . . Nigel Nicolson, *Long Life: Memoirs*, Weidenfeld and Nicolson, 1997, p185

p.212 *one of the greatest* . . . *Evening News*, 30 June 1933

p.214 *Not at all* . . . Mrs Greville, in Charles Ritchie, *The Siren Years*, Macmillan, 1974, p99

p.214-5 *Much talk about* . . . Sir Robert Bruce Lockhart, from Kenneth Young (ed.), *The Diaries of Sir Robert Bruce Lockhart, 1915-1938* (14 September and 17 October 1934), Macmillan, 1973

p.218 *have not yet* . . . *The English Review*, July 1936

p.220 *forthcoming and agreeable* . . . The Marquess of Londonderry, *Ourselves and Germany*, Penguin, 1938, p73 and p93

p.220 *man of arresting* . . . Lady Edith Londonderry, quoted in Anne De Courcey, *Society's Queen*, Phoenix, 1992, p331

p.220 *Lady Londonderry will* . . . letter from Unity Mitford to Diana Mosley (8 February 1936), from Charlotte Mosley (ed.), *The Mitfords: Letters Between Six Sisters*,

p220 *Londonderry just back* . . . Harold Nicolson in Nigel Nicolson (ed.), *Harold Nicolson: Diaries and Letters 1930-1939* (20 February 1936), Phoenix, 2005, p157. Reproduced with the permission of the Harold Nicolson Estate.

p221 *a fat, unattractive* . . . Elsa Maxwell, *RSVP*, Little, Brown and Company, 1954, p8

p.224-225 *jolly, plain* . . . Sir Henry Channon, in Robert Rhodes James (ed.), *Chips: The Diaries of Sir Henry Channon* (5 April 1935), Phoenix, 1996 p227 *Story goes* . . . Sir Robert Bruce Lockhart, from Kenneth Young (ed.), *The Diaries of Sir Robert Bruce Lockhart*, Macmillan, 1973, p331

p.228-9 *The crown always* . . . Sir Henry Channon in Robert Rhodes James (ed.), *Chips: The Diaries of Sir Henry Channon* (13 January 1940), Phoenix, 1996, p231

Chapter eight

p.232 *My impression* . . . Sir Alan Lescalles, in Duff Hart-Davis (ed.), *King's Counsellor: Abdication and War: The Diaries of Sir Alan Lescalles* (5 March 1943), Weidenfeld and Nicolson, 2006

p.234 *scorns the English* . . . Bella Fromm, *Blood and Banquets: A Berlin Social Diary*, Carol Publishing Group, 1990, p205-6

p.236 *The Channons* . . . Harold Nicolson from Nigel Nicolson (ed.), *Harold Nicolson: Diaries and Letters 1930-1939* (20 September 1936), Fontana Books, 1969. Reproduced with the permission of the Harold Nicolson Estate.

p.236. *Yes, I should find* . . . ibid., letter to Vita Sackville-West, 12 June 1936

p.238 *Cliveden, I admit* . . . ibid., letter to Vita Sackville-West, 28 June 1936

p.240. *Received by Ribbentrop* . . . Sir Henry Channon in Robert Rhodes James (ed.), *Chips: The Diaries of Sir Henry Channon* (5 April 1935), Phoenix, 1996

p.240 *There were Rolls* . . . Beverley Nichols, *All I Could Never Be*, Jonathan Cape, 1949, p274

p.243 *I have never seen* . . . letter from Harold Nicolson to Vita Sackville-West (11 June 1936), from Nigel Nicolson (ed.), *Harold Nicolson: Diaries and Letters 1930-1939*,

Fontana Books, 1969. Reproduced with the permission of the Harold Nicolson Estate.

p.244 *She looked old* . . . Virginia Woolf, 'Am I a Snob?', from Jeanne Schulkind (ed.), *Virginia Woolf: Moments of Being*, Pimlico, 2002, p74

p.245 *Huh* . . . Rosina Harrison, *Gentlemen's Gentlemen: My friends in service*, Arlington Books, 1976, p85, republished by Sphere as *Gentlemen's Gentlemen: from Boot Boys to Butlers*, 2015. Reproduced by kind permission of Sphere.

p.245 *It is evident* . . . Harold Nicolson from Nigel Nicolson (ed.), *Harold Nicolson: Diaries and Letters 1930-1939* (2 April 1936), Phoenix, 1996. Reproduced with the permission of the Harold Nicolson Estate.

p.249 *bright and witty* . . . Cecil Beaton in Richard Burkle (ed.), *Self Portrait with Friends: the Selected Diaries of Cecil Beaton, 1926-1974,* Weidenfeld and Nicolson, 1979, p47

p.252 *I forget* . . . letter from Harold Nicolson to Vita Sackville-West (9 December 1936), from Nigel Nicolson (ed.), *Harold Nicolson: Diaries and Letters 1930-1939*, Fortune Books, 1969. Reproduced with the permission of the Harold Nicolson Estate.

p.253 *From being the beloved* . . . Sibyl Colefax quoted in Kirsty MacLeod, *A Passion for Friendship: Sibyl Colefax and her Circle*, Michael Joseph, 1991, p149

p.253 *We all acclaim* . . . letter from Mrs Margaret Greville to King George VI, 11 December 1936. From the Royal Archives.

p.254. *The attitude of* . . . Sir Alan Lascelles in Duff Hart-David (ed.), *Abdication and War: The Diaries of Sir Alan Lascelles*, Weidenfeld and Nicolson, 2006, p414

p.255 *Where are the friends* . . . Osbert Sitwell, 'Rat Week', *An*

Essay on the Abdication, Michael Joseph, 1986. Reproduced with kind permission of David Higham Associates.

p.256 *The other day* . . . letter from Queen Mary to Prince Paul of Yugoslavia, 16 December 1936. Reproduced with kind permission from The Prince Paul of Yugoslavia papers, The Bakhmeteff Archive of Russian and East European History and Culture, Rare Book and Manuscript Library, Columbia University, New York.

p.257 *She was very upset* . . . Rosina Harrison, *My Life in Service*, Cassell, 1975, p214

p.257 *Really, she seems* . . . Lady Nancy Astor in Adrian Fort, *Nancy: The Story of Lady Astor*, Vintage Books, p248

p.258 *In England* . . . Richard Collier, *The Rainbow People*, Weidenfeld and Nicolson, 1984, p170

p.258 *HRH is wearing* . . . letter from Mrs Margaret Greville to Lord Reading, British Library, Mss Eur F118/27/27-105

p.261 *I have no intention* . . . Elephant story from Mark Amory, *Lord Berners: The Last Eccentric*, Chatto and Windus, 1998, p171

Chapter nine

p.271 *I discussed* . . . The Marquess of Londonderry, *Ourselves and Germany*, Penguin, 1938, p73

p.273 *extend the hand* . . . ibid., p27-8

p.273-4 *The more positive 'isms'* . . . *October, 1938* . . . The Marchioness of Londonderry, *Retrospect*, Frederick Muller Ltd, 1938, p256

p.274 *I am completely* . . . letter from Lord Londonderry to Hermann Goering, November 1939, quoted in Anne De Courcy, *Society's Queen: The Life of Edith, Marchioness of Londonderry*, Phoenix, 1992, p352-3 p.278 . . . *Dear Ivy Chamberlain* . . . Beverley Nichols, *All I Could Never Be*, Jonathan Cape, 1949, p20

p.278 *She is nothing* . . . Harold Nicolson, from Nigel Nicolson (ed.), *Harold Nicolson: Diaries and Letters 1930-1939* (20 July 1937), Fontana, 1969. Reproduced with the permission of the Harold Nicolson Estate.

p.279 *I have had* . . . Margot Asquith, *Autobiography*, Penguin, 1920, p128

p.279 *The Nazis* . . . Bella Fromm, *Blood and Banquets: A Berlin Social Diary* (8 October 1933)

p.283 *A visit* . . . from a scrapbook in the archives at Polesden Lacey, 1930s

p.283 *We both felt* . . . letter from Queen Elizabeth to Edith, Marchioness of Londonderry, 3 March 1938, Londonderry Papers, PRONI, D. 3099/3/13/5/15

p.285 *Lady Cunard is* . . . letter from Queen Elizabeth to Edith, Marchioness of Londonderry , 31 May 1937, PRONI, Londonderry Papers, D. 3099/13

p.285 *Give a canary* . . . Lord Berners quoted in Mark Amory, *Lord Berners: The Last Eccentric*, Chatto and Windus, 1998, p163

p.288 *A great London hostess* . . . Elsa Maxwell quoted in Tilar J. Mazzeo, The Hotel on the Place Vendôme, HarperPerennial, 2014, p52

p.288 *was not beautiful* . . . ibid.

p.289-90 *I do not believe* . . . Harold Nicolson in Nigel Nicolson (ed.), *Harold Nicolson: Diaries and Letters 1930-1939* (10 April 1939), Fontana, 1969. Reproduced with the permission of the Harold Nicolson Estate.

p.290 *War was not* . . . Lord Bob Boothby, *Recollections of a Rebel*, Hutchinson, 1978, p78

p.292 *There is no one* . . . Sir Henry Channon in Robert

Rhodes James (ed.), *Chips: The Diaries of Sir Henry Channon* (4 August 1939), Phoenix, 1996

p.293 *It is impossible* . . . ibid., 24 August 1939

Chapter ten

p.295 *as frail as a pack of cards* . . . letter from Diana Cooper to John Julius Norwich from *Darling Monster: The Letters of Lady Diana Cooper to her son John Julius Norwich, 1939-1952*, Chatto and Windus, 2013, p68

p.296-7 *In the Dorchester* . . . Charles Ritchie, *The Siren Years*, Macmillan, 1974, p68

p299 *Dined at the Dorchester* . . . ibid., p73

p.304 *Today Plymouth* . . . Nancy Astor quoted in the *Western Morning News*, 7 April 1941

p.307 *Excitement is* . . . *New York Journal-American*, Hearst Newspapers, 9 February 1942, quoted in John Lucas, *Thomas Beecham: An Obsession with Music*, The Boydell Press, 2008, p279-9

p.308 *Emerald was gay* . . . Sir Henry Channon in Robert Rhodes James (ed.), *Chips: The Diaries of Sir Henry Channon* (16 November 1942), Phoenix, 1996

p.311 *Dear Sibyl* . . . letter from Lord Berners, quoted in Mark Amory, *Lord Berners: The Last Eccentric*, Chatto and Windus, 1998, p187-8

p.312-3 *Dined with the Masseys* . . . Charles Ritchie, *The Siren Years*, Macmillan, 1942

p.313-4 *it was too pathetic* . . . letter from Queen Elizabeth to Osbert Sitwell, 13 September 1942, quoted in William Shawcross (ed.), *Counting One's Blessings: The selected letters of Queen Elizabeth, the Queen Mother*, Pan Macmillan, 2012, p324 p.314 *That damned Ribbentrop* . . . Beverley Nichols, *All I Could Never Be*, Jonathan Cape, 1949, p22-24

p.319-320 *Laura Mae Corrigan* . . . *Time Magazine*, 5 October 1942

p.321 *Everyone was there* . . . Noel Coward in Graham Payne and Sheridan Morley (eds.), *The Noel Coward Diaries*, Macmillan, 1983, p25

p.322 *I am grateful* . . . Lady Nancy Astor in a speech at Southport on 1 August 1942, quoted in Adrian Fort, *Nancy: The Story of Lady Astor*, Vintage, 2013, p294

p.324 *There is still* . . . The Marchioness of Londonderry, *Retrospect*, Frederick Muller Ltd, 1938, p253

p.326 *the war* . . . letter from Lord Londonderry to Lady Desborough, February 1945, quoted in Anne De Courcy, *Society's Queen: The Life of Edith, Marchioness of Londonderry*, Phoenix, 1992, p365

Chapter eleven

p.334 *He took most* . . . Lord Boothby, *Recollections of a Rebel*, Hutchinson, 1978, p69

p.334-5 *I haven't seen her for years* . . . Lord Berners, quoted in Mark Amory, *Lord Berners: The Last Eccentric*, Chatto and Windus, 1998, p229

p.338 *an extraordinary* . . . *Daily Mail*, 12 July 1948

p.338 *Those who loved* . . . *The Times*, 17 July 1948

p.339 *When I arrived* . . . Nigel Nicolson, 'Hostess with the Mostess', *The Spectator*, 27 May 1994

p.340 *No, I am not* . . . Sibyl Colefax, in James Lees-Milne, *Diaries 1942-1954* (1 September 1948), John Murray Press, 2006, p258

p.340 *poor little Coalbox* . . .

p.341 *Sibyl genuinely* . . . Kenneth Clark, *Another Part of the Wood*, John Murray Press, 1974

p.345 *When I last* . . . Beverley Nichols, *The Unforgiving Minute*, W.H. Allen, 1978, p150

p.347 *still full of vitality* . . . Noel Coward, *The Noel Coward Diaries* (1 May 1955), edited by Graham Payne and Sheridan Morley, Macmillan, p265

p.350 *I went into* . . . Rosina Harrison, *Rose: My Life in Service*, Cassell, 1975, p260

Chapter twelve

p.351 *Giving parties* . . . Elsa Maxwell, *RSVP*, Little, Brown and Company. Reproduced with kind permission of the Permissions Company Inc.

p.354 *What I really like* . . . Nancy Astor, quoted in Adrian Fort, *Nancy: The Story of Lady Astor*, Vintage, 2013, p214

p.357 *A social Napoleon* . . . Beverley Nichols, *All I Could Never Be*, Jonathan Cape, 1949, p13

p.360 *Laura was a* . . . Elsa Maxwell, *RSVP: Elsa Maxwell's Own Story*, Little, Brown and Company, p22. Reproduced with kind permission of the Permissions Company Inc.

p.361 *As a little girl* . . . Laura Corrigan quoted in Pamela Horn, *Country House Society: The Private Lives of England's Upper Class*, Amberley Publishing, 2013, p50

Every reasonable effort has been made to contact the copyright holders, but if there are any errors or omissions, John Murray Press will be pleased to insert the appropriate acknowledgement in any subsequent printing of this publication.

For a full list of further reading please visit www.tworoadsbooks.com/non-fiction/queen-bees-sian-evans/

Picture acknowledgements

Alamy: 2 above/© National Trust Photo Library/painting by John Singer Sargent 1908/photo John Hammond, 2 below/© SOTK2011, 4 above right/War Archive/painting by Philip de Laszlo 1918, 5 above right/© Man Ray/Courtesy Everett Collection, 6 above/ © V&A Images. © The Cecil Beaton Studio Archive at Sotheby's: 3 below, 4 below left, 5 below left, 8 below left. Getty Images: 5 above left/photo W.G. Phillips, 6 below/Fox Photos, 7 above/The LIFE Picture Collection/photo Hans Wild. © David Low/Solo Syndication: 7 below. © Mirrorpix/Bridgeman Images: 8 above left. © National Trust/Richard Holttum: 1 below. © National Trust Images: 1 above/painting by Emile-Auguste Carolus-Duran 1891/photo John Hammond, 4 above left/painting by Philip de Laszlo 1927/photo John Hammond, 8 above right. Private Collection; 3 above/ *The Hall of Argyll House*, painting by Sir John Lavery (1856-1941).

Every reasonable effort has been made to contact the copyright holders, but if there are any errors or omissions, John Murray Press will be pleased to insert the appropriate acknowledgement in any subsequent printing of this publication.

Acknowledgements

—————

A great many people were extremely helpful and generous in sharing their knowledge and expertise while I was researching and writing this book. I would especially like to thank the following individuals, who contributed in so many ways:

Diane Banks, Angela Barrett, Grant Berry, Vicky Bevan, Philip Baldwin, Pam Burbridge, Pamela Clarke, Roger Coleman, Damian Collins MP, Alison Dalby, Paul Dearn, Harvey Edgington, Sarah Evans, Mark Fifield, Cara Wallace, Clare Gogerty, Cathy Gosling, Susannah Handley, Kate Hewson, Lisa Highton, David Kitt, Avril Loughlin, Sue Lovett, Jonathan Marsh, Steve Price, Nigel Porter, Polly Powell, Chris Rowlin, John Stachiewicz, and Lauren Taylor.

Index

About the author

———

Cultural historian Siân Evans has worked for the National Trust, the V&A and the Design Museum, and is the author of several works of social history including *Mrs Ronnie: The Society Hostess Who Collected Kings*, *The Manor Reborn* and *Life Below Stairs*.

Siân lives in London.

Stories . . . voices . . . places . . . lives

We hope you enjoyed *Queen Bees*.
If you'd like to know more about this book
or any other title on our list, please go to
www.tworoadsbooks.com

For news on forthcoming Two Roads titles,
please sign up for our newsletter.

enquiries@tworoadsbooks.com

TwoRoadsBooks